"Shellum combines solid research and narration skills in this detailed examination of the service of African American regular army enlisted soldiers and their officers in early 1900s California."

—THOMAS D. PHILLIPS, coauthor of *The Black Regulars, 1866–1898*

"*Buffalo Soldiers in California* is Brian Shellum's latest effort to reveal the untold stories of Charles Young and the Buffalo Soldiers. Brian has labored hand-in-hand with my family members to shed new light on Young's exemplary achievements in San Francisco and at Sequoia National Park. Brian's research has directly supported the Brigadier General Charles Young Foundation's efforts to promote his legacy."

—RENOTTA YOUNG, descendant of Charles Young and CEO of the Brigadier General Charles Young Foundation

"I found Brian Shellum's meticulously researched and expertly written history of the Buffalo Soldiers at the Presidio in San Francisco particularly fascinating as it highlights Captain Charles Young's remarkable year at Sequoia National Park and my hometown of Three Rivers. It is a legacy I have long been aware of, but I now have such greater understanding and appreciation of all that Young accomplished, and the intelligent, kind man of great integrity he truly was."

—JAY O'CONNELL, author of *Co-operative Dreams: A History of the Kaweah Colony*

"As a first-generation Californian, I came of age not knowing a thing about the contributions of African Americans in my home state. It wasn't included in our primary or secondary education. For this reason, I am extremely grateful and humbled by Brian Shellum's effort in putting together such an amazing literary work, telling the story of great African American patriots, the Buffalo Soldiers, who served our country with bravery, distinction, and honor during the nineteenth century. . . . Shellum's inspiring book is a must-read for all Americans and, in particular, those of African American heritage."

—GLORIA RICHARD, descendant of Trumpeter Frank McKenzie, I Troop of the Ninth U.S. Cavalry

I0895785

"Brian Shellum has done a most admirable job in portraying the life of Colonel Young and his soldiers as he followed them in their later years. In addition, his inclusion of Colonel Pearson, another early-day resident of Three Rivers, went a long way to complete this history and give it extra meaning. I look forward to reading it and adding this book to my personal library."

—SOPHIE BRITTON, author of *Pioneers in Paradise: A Historical Biographical Record of Early Days in Three Rivers, California*

"Granddaddy Peggy was proud to have served with Colonel Young and spoke of him and the Buffalo Soldiers often. . . . Thank you, Brian Shellum, for providing so much information about Granddad."

—PAM D. JONES, descendant of Cook Abner Jones, I Troop of the Ninth U.S. Cavalry

"Historian Brian Shellum documents a too-little-known chapter in the lives of pioneering African American Army officer Charles Young and the Buffalo soldiers he commanded. . . . These soldiers, who helped Young develop his effectiveness as a cavalry officer, are given their own voice through their personal memories and those of others who knew them."

—FLOYD THOMAS, curator emeritus of the National Afro-American Museum and Cultural Center

"*Buffalo Soldiers in California* establishes Brian Shellum as the leading scholar on the military career of Colonel Charles Young, and this book provides important insight into San Francisco's race relations at the turn of the twentieth century, the day-to-day life of Buffalo Soldiers in a western urban city, and the largely unknown role of Black soldiers as both 'guardians' and a superintendent of Sequoia and General Grant National Parks. Most critically, Shellum reveals an important phase in the life of a remarkable man and an important Black leader."

—ALBERT S. BROUSSARD, author of *Black San Francisco: The Struggle for Racial Equality in the West, 1900–1954*

PRAISE FOR BRIAN SHELLUM'S *Black Officer in a Buffalo Soldier Regiment: The Military Career of Charles Young*

"During a long and distinguished career—from being the first African American captain in the regular army and first to be in charge of a national park, to serving in the Philippines, chasing Pancho Villa in Mexico, and representing the United States in Liberia—Charles Young succeeded in spite of the Jim Crow prejudices permeating the American military of his time. His is a remarkable and inspiring story, though often overlooked. In this well-researched book, Brian Shellum finally gives Young the historical attention he deserves."

—DAYTON DUNCAN, coauthor of *The National Parks: America's Best Idea*

"Shellum's book is a welcome addition to recent studies of the Black military experience. . . . This is an enjoyable, commanding, and well-researched work."

—BRUCE A. GLASRUD, *Journal of American History*

"Brian Shellum is to be congratulated for providing a first-rate biography of a proud and competent officer serving during a difficult period of his country's history."

—THOMAS R. BUECKER, *Nebraska History*

"Brian Shellum has filled an important void in African American biography and American military history."

—RONALD G. COLEMAN, *Utah Historical Quarterly*

"This is a solid study of an important figure in American history. It is easy to recommend to those with an interest in military affairs, biography, and the African American experience."

—CLAUDE CLEGG, *Register of the Kentucky Historical Society*

BISON BOOKS

# BUFFALO SOLDIERS IN CALIFORNIA

## Charles Young and the Ninth Cavalry, 1902–1904

BRIAN G. SHELLUM

*University of Nebraska Press* | LINCOLN

© 2024 by the Board of Regents of the University of Nebraska. All rights reserved.

The University of Nebraska Press is part of a land-grant institution with campuses and programs on the past, present, and future homelands of the Pawnee, Ponca, Otoe-Missouria, Omaha, Dakota, Lakota, Kaw, Cheyenne, and Arapaho Peoples, as well as those of the relocated Ho-Chunk, Sac and Fox, and Iowa Peoples.

∞

Library of Congress Cataloging-in-Publication Data
Names: Shellum, Brian G., author.
Title: Buffalo soldiers in California: Charles Young and the Ninth Cavalry, 1902–1904 / Brian G. Shellum.
Other titles: Charles Young and the Ninth Cavalry, 1902–1904
Description: Lincoln: University of Nebraska Press, 2024. | Includes bibliographical references and index.
Identifiers: LCCN 2023040996
ISBN 9781496238511 (paperback)
ISBN 9781496239907 (epub)
ISBN 9781496239914 (pdf)
Subjects: LCSH: Young, Charles, 1864–1922. | United States. Army—African American officers—Biography. | United States. Army. Cavalry, 9th. I Troop—Biography. | Presidio of San Francisco (Calif.)—Biography. | National parks and reserves—California—History—20th century. | United States. Army—Civic action—History—20th century. | United States. Army. Cavalry, 9th. I Troop—Registers. | United States. Army—African American troops—Biography. | California—History, Military—20th century. | BISAC: HISTORY / United States / State & Local / West (AK, CA, CO, HI, ID, MT, NV, UT, WY) | HISTORY / Wars & Conflicts / General
Classification: LCC E185.63 .S485 2024 | DDC 355.0092 [B]—dc23/eng/20240423
LC record available at https://lccn.loc.gov/2023040996

Set in Lyon Text by A. Shahan.

For my sister
Karen Winn

# Contents

# Illustrations

# Acknowledgments

As in the past, I owe the lion's share of thanks to my wife, Paula, for granting me the time and encouragement to complete *Buffalo Soldiers in California*, my fifth book. She has been my chief supporter along the way. I thank my daughter, Kara, and my son, Greg, for inspiring and encouraging me as only children can. I recall the first time we walked into a bookstore seventeen years ago and saw my first book on the shelf. My son walked up; removed the book, which was displayed with its spine out; and made room for it on the shelf with the cover showing. I'll never forget that gesture.

I wrote much of this book during the COVID-19 epidemic that began in 2019. Despite being vaccinated, I had mild cases of COVID twice, and during my forced periods of quarantine, I accomplished a lot of writing. Travel restrictions and the closure of public archives made the research process more difficult. I was fortunate to have good contacts at closed facilities and good access to online resources.

Besides the National Archives, several organizations and individuals helped me with research materials for this book. The National Afro-American Museum and Cultural Center in Wilberforce, Ohio, has been a rich source of original research materials, and I thank director Dr. Chuck Wash and my old friend Dr. Floyd Thomas for their continued support. The curator at Sequoia National Park, Dr. Ward Eldridge, has been a wonderful source of information over the twenty years I have known him, and I wish him well in retirement. Guy Washington, a former ranger at the Presidio with whom I have worked on researching Buffalo Soldiers for the past two decades, shared his files and contacts with me. Some of those files were compiled by Justine Lai, with whom I worked many years ago digitizing photographs in Akron, Ohio. Amanda Williford, the curator at the Golden Gate National Recreation Area, provided some great photos for the book. Tom Marshall and Nancy Brunson at the Three Rivers Historical Museum in California opened the archives to me at a time when it was closed to the public due to COVID. Three Rivers historian Sophia Britten helped me with the local history as well as sharing the stories of her husband's father, Ranger Ernest Britten. Laura Brooks, of Paso Robles, California, shared the files of her mother, Dorothy Lowe, who wrote about the Camp Atascadero maneuvers. The West Point Library's Special Collections have been a valuable source of information on West Pointers, and Susan Lintelmann was always quick to respond to requests.

I was fortunate to have a group of dedicated readers who reviewed my various drafts. Tom Phillips, co-author of *The Black Regulars*, offered invaluable insight into the lives of Blacks in the military and was the first to read the chapters of my book. I have already mentioned Floyd Thomas, who reviewed and commented on my drafts. Jay O'Connell, a TV producer and author, provided pages of comments and gave me important insight on the local history of Three Rivers. My sister Rolynn Anderson, a former English teacher who writes fiction, evaluated my second draft and provided ways to improve my structure and organization. Park Ranger Shelton Johnson, an old friend, provided input on my draft manuscript and gave me important additional information about Yosemite National Park. Finally, Dr. Albert Broussard reviewed my draft and provided critical insights on the lives of African Americans in San Francisco in his books.

The descendants of three members of I Troop, Ninth Cavalry who served in California gave me invaluable support. Renotta, Rhavie, and Lawrence Young are all descendants of Charles Young and are good friends with whom I have worked on the board of the Brigadier General Charles Young Foundation. Renotta and Lawrence grew up with Charles Young's two children, who were their first cousins, and gave me fascinating insight to the "Young Doctrine." Another descendant, Pam Jones, is a granddaughter of Young's cook, Abner Jones, and provided stories and photos of his life after the army. And Gloria Richard's great uncle, Frank McKenzie, was Young's trumpeter. Gloria provided me with a priceless photo and detailed information on McKenzie's family life.

I also thank the following organizations for their support: Colorado Springs Fine Arts Center, Huntington Library, Nebraska State Historical Society, Ohio Historical Connection, Omega Psi Phi Fraternity, National Park Service, Uintah County Library Regional History Center, Utah State Historical Society, West Point Association of Graduates, and Wyoming State Archives. Other individuals who assisted and encouraged me along the way include Michael Alexander, Rainey Astin, Teresa Baker, Geneva Brett, Vincent Brooks, Don Burger, Jason Carr, Jeffrey Carter, Robert Cherney, Roger Cunningham, Mark Donnelly, Tom Engberg, Charles Frank, Bill Gwaltney, Stephen Haller, Michael Harris, Paul Hardwick, Mark Harrington, Richard Hartman, Steven Heffelfinger, Edwin Henderson, Dru Holley, Gregory Irwin, Bruce Johnson, Joy Kinard, Don Kohrs, Axel Krigsman, James McKinnon, James Edward Mills, George Palmer, Matt Parks, Rik Penn, Antony Powell, Emma Powell, Steve Rawlick, Dick Riney, Michael Roberts, Kevin Samsel, Kris Warren Samsel, Doc Settles, Liv Sheldon, Susan Shumaker, Frank Simkonis, Mike Smith, Scott Stephenson, and Robert Stewart.

# BUFFALO SOLDIERS IN CALIFORNIA

# Introduction

When Charles Young stepped ashore at the Presidio of San Francisco in 1902, he was a proven combat veteran and experienced troop commander. He commanded I Troop, Ninth U.S. Cavalry, arguably the best unit in one of the finest regiments in the U.S. Army. Yet the corrosive effect of thirteen years' serving as a Black officer in a white officer corps had left him bitter and lonely. He left California two years later a changed man with a better outlook, and this book explores his transformation.

This narrative follows the journey of Capt. Charles Young and the Ninth U.S. Cavalry in California from 1902 to 1904. Young, the senior of three Black officers then serving in the Regular Army, had proven himself in combat during two years of brutal guerrilla warfare in the Philippine-American War. His success in that conflict earned the Ninth Cavalry the plum assignment at the Presidio of San Francisco, one of the most sought-after military postings in the country.

Consider Young's accomplishments in the thirteen years between his graduation from West Point in 1889 and his arrival in San Francisco: he served in the West during the closing battles of the Indian Wars, established the first Black officer training program at Wilberforce University, was appointed a major to command an Ohio volunteer battalion during the Spanish-American War, and fought as a troop commander in the Philippine-American War. He had learned from each of these challenging assignments and compiled an impressive record.

The reader will discern several reoccurring themes or threads throughout this book. During his army career, firmly placed in the Jim Crow era, Young lived socially isolated in an officer corps uncomfortable with an African American in its ranks. Despite this, he used his natural talents and professional growth to persevere and prosper. The army deliberately shuffled Young between the few assignments it considered suitable for a Black officer in a white man's officer corps: the Buffalo Soldier regiments, an African American university, and diplomatic posts in Black republics. Fortunately for Young, the Ninth Cavalry was among the best in the Regular Army, and the detached duty assignments made him more competitive for promotion. Using the experience gained from these varied positions, Young established himself as an exceptional cavalry officer with a strong record and important mentors.

Though better known today, Charles Young remains virtually unknown to many Americans, African Americans included. Reflect on his extraordinary achievements: third Black graduate of West Point, first African American superintendent of one of our national parks, first Black U.S. military attaché, first African American officer to command a cavalry squadron, and highest-ranking Black Regular Army officer in his lifetime. Unlike the two Black academy graduates before him, Young went on to a long and distinguished military career and achieved the rank of colonel. For nearly thirty years, he was the standard-bearer for his race in the officer corps.

Racial prejudice as well as medical problems on the eve of World War I prevented Young from commanding troops in Europe and becoming the first African American general. Rather than heed the 1917 promotion board's recommendation to waive Young's medical conditions so he could continue on active duty, President Woodrow Wilson and Secretary of War Newton Baker caved to pressure from racist southern senators and shuffled him off to retirement. The U.S. Army rectified that injustice one hundred years after his death with his posthumous promotion to brigadier general in 2022.

*Buffalo Soldiers in California* is intended to further the process of rescuing Charles Young from historical obscurity and restoring the prestige and recognition he enjoyed in his lifetime. It is also intended to shed light on the lives of the Buffalo Soldiers who helped him attain his measure of greatness. Young's success depended on the professionalism and dedication of his enlisted men, and they served him well.

Young's success in the Ninth Cavalry would not have been possible without the competence and commitment of the noncommissioned officers and soldiers he led. Many of the veteran sergeants of I Troop were already serving with the Ninth Cavalry when Young arrived as a newly minted second lieutenant in 1889, and they helped foster his education as a cavalry leader. Yet many of the Buffalo Soldiers of I Troop were younger members of a new generation of Black soldiers who joined the army in the wake of the Spanish-American War. Young provided the inspired leadership that molded both cohorts into an efficient fighting force in the Philippines but found new challenges awaiting him in peacetime duty in California.

This narrative discusses in detail the experiences of the enlisted soldiers before, during, and after their military service in California. This book begins and ends with the story of the enlisted soldiers of I Troop, Ninth Cavalry, whom Young referred to as that "rowdy gang of mine." As much as possible, I have focused on the stories of the enlisted troopers who were the backbone of the Buffalo Soldier regiments.

In addition to official army records and contemporary newspaper accounts, many of the details of the lives of the Buffalo Soldiers of I Troop came directly from recollections of the soldiers themselves. Several of Young's cavalry troopers belonged to a second generation of more educated Black soldiers who later wrote letters documenting their thoughts and experiences. Several local Californians who befriended Young during his time at Sequoia National Park also wrote diaries. And a few descendants of the Buffalo Soldiers who settled in California shared stories and photographs passed down from veterans of I Troop who died as recently as the 1970s.

*Buffalo Soldiers in California* opens with an introduction to Young's rowdy gang and describes the background of the key officers and enlisted soldiers of I Troop. The narrative then covers the process of the Ninth Cavalry's settling into a garrison routine and facing the challenges of being stationed in a large city. Succeeding chapters cover two summers of patrolling the Sequoia, General Grant, and Yosemite National Parks, as well as the mission of training the California National Guard. The book ends with a postscript covering the lives of the officers and men after leaving the Presidio, focusing on those who decided to stay in California after their army service. Finally, an appendix provides detailed biographies of every member of I Troop who served in California.

This book is intended for the reader interested in the service of African American soldiers in the first decade of the twentieth century. Much has been written about the Buffalo Soldiers in the post–Civil War era who played a prominent role in the Indian Wars in the West and the Spanish-American War at the turn of the century. Much less is known about the service of Black regulars in the early years of the twentieth century after the Philippine-American War.

Young served in the Regular Army at a time when it was transitioning from a western frontier force to a modern military. Young and the Ninth Cavalry were important actors in this transformation of what historian Edward M. Coffman called the Old Army. And one of the important missions given to the U.S. Army after 1890 was to protect America's three national parks: Yellowstone, Sequoia and General Grant, and Yosemite. The troopers of the Ninth Cavalry surpassed expectations during two seasons of park patrolling, and Captain Young became the first Black national park superintendent at Sequoia in the summer of 1903.

In this first detailed account of the Buffalo Soldiers' experiences in California outside of the army after the turn of the century, readers learn the former soldiers of I Troop found opportunities in California. They landed jobs, bought homes, got married, had families, and, to a certain extent, thrived in California after their military service. They personified the motto of the Ninth Cavalry: "We Can, We Will."

# 1

## Rowdy Gang of Mine

How many pleasant memories it awakened of that beloved rowdy gang of mine, I Troop, 9th Cavalry.
—Letter from Charles Young, October 15, 1916

While chasing Pancho Villa in Mexico as part of the Punitive Expedition in 1916, Maj. Charles Young received a letter from Joseph "Joe" Clark of Baltimore, Maryland, one of his former enlisted men from I Troop, Ninth U.S. Cavalry. They had served together fifteen years earlier. Clark's onetime troop commander had read the letter, which arrived in April, and tucked it into his overcoat pocket. Since the weather in Mexico turned warm in the summer, Young had no occasion to wear his overcoat until October when the fall chill arrived. When he rediscovered the letter, he wrote his former soldier a long-overdue reply.[1]

Young reminisced: "How many pleasant memories it awakened of that beloved rowdy gang of mine, I Troop 9th Cavalry." He had served as the captain and commander of I Troop from 1899 until 1915. During that time, his troop saw service at Fort Duchesne, Utah; the Philippine Islands; the Presidio of San Francisco, California; and Fort D. A. Russell, Wyoming. Young also served detached duty assignments as the military attaché to Haiti and Liberia during this period.[2]

On the second page of his letter, Young mentioned a group of former troopers that had served with him in the Philippines and at San Francisco, discussing the men's fortunes after leaving the army. He wrote:

> Glad to hear from you over more, that you are alive, married and getting along well. Most of the "I" Troopers who have gone out in civil life are doing fine, I'm proud to say. Let's see: there's "Swamp" Pierce, Nicholas, Dee Smith, Malone, Norman, Peggy and Wirt Langley, not to forget Leo Frye, all living and married in San Francisco alone, and getting along. Henry Whitfield alone of all those boys out there did bad. But Whitfield was not a bad boy in spite of the fight you two lads had. In fact it was for fighting he went to the "Pen." But you know it is never too late for a boy to make up his mind to find the straight clean thing in life and do it.

That Major Young, while chasing Villa's rebel forces in Mexico, would take the time to respond to a letter from a private who had served a single three-year enlistment in his troop, is noteworthy. Joe Clark had served well in the army, receiving a good character rating from Young at the end of his enlistment. But Young's response to his former I Troop private is not surprising since he spent his entire three-decade career in the army mentoring Black soldiers.

Who were the members of this "rowdy gang" Young mentioned in the letter from Mexico? Their names are important and are discussed in the chapters to follow. Young's beloved troopers, named in order from the letter, included Samuel "Swamp" Pierce, William H. Nicholas, Dee Smith, John L. Malone, James Norman, Abner "Peggy" Jones, Wirt L. Langley, Leo Frye, and Henry Whitfield.

What forged these soldiers' loyalty and identity under Young's leadership? How did Young build relationships and shape the lives of his rowdy gang while stationed at the Presidio of San Francisco? Why did they settle in the Bay Area after their service in the U.S. Army? And, finally, what were their experiences in California after their military service? To answer these questions, it is first necessary to examine the service of Charles Young and his Buffalo Soldiers in the Golden State from 1902 to 1904.

# 2

## Time, Place, Men

> The army transport *Sheridan*, which arrived Thursday night from Manila, passed quarantine yesterday morning, and about 4 o'clock in the afternoon docked at the transportation wharf. She brought 503 members of the Ninth (Colored) Cavalry.
> —*San Francisco Call*, November 1, 1902

During the month of October 1902, the Ninth U.S. Cavalry Regiment, consisting of the headquarters, band, and twelve troops of cavalry, disembarked at the Presidio of San Francisco aboard military transports from the Philippine Islands. The 7,456-mile trip by water took about thirty days and included a five-day stay at Mariveles, a quarantine station in the Philippines; a short stopover in Nagasaki, Japan; and, finally, the long leg home across the Pacific to the West Coast of the United States. The debarkation of the Buffalo Soldiers marked the beginning of their two-year stay at the Presidio, where they would prove the equal of any other Regular Army unit in the service.[1]

### *Arrival*

The Buffalo Soldiers landed in San Francisco after completing a two-year deployment to the Philippine Islands, where they fought insurgents during the Philippine-American War. The United States seized the islands from Spain during the Spanish-American War in 1898 and, in the Treaty of Paris, paid $20 million for possession of the Philippines. Instead of giving the

Filipinos the independence they longed for, the United States added the island to its new overseas empire and had to fight a prolonged insurgency to retain it. The Ninth Cavalry was one of the Regular Army regiments the War Department rotated through the Philippine Islands that fought in the Philippine-American War from 1899 to 1902.[2]

The Ninth Cavalry was one of the four storied Buffalo Soldier regiments in the standing army. These units originated in post–Civil War legislation to set the size of the peacetime army and establish Black Regular Army regiments. The service of nearly 200,000 Black volunteers during the Civil War, who fought in all the major theaters of combat and suffered more than 36,000 dead, earned Blacks the right to serve in the Regular Army in the postwar era. This was a major triumph for African Americans who, so recently freed from their slave shackles in the South, sacrificed so much during the Civil War.[3]

The Ninth and Tenth U.S. Cavalry Regiments, along with the Twenty-Fourth and Twenty-Fifth U.S. Infantry Regiments, established a creditable record after their formation, boasting a higher esprit de corps, better reenlistment rates, and lower desertion rates than those of their white counterparts. These four Buffalo Soldier regiments composed only 10 percent of the post–Civil War Regular Army's strength, yet they played a key role in the Indian Wars on the western frontier. They added laurels to their sterling record in the subsequent Spanish-American and Philippine-American Wars.[4]

Contingents of the Ninth Cavalry came to San Francisco on two separate U.S. Army Transport (USAT) ships in October 1902. The regimental staff, band, and F, G, H, K, L, and M Troops arrived aboard USAT *Logan* in mid-October 1902 and, after a short quarantine, went into a temporary camp in the Infantry Cantonment on the eastern edge of the Presidio near the Lombard Street entrance. The staff, band, and F, G, and H Troops stayed about a week before departing for Fort Walla Walla, Washington, while the K, L, and M Troops, composing most of the Third Squadron, marched to the Presidio's main post, where they moved into the barracks in late October.[5]

The second component of the Ninth, comprising A, B, C, D, E, and I Troops, arrived aboard USAT *Sheridan* the last day of October 1902. All went into the Infantry Cantonment after a short period of quarantine.

Captain Young and I Troop later moved into the barracks to complete the Third Squadron that garrisoned the Presidio. A, B, C, and D Troops departed on special trains with the First Squadron staff in early November for its new station at the Monterey Military Reservation in Monterey, California, and E Troop left for Fort Walla Walla as the last element of the Second Squadron. This completed the rotation of the Ninth Cavalry to its new West Coast garrison assignments.[6]

When the Ninth arrived in San Francisco, it had an aggregate strength of 1,142 officers and men. The regiment comprised twelve troops of about ninety men each, further divided into three squadrons of four troops each. The regiment and three squadrons each had a small headquarters consisting of a handful of officers and senior noncommissioned officers. Only the Third Squadron, commanded by Maj. Joseph Garrard and comprising I, K, L, and M Troops, remained to garrison the Presidio of San Francisco for the next two years. Commanding I Troop was Capt. Charles Young, the senior Black Regular Army officer at the time and, of the three, the only graduate of the U.S. Military Academy at West Point, New York.[7]

### *Choice Post*

The Third Squadron earned the plum assignment at the Presidio because of the leadership of Young and the success of his soldiers in the Philippines. Maj. Gen. Robert P. Hughes commanded the Department of California, headquartered in San Francisco, when the Ninth Cavalry arrived in 1902. General Hughes had served in the Philippine Islands before this time and been impressed with the service of the Ninth Cavalry and especially Captain Young's troop. Hughes visited Young's I Troop at Blanca Aurora in 1901 and praised the way it had defeated the local insurgency and pacified the residents.[8]

Sgt. William H. Nicholas, a member of I Troop, described General Hughes's visit in a letter. According to Nicholas:

> On or about August 15, 1901, General Hughes was up to inspect the work done by Captain Young. He said to Captain Young: "I have for 3 years been trying to get officers and men to accomplish just this; you are the first one who has been able to locate Blanca Aurora and carry out my orders, and I shall certainly do all that is in my power to recommend

you to the War Department for your good performance of duty as an army officer. I will also see to it that you and your men shall be stationed at some choice post in the U.S. when you return there."

As the department commander with his headquarters in San Francisco in 1902, he was in a position to request that Young's squadron of the Ninth Cavalry be stationed at the Presidio.[9]

Young and his Black troopers were delighted to be assigned to such a choice post. The Presidio of San Francisco was a fort established by the Spanish in 1776 on the headlands above the Golden Gate. The coastal presidio marked the northernmost limit of the American empire established by the Spanish and later transferred to Mexican control in 1821. The Presidio of San Francisco passed to U.S. command during the Mexican-American War in 1846. Thereafter, it was continually garrisoned by U.S. Army soldiers.[10]

In 1902 San Francisco was a city where whites, for the most part, treated Blacks civilly while denying them certain employment opportunities and proportional political power. According to the 1900 U.S. Census, 1,654 Blacks—along with 13,954 Chinese and 1,781 Japanese—lived in the city with a total population of 342,782 people. African Americans in San Francisco gained access to public transportation in 1867, won the right to vote (males only) in 1869, and fought successfully for desegregated schools in 1875. Despite the absence of segregation laws, Blacks still faced significant limitations to what they could expect in housing and civil rights in the city.[11]

According to the *San Francisco Chronicle*, the city had no "regular Negro Quarter"; rather, it had a "peculiar Negro colony." Blacks, "through the unusual conditions here, have turned to the trades and professions, and many have entered into business." The Chinese had already filled the ranks of the servant class, so many Blacks who came in the days after the gold rush of 1849 turned their attention to other pursuits. This resulted, according to the report, in a "small but select class of negroes in the city, some engaged in responsible positions, others in business for themselves." And because real estate was more reasonable across the bay in Oakland, many built homes there. There were still limits to expectations, but far better conditions existed in San Francisco than in Los Angeles, which by then had twice the number of Black residents.[12]

According to J. S. Francis, the editor of the Black weekly newspaper *Western Outlook*, no strong color line was drawn in San Francisco. He noted Blacks had "been allowed to rent in most parts of the city and have been given their chance when they have been willing and able to take it." He noted this was in part due to the "conscious effort on the part of influential members of the race, who have had a certain authority in the matter of regulating immigration." They discouraged the "undesirable element" and welcomed those with "education and general ability."[13]

Considering the conditions, Young and his troopers must have been pleased to enjoy U.S. society again after two years of fighting in the Philippines. San Francisco was a thriving city, the ninth largest in the United States, and by the turn of the century, it had transformed from a lawless frontier town to a major American metropolis. San Francisco served as a leading social, cultural, and economic center for African Americans and had the largest Black population in California until surpassed by Los Angeles in 1900. Lucky for Young and his men, they lived in the city by the bay before it was leveled by the great earthquake of 1906.[14]

Captain Young would soon become familiar with the Barbary Coast, the infamous entertainment district in San Francisco. The Barbary Coast was linked to the waterfront by Pacific Avenue and Broadway Street, and bounded by Stockton, Kearney, Broadway, and Washington Streets. In this area, from "late afternoon until dawn all of the dives were thronged with a motley crew of murderers, thieves, burglars, gamblers, pimps, and degenerates of every description, practically all of whom were busily gunning for the sailors, miners, countrymen, and others who visited the district through curiosity or in search of women and liquor." The Black soldiers of the Ninth would soon become all too familiar with the Barbary Coast.[15]

### *Men of I Troop*

In selecting the Ninth Cavalry Regiment for the plum assignment in San Francisco, General Hughes credited the effectiveness of Captain Young in the Philippine Islands. Yet no troop commander functions in a vacuum. Without an effective first sergeant, successful sergeants, competent corporals, and proficient privates, no cavalry troop can master the rigors of combat or maintain its readiness in garrison. Therefore, it is important to examine who Captain Young and his men were, where they came from, and what made them such an effective team.

A brief narrative of the backgrounds of the members of I Troop provides clues to their effectiveness as a unit. Many had served and fought together for many years as a cohesive cavalry troop. A record of their experiences also serves as a primer of the history of the Buffalo Soldiers, since the members of I Troop had been assigned to all four regiments at various times after the Ninth's establishment in 1866. For more detailed information on certain individuals, short biographies of the I Troop members are provided in appendix B.

### CAPT. CHARLES YOUNG

As noted previously, the commander of I Troop, Capt. Charles Young, was one of only three Black officers then serving in the Regular Army and the only West Point graduate among them. Born enslaved in Mays Lick, Kentucky, in 1864, just one year before the end of the Civil War, Charles Young enjoyed a remarkable early life. His parents escaped enslavement when Charles was six months old, and he grew up in Ripley, Ohio. Young's father, Gabriel Young, served in the Fifth U.S. Colored Heavy Artillery Regiment during the Civil War and passed on to his son an affinity for horses, a love of the army, and a passion for what military service could do for a Black man. He was one of the Black volunteers who paid the price for Buffalo Soldiers to serve in the postwar era. His mother, Arminta Young, was educated and instilled in her son the importance of education and a love of music.[16]

After graduating from an integrated high school and teaching in a Black school in Ripley for a few years, Young won a nomination in 1884 to the U.S. Military Academy at West Point. Enormous hardships, academic challenges, and social ostracism dogged him at West Point, yet he succeeded through a combination of focused intellect, hard work, and a sense of humor. Upon graduation in 1889, the army assigned 2nd Lt. Charles Young to the Ninth U.S. Cavalry, one of the Buffalo Soldier regiments. Young initially served as a second lieutenant assigned to B Troop, and after promotion to first lieutenant in 1896, he was reassigned to I Troop in 1897.[17]

Young acquired some considerable military skills in the thirteen years between his commissioning and arrival at the Presidio. He served on various western frontier posts, at Wilberforce University in Ohio as a professor of military science and tactics, as a commander of a Black Ohio National Guard battalion during the Spanish-American War, and in combat against guerrillas in the Philippine-American War. He established a reputation as an exceptional leader of men and a master of cavalry tactics. Still a bachelor at the age of thirty-eight, Young was at the peak of his company-grade career in 1902.[18]

Captain Young was admired and loved by his Buffalo Soldier troopers, as evidenced by their letters and written accounts. A strict disciplinarian and tough taskmaster, he worked his Black soldiers relentlessly and tolerated no slackers. According to Sergeant Nicholas, upon assignment to the troop, Young "drilled in every form of army tactics, mounted and dismounted, bareback and in the saddle. Sham battles every day, save Sundays and holidays, and at the expiration of one year, every man could ride a horse at break-neck speed taking hurdles, ditches, also crossed stirrups 'Cossack Style,' in fact in every style and fashion to the satisfaction of any cavalry officer in the U.S. Army." He turned I Troop into one of the best outfits in the Ninth Cavalry, earning the grudging respect of every white officer in the regiment.[19]

Apart from Booker T. Washington and W. E. B. DuBois, no other African American at the time possessed more name recognition in the Black press than Charles Young. Both African American West Point graduates before him had fallen: Henry O. Flipper to trumped-up court-martial charges and John H. Alexander to untimely heart disease. After Young, no Black man graduated from West Point for nearly fifty years. Young succeeded in a white man's officer corps, and the Black press eagerly followed his successes from the halls of West Point to the jungles of the Philippines. His name appeared early and often in the white San Francisco newspapers, a sign of his popularity, and continued to do so for the next two years.

### FIRST LT. SAMUEL B. PEARSON

The only other officer in I Troop when it stepped ashore in San Francisco—and the only white man in the unit—was 1st Lt. Samuel Burnette "Sammy" Pearson. Born in San Diego, California, in 1870, Pearson enlisted in the army in 1897 and served in the First U.S. Cavalry as a private, corporal, and sergeant, seeing action during the Spanish-American War in Cuba in the Santiago campaign. He passed his 1899 commissioning examination, earning the bars of a second lieutenant, and was assigned to the Ninth U.S. Cavalry. Pearson's first officer assignment, as a "shavetail" in the soldier slang, was at Fort Duchesne, Utah, with K Troop, Ninth Cavalry.[20]

After his arrival at Fort Duchesne, Pearson began a tight professional relationship and close personal friendship with Young that lasted their lifetimes. He became one of Young's closest white friends. Pearson later commented: "I was his lieutenant for several years and knew him more intimately probably than most others did, and we used to have many intimate personal talks together when he would tell me some of his aspirations and endeavors, and I know that no officer under whom I ever served ever showed me more courtesy and consideration than did Young and I loved him for what he was."[21]

In 1901 while campaigning in the Philippines, newly promoted First Lieutenant Pearson volunteered to serve under Young in I Troop. Sergeant Nicholas reported: "First Lieutenant S.B. Pearson, Ninth Cavalry, made application to the regimental commander to be transferred to Captain Young's troop and assigned to duty as First Lieutenant under Captain Young, of whom he was very fond." Most white officers avoided service with Young, so Pearson's request to serve under the Black officer is remarkable.[22]

Young had shown proof of his friendship with Pearson in the way he treated Pearson's wife, Margaret, whom Samuel had married in 1900 at Fort Duchesne, Utah. Pearson's wife joined him in 1901 in the Philippines at a safe garrison where officers' wives were permitted to join the troop. According to Nicholas: "Lieutenant Pearson's wife was with him and in the meantime became sick with tropical fever. Captain Young gave over his more desirable quarters to Mrs. Pearson and occupied some that were less livable for himself." Pearson admitted that more than once Young gave his quarters to him and his wife with the excuse that "he was a bachelor and never stayed at home anyway except to sleep and any old place would do for that."[23]

Captain Young had a capable first lieutenant in Pearson, one who had experienced both sides of the enlisted-officer divide. Pearson had seen combat in both Cuba and the Philippine Islands and was respected by his African American troopers in the Ninth Cavalry, as evidenced by the endorsement of Sergeant Nicholas. He was the only white officer in I Troop, yet he was ideally suited by temperament to serve under Young in California.

### FIRST SGT. WILLIAM S. JONES

The first sergeant in I Troop when it returned from the Philippines was the old veteran William S. "Jasper" Jones. Born enslaved in Manassas, Virginia, in 1864, the same year as Captain Young, he was the key to good order and discipline in the troop. Jones enlisted in the army in 1882 as an eighteen-year-old in Pittsburgh, Pennsylvania, listing his civilian occupation as laborer. He was initially assigned to K Troop, Ninth Cavalry, stationed in Indian Territory (later Oklahoma). He ended his first five-year enlistment as a troop trumpeter at Fort D. A. Russell, Wyoming.[24]

Jones inked the paperwork for a second enlistment in 1887 and continued as a trumpeter with K Troop. Since Jones signed up for a consecutive enlistment, he was rewarded with a monthly bonus in his pay. While serving at Fort Robinson, Nebraska, he witnessed the arrival of the newly commissioned Second Lieutenant Young in 1889. They served together until Young moved with his troop to Fort Duchesne, Utah, in 1890. Trumpeter Jones completed his second enlistment in November 1890, just a month before the Ninth Cavalry participated in the Pine Ridge Campaign and Wounded Knee, the tragic end of the Indian Wars.[25]

Jasper Jones took his first and only break in military service during the next four years, remaining at Fort Robinson, perhaps employed as a teamster, or "mule skinner," for the army. Civilian life did not suit him, and in 1894 he enrolled again in the army at Fort Robinson and was assigned to I Troop, the unit in which he served for the rest of his military career. Jones joined the troop at Fort Washakie, Wyoming, the only U.S. military post ever named after a Native American. Chief Washakie of the Eastern Shoshones always placed peace and the welfare of his people above all other concerns.[26]

Sergeant Jones deployed to Florida in 1898 with I Troop during the Spanish-American War. The troop remained in port at Tampa with most of the Third Squadron and never saw action in Cuba. Captain Young, then commanding the Ninth Ohio Volunteer Infantry, likewise missed the action in Cuba. In 1899 after the war, the two reunited at Fort Duchesne, Utah, where Young reenlisted and recommended Jones as the first sergeant of I Troop, a leadership position he held for the next fourteen years.[27]

As first sergeant, nicknamed "top sergeant" or "top" in the soldier slang, Jones wore three chevrons with a diamond on his upper shoulder sleeve, making him the senior noncommissioned officer in the troop. Young and Jones shipped off to the Pacific in 1901 and fought together in a brutal guerrilla war for two years. Captain Young reenlisted First Sergeant Jones in the Philippine Islands in 1902, and he continued as the top sergeant in I Troop stateside.[28]

### QUARTERMASTER SGT. GEORGE BROWN

The second-ranking noncommissioned officer in I Troop was Quartermaster (QM) Sgt. George Brown. Born in 1856 in Rutherford County, Tennessee, in the pre–Civil War South, he enlisted as a twenty-two-year-old former hostler in Nashville in 1879. Brown served initially with the Twenty-Fourth Infantry, which was then stationed in Texas monitoring the Comanches and Kiowas. He completed his first enlistment with Company F, Twenty-Fourth Infantry in 1884 at Fort Elliott, Texas.[29]

After a two-week break in service as a civilian, Brown reenlisted in 1884 at Fort Leavenworth, Kansas, and was assigned to I Troop, Ninth Cavalry, the unit with which he would serve for all but the last part of a very long career. Since he signed up again within three months, he earned a bonus increase in his pay for consecutive assignments. Initially stationed at Fort Reno, Indian Territory, Brown later moved with I Troop by horse and rail to Fort Niobrara, Nebraska, in 1885 when the regiment took up its new station in the Department of the Platte.[30]

Private Brown closed out his second enlistment in 1889 at Fort Robinson and reenlisted a week later, again earning a bonus in monthly pay. He continued to serve with I Troop and was on hand when Second Lieutenant Young arrived at the post in 1889. The regiment was still mourning the April 1889 death of Col. Edward Hatch, who had commanded the Ninth since its creation in 1866. During his third enlistment, Brown assumed the duties of trumpeter, serving alongside Trumpeter Jasper Jones in I Troop at Fort Robinson. He was with I Troop when it marched in December 1890 to support the Seventh U.S. Cavalry at Wounded Knee, South Dakota, during the Indian Wars.[31]

Trumpeter Brown completed his enlistment at Fort Robinson in 1894 and signed up for another tour after a few days' break as a civilian. He moved with I Troop to its new station at Fort Washakie, Wyoming, soon after he reenlisted. During his fourth term, Brown was appointed the troop farrier, responsible for trimming and shoeing the I Troop horses. He ended his enlistment at Fort Washakie in 1897 as a farrier and signed up again without a break in service.[32]

Brown deployed in 1898 with I Troop to Tampa, Florida, during the Spanish-American War but saw no action. When I Troop redeployed west after the war, it took up its new duty station at Fort Duchesne, Utah. Brown was appointed the troop quartermaster sergeant in 1898 and was still serving as such when Young arrived in the troop the fall of 1899. As quartermaster sergeant, Brown was responsible for the troop's transportation, animals, forage, fuel, clothing, equipage, barracks, storehouses, and property. His badge of rank was three chevrons topped by a horizontal bar, and the soldiers called him "QM" in the army slang. Brown served as quartermaster sergeant throughout the Philippine campaign, returning with I Troop to San Francisco in 1902.[33]

### TRUMPETER FRANK MCKENZIE

Trumpeter Frank McKenzie was one of two bandsmen assigned to I Troop when it landed in San Francisco in 1902. Born at Fort Wingate, New Mexico Territory, in 1874, McKenzie was eighteen when he enlisted at Fort Robinson, Nebraska, in 1892. His birthplace and place of enlistment point to his military lineage: his father, Edward McKenzie, was also a Buffalo Soldier. And the enlistment officer assigned the younger McKenzie to E Troop, Ninth Cavalry, the same regiment in which his father had served for the past nineteen years.[34]

Frank's father was already an old soldier when his son enlisted. Born in New Orleans, Louisiana, in 1845, Edward McKenzie joined the Buffalo Soldiers shortly after they were formed, enlisting in Company E, Fortieth U.S. Infantry in Boston, Massachusetts, in 1866. When the four Black infantry regiments combined into two following an army force structure reduction in 1869, he became a founding member of the new Company G, Twenty-Fourth Infantry. He ended his first enlistment in 1869 as a private serving as part of the occupation of the South on Ship Island, Mississippi.[35]

After a short break in service to visit home, the elder McKenzie signed up again in Boston in 1870 for a five-year tour and was assigned to Company E, Twenty-Fourth Infantry. He ended his second enlistment in 1875 as a corporal at Fort Concho, Texas. After a two-month break in service, he showed up at the enlistment center at San Antonio to sign up again, listing his occupation as laborer. The enlistment officer assigned him to I Troop, Ninth Cavalry, the unit in which he would serve for the balance of his long career. He was serving as a sergeant on this fifth enlistment when his son, Frank, joined the Ninth in 1892.[36]

The younger McKenzie, originally assigned to E Troop, transferred in 1895 to I Troop, Ninth Cavalry, where his father still served as a sergeant. Frank completed his first enlistment in 1897 at Fort Washakie, Wyoming, as the troop trumpeter and reenlisted for another tour. He was with the troop to celebrate the retirement of his father Christmas Eve 1897 after thirty-one years as a Buffalo Soldier, the last twenty-two years in I Troop. Frank McKenzie continued to serve in I Troop, Ninth Cavalry for the next ten years.[37]

Trumpeter McKenzie deployed with I Troop to Tampa, Florida, in 1898 during the Spanish-American War but saw no combat. After the unit moved to its new station at Fort Duchesne, Utah, he was there to welcome Lieutenant Young to I Troop in 1899. He reenlisted in 1900 and deployed the following year to the Philippines. McKenzie still served as the trumpeter, known as the "windjammer" in the soldier slang, when the troop redeployed to California in 1902.[38]

### SADDLER ALFRED MAJOR

Alfred Major was one of the longest-serving men in the Ninth Cavalry when he arrived with I Troop in San Francisco. Born in 1857 in Accomack County, Virginia, Major enlisted in 1879 in Baltimore, Maryland, listing his occupation as sailor. He was born free, the son of a sailor who was often away at sea and a mother who worked as a washerwoman. Major enlisted two days before his older brother, John, and both were assigned to C Troop, Ninth Cavalry by the enlisting officer. His brother deserted in 1881, but Alfred Major served out his first term in 1884 at Fort Sill, Indian Territory.[39]

After a two-week visit to the East Coast, Major enlisted again in 1884 in Washington DC, thus retaining his reenlistment bonus and higher pay.

The enlistment officer assigned him to I Troop, Ninth U.S. Cavalry, still stationed in Indian Territory. He rotated with the regiment in the summer of 1885 when it moved north to Fort Robinson, Nebraska. The Ninth Cavalry then took on the mission of monitoring the Lakotas and fighting the closing battles of the Indian Wars.[40]

Major reenlisted in early February 1889 at Fort Robinson as the troop saddler, the man responsible for maintaining the unit's tack. Thirty-two years old and in his third enlistment, he was serving at Fort Robinson when 2nd Lt. Charles Young arrived from West Point in November 1889. Major signed up again in 1894 and accompanied his unit to Fort Washakie, Wyoming, during a periodic rotation of Ninth Cavalry troops. He deployed with I Troop to Tampa during the Spanish-American War but saw no combat and moved with his troop to Fort Duchesne, Utah, after the conflict.[41]

Soon after his fifth enlistment in early 1899 at Fort Duchesne, he turned forty-two, having served twenty-years in the army. Major would have been called "old issue," army slang for a very old soldier, by the younger soldiers in the troop. He was present when First Lieutenant Young arrived at Fort Duchesne to report to his new assignment with I Troop in the fall of 1899. Major was seven years older than Young, yet both were superb riders and shared a love of horses.[42]

Major shipped out to the Philippine Islands with I Troop in 1901 and served as the saddler throughout the campaign. The Ninth Cavalry took their horses with them to the Philippines, but much of the campaigning was done on foot because of the terrain and mission. The horses suffered terribly from disease on the islands and had to be left behind when the Ninth redeployed to the United States. According to Sergeant Nicholas, I Troop "lost 75 per cent of the horses and mules to the disease Surra." This disease of domesticated animals is transmitted by biting insects and causes uncontrollable bleeding. Major reenlisted in the Philippines and returned to San Francisco in late 1902 with I Troop, still the saddler.[43]

### SGT. WILSON CARY

Sgt. Wilson Cary served as one of I Troop's six sergeants on arrival in San Francisco. Born in 1876 in Orange, Virginia, he was one of the second generation of Buffalo Soldiers born after the Civil War. Cary enlisted in Baltimore, Maryland, in 1898, just two months before the outbreak of the Spanish-American War, and was assigned to K Troop, Tenth U.S. Cavalry. He fought with the Tenth in Cuba and participated in the Santiago campaign. Cary was discharged in February 1899 during the postwar reduction of the army.[44]

Cary returned to civilian life briefly, then he reenlisted in Cincinnati, Ohio, in 1899. The enlistment officer assigned Cary to I Troop, Ninth Cavalry. Since he signed the paperwork for another enlistment within three months of his discharge, he retained his reenlistment bonus and earned additional pay for the consecutive years served after his initial enlistment. The army provided transportation back to the point of the soldier's initial enlistment, so many soldiers considered this a paid leave to visit family and friends. Once the ex-soldier ran out of money, he reenlisted, and the army funded his return, often to the same unit he had just left.[45]

Cary arrived at his new posting at Fort Duchesne at about the time Young joined I Troop as a first lieutenant in 1899. The troop was then commanded by Capt. John F. Guilfoyle, who had been assigned to the Ninth Cavalry since his graduation from West Point in 1877. Guilfoyle, saddled with the responsibilities commanding the post at Fort Duchesne, turned over I Troop to Young. Sergeant Nicholas remembered Guilfoyle saying of Young: "He is an intelligent officer, and I am going to give him full command of the troop to do as he sees fit."[46]

Captain Young and First Sergeant Jones recognized Cary's leadership potential. He deployed with I Troop to the Philippine Islands, served with distinction under challenging circumstances, and was rewarded with the stripes of a sergeant. Captain Young gave Sergeant Cary an excellent character rating when he ended his term in 1902 and personally signed his reenlistment papers. By the time of their deployment to San Francisco, Cary served as one of I Troop's six sergeants.[47]

### SGT. WILLIAM H. NICHOLAS

Sgt. William H. "Nick" Nicholas was another of Young's sergeants in I Troop on its return from the Philippines. Born in 1876 in Charlottesville, Virginia, Nicholas enlisted in Richmond, Virginia, in 1897, recording his occupation as messenger. The enlistment officer, who described Nicholas as a "light mulatto," assigned him to I Troop, Ninth Cavalry, then stationed at Fort Washakie, Wyoming. He deployed with the regiment to Florida at the outbreak of the Spanish-American War, but I Troop remained at the Port of Tampa and never saw action.[48]

Nicholas entrained with I Troop when it returned to its new peacetime station at Fort Duchesne in 1898. Soon after the arrival of Lieutenant Young in 1899, Nicholas was promoted to corporal and appointed his troop clerk. Along with Sergeant Cary, Nicholas was among the second generation of better-educated Buffalo Soldiers born after the Civil War. Young promoted Nicholas to sergeant and reenlisted him for another term in 1900.[49]

Nicholas deployed with I Troop to the Philippines and served as a sergeant for Captain Young through two years of tough campaigning. He later provided a detailed account of some of the most challenging combat actions on the island of Samar, especially the weeklong running gun battle the troop fought in boats up the Gandara River. It was this action and Young's subsequent peaceful pacification of the local population that so impressed General Hughes and influenced the troop's assignment to the Presidio of San Francisco in 1902.[50]

### SGT. SAMUEL PIERCE

One of the younger noncommissioned officers to arrive with I Troop in San Francisco was Sgt. Samuel "Swamp" Pierce. Pierce was born in 1881 in Washington DC, where he enlisted at age seventeen in 1898, lying about his age. Like Cary and Nicholas, he was among the new generation of better-educated Buffalo Soldiers born after the Civil War. Assigned to I Troop, Ninth Cavalry by the enlistment officer, he joined the unit at Fort Washakie, Wyoming. He deployed to Florida in April 1898 during the Spanish-American War and, like the rest of I Troop, saw no action in Cuba.[51]

After the war, Pierce moved with his unit to the new posting at Fort Duchesne, Utah. He was still a private in the fall of 1899 when I Troop welcomed Lieutenant Young to the post. Shortly after he took over the troop, Young recognized Pierce's leadership ability, and by the end of his first enlistment, he wore the two chevrons of a corporal on his upper sleeves.[52]

Corporal Pierce reenlisted in 1901 at Fort Duchesne and deployed with I Troop to the Philippines; there, he acquired the nickname "Swamp," which is attributed by Young in his 1916 letter to Joe Clark. By the time the troop redeployed to San Francisco, Pierce wore the three stripes of a sergeant. Beginning at Fort Duchesne and continuing through their service together in the Philippines, Sergeants Pierce and Nicholas formed a friendship that lasted their lifetimes.[53]

### SGT. JOHN L. MALONE

Sgt. John L. Malone, born in 1873 in Mocksville, North Carolina, was one of Young's former sergeants when they landed in California. Malone enlisted as a twenty-one-year-old in 1894 in Jonesborough, Tennessee, listing his occupation as farmer. The enlistment officer assigned Malone to I Troop, Ninth U.S. Cavalry, and he joined the troop at Fort Washakie, Wyoming, where he completed his first term as a private.[54]

Malone, who listed his height as six feet when he reenlisted at Fort Washakie in 1897, deployed with I Troop to Florida during the Spanish-American War. After seeing no combat, he spent several months recuperating from a tropical illness in a military hospital. He redeployed with his troop to its new peacetime garrison at Fort Duchesne in late 1898, where Young appointed him a corporal in 1900. By the end of his second term in November 1900, he wore the three chevrons of a sergeant.[55]

Sometime before he deployed with Young and I Troop to the Philippines in 1901, Malone was busted to private and served as such throughout two years of campaigning on the island. He was still a private when he redeployed to San Francisco in late 1902, though soon after arrival he earned his sergeant stripes again.[56]

### CPL. GEORGE W. FEARINGTON

Cpl. George W. Fearington was another of I Troop's young noncommissioned officers on arrival in California. Born in 1874 in Durham, North Carolina, Fearington enlisted in Lexington, Kentucky, in 1892, registering his occupation as laborer. The enlistment officer assigned Fearington to I Troop, Ninth Cavalry, which was then situated at Fort Robinson, Nebraska.[57]

Fearington ended his first enlistment with I Troop at Fort Washakie in 1897 as a private. He signed up for another term, and by the end of his enlistment at Fort Duchesne in 1900, Captain Young rewarded Fearington with the two stripes of a corporal. He redeployed with I Troop to California after serving for two years in the Philippines as a noncommissioned officer wearing corporal stripes.[58]

### COOK JOSEPH R. TAYLOR

One of two cooks in Young's troop when it arrived in San Francisco, Joseph R. Taylor was born in 1874 in Whitfield, Alabama. He enlisted in 1898 in Tuskegee, Alabama, listing his occupation as carpenter. The Black recruiting officer, Chaplain George W. Prioleau of the Ninth Cavalry, assigned Taylor to I Troop. Captain Young and Chaplain Prioleau were close friends, both having served at Wilberforce University together. Private Taylor joined his new troop at Tampa, where it was stationed during the Spanish-American War.[59]

Taylor traveled to the troop's new home station at Fort Duchesne, Utah, after the war and deployed with the regiment to the Philippines. Captain Young reenlisted him in the midst of the hard fighting up the Gandara River on Samar Island. At some point during his Philippine service, Young designated Taylor one of the troop's cooks, earning him the pay and privileges of a noncommissioned officer, a position he held upon arrival in California.[60]

### PRIVATES OF I TROOP

Another of the enlisted soldiers of I Troop who arrived in San Francisco in 1902 with I Troop was Pvt. Dock Smelly. Born in Randolph, Alabama, in 1877, Smelly enlisted in Cleveland, Ohio, in 1898. The enlisting officer assigned Smelly to I Troop, Ninth Cavalry. He may have seen something special in Smelly, despite his five-foot-four size and unfortunate name; he turned out to be a fine soldier and superb athlete.[61]

Smelly joined the unit at Fort Washakie, Wyoming, and deployed with I Troop to Tampa, Florida, where he remained during the Spanish-American War. After I Troop's move to Fort Duchesne, Utah, Lieutenant Young reenlisted Private Smelly for another term. He served during the unit's deployment in the Philippines and was a member of the contingent sent back to San Francisco for two months in 1901 to care for the troop's horses. By the time the Ninth arrived in San Francisco, he was a candidate for a future leadership position and one of the finest horsemen in I Troop.

One other enlisted soldier to land with I Troop in San Francisco was Pvt. Herbert Taylor. Born in 1880 in Dinwiddie County, Virginia, Taylor first served as a volunteer during the Spanish-American War. He was a member of Company F, Sixth Virginia Volunteer Infantry, which mustered into federal service in 1898, too late to see action during the war. After his unit mustered out in 1899, he enlisted in the army in Richmond, Virginia. He was one of at least six soldiers in I Troop who had served during the Spanish-American War as a volunteer and, once the war ended, decided to join the Regular Army.[62]

The recruiting officer assigned Taylor to I Troop, Ninth Cavalry, then at Fort Duchesne, Utah. Taylor was present at Fort Duchesne when the U.S. Census of 1900 was tallied, and he reported to the enumerator, 2nd Lt. Samuel Pearson, that both his parents were born in Africa. Nothing is known about how and when Taylor's parents arrived in the United States, but he was the only soldier registered in I Troop who was a first-generation American of African descent.[63]

Private Taylor completed his enlistment at Tabaco in the Philippines and was discharged in February 1902. He enlisted again four days later in the shadow of the Volcano Mayon, which had erupted five years earlier, killing more than thirteen hundred people. Assigned again to I Troop, he continued to serve as a private when the Ninth Cavalry rotated back to the United States later the same year.[64]

One of the most unlikely soldiers to arrive in San Francisco with I Troop was Pvt. Abner "Peggy" Jones. Born in Columbus, Ohio, in 1883, Jones never wanted to be a soldier. He began his life in the army as a civilian cook for 1st Lt. Charles Young sometime before his arrival at Fort Duchesne, Utah, in 1899. It is possible Young employed him during his service with the Ninth Ohio Volunteers during the Spanish-American War, since the unit mustered into service in Columbus.[65]

Captain Young took Jones with him as his civilian cook when he deployed from Fort Duchesne, Utah, to the Philippines in 1901. Having no training as a soldier, Jones fell from the ship in the Philippines and had to be fished out of the water. Because the army forbade the employment of U.S. civilians in the war zone, Young had to enlist Jones as a private in the army in May 1901 in Calbayog, Philippine Islands. Sergeant Nicholas noted in a letter that Young assumed guardianship of Jones to enlist him in the Philippines, since he was not yet eighteen years old.[66]

According to Sergeant Nicholas, as a soldier, Jones continued to serve as Young's cook. But by 1902 in San Joaquin, per Nicholas, "he became somewhat undisciplined and the Captain ordered First Sergeant Jasper Jones to put him to straight and full duty." Captain Young thereafter employed a Chinese cook, who, Nicholas pronounced, "was an excellent one." The other soldiers in I Troop disliked soldiers who worked for officers, referring to them derisively as "dog robbers," thus Private Jones's demotion to the ranks was likely a painful one. Jones arrived in San Francisco in 1902 on the lowest rung of the enlisted ladder in I Troop.[67]

When Charles Young's I Troop landed stateside in October 1902, it was considered one of the best-led and most proficient cavalry units in the Ninth Cavalry. Commanded by the only Black graduate of West Point who was still serving and led by a cadre of long-serving Buffalo Soldier noncommissioned officers, I Troop had proven itself in combat in the Philippines and garnered an assignment to the Presidio for its efforts. Captain Young and I Troop would add laurels to their martial achievements during the next two years in California.

# 3

## Settling In

> The Ninth Cavalry is a colored regiment, and Troop I is commanded by Captain Young, the only colored graduate of West Point in the service.
> —*San Francisco Chronicle*, November 8, 1902

The year 1902 marked the first time the War Department garrisoned the Presidio of San Francisco with African American troops. This was also the first occasion the Buffalo Soldiers had been stationed in a major metropolitan area on the West Coast. Young and his troop were on notice to comport to a garrison routine that the military leadership of the post as well as the people and press of San Francisco would intensely scrutinize.

### *I Troop Organization*

The organization and strength of a cavalry troop in 1902 was straightforward. At full strength, a cavalry troop, like an infantry company, was authorized one captain, one first lieutenant, and one second lieutenant. The captain, referred to as the "Old Man" by the soldiers, commanded the troop while assisted by his lieutenants. Cavalry troops routinely served shorthanded, with officers away on detached duty, which was any duty away from their assigned troop and regiment. When I Troop arrived in San Francisco, Young filled the captain's billet, Pearson served as the first lieutenant, and the second lieutenant position in the troop was vacant and remained so for the next two years.[1]

A cavalry troop in 1902 had sixty-five enlisted men: one first sergeant, one quartermaster sergeant, six sergeants, six corporals, two cooks, two farriers and blacksmiths, one saddler, one wagoner, two trumpeters, and forty-three privates. Among the noncommissioned officers, the first sergeant ran the troop for the commander, the quartermaster sergeant kept track of the unit's property, the sergeants led the six sections, and the corporals handled the squads. In support of the troop, cooks prepared meals, farriers shoed the horses' hooves, blacksmiths forged horseshoes, saddlers cared for the saddles, wagoners operated the wagons, and trumpeters regulated the day with calls. The privates obeyed orders and endured countless hours of stable duty, guard duty, drills, training, and inspections.[2]

The two assigned cooks deserve special mention since the status of their profession in the U.S. Army had recently changed. For most of the nineteenth century, cooking duties had rotated among the soldiers in the troops with predictably bad results. This changed as a lesson learned during the Spanish-American War, where the lack of food safety contributed to thousands of illnesses and deaths. In 1899 Congress authorized two cooks per troop, and they received training and sergeants' pay and privileges, which included stripes on their uniform trouser legs. After 1899 cooks had a profession and soldiers better food. The I Troop cooks had a copy of the *Manual for Army Cooks*, published in 1896, full of methods and recipes.[3]

First Sergeant Jones used Trumpeter McKenzie's M1892 trumpet (G trumpet with F slide) to control the rhythm of the daily life of the I Troop's soldiers. The trumpeter started the day with reveille, followed by assembly, surgeon's call, and breakfast call. After breakfast he would deliver the familiar calls for reports, roll calls, guard mounts, stable call, mounted drill, and other details. He would signal dinner call at lunchtime, stable call again in the afternoon, and, at the end of the duty day, attention, assembly, and retreat. After supper, taps would signal lights out and time for the soldiers to sleep. Like the cooks, the trumpeter received higher pay than the privates and wore leadership stripes on his trouser legs.[4]

By army regulation, company noncommissioned officers were chosen "by the regimental commander upon the recommendation of the troop commander." However, most troops operated separately, and the troop commander made the day-to-day decisions on noncommissioned officer leadership positions. Captains such as Young often served more than a decade as a troop commander and knew their men extremely well.[5]

The first sergeant ran the day-to-day operations of a cavalry troop. He and the sergeants and corporals in the troop, known collectively as the noncommissioned officers, or noncoms, did much to shape the effectiveness of a unit. While Young might command the troop, as a commissioned officer, he was separated from his enlisted soldiers by a strict and well-understood social barrier. The first sergeant, on the other hand, came up through the ranks from private to corporal to sergeant and knew the soldiers and their lives intimately.

The pay of new enlisted soldiers was meager; privates collected only thirteen dollars a month, which was the same rate paid to Union privates in the Civil War. Trumpeters also made thirteen dollars monthly, though a chief trumpeter collected twenty-two dollars. Next in line came wagoners, who received fourteen dollars a month, and corporals, saddlers, blacksmiths, and farriers, who were paid fifteen dollars a month. Cooks, so recently elevated in status, collected eighteen dollars a month, the same wage as a sergeant or quartermaster sergeant. And the highest-paid noncommissioned officer in the company was the first sergeant, who was paid the sum of twenty-five dollars each month.[6]

Yet one must add to this base pay the other benefits soldiers serving in the army received. The army provided the soldier a barracks in which to live, food to eat, uniforms to wear, medical treatment, access to the old soldiers' home, and burial services for those who died on active duty. Longer-serving soldiers earned additional pay, called retained pay, for consecutive years served after their initial enlistment if they reenlisted within three months of the end of their last term. And an enlisted man who served thirty years could retire and receive 75 percent of his pay in the rank in which he retired for the rest of his life.[7]

The monthly pay of the first-term privates in I Troop was far from princely at thirteen dollars in cash. Still, a Black cavalry private earned the same as his white infantry and artillery counterparts at the Presidio, something quite unheard of elsewhere in society. According to one source, the soldier's monthly pay of thirteen dollars could go far at a time of ten-cent beer, twenty-five-cent whiskey, nickel cigars, quarter dances, and a two-dollar session with a prostitute.[8]

### *Reorganization*

One of the first things the Ninth Cavalry undertook upon arrival in October 1902 was to reorganize and refit. After the Philippine-American War, returning stateside army units were forced to stand down, release soldiers eligible for discharge, and fill the gaps created in the enlisted ranks. So the first task Captain Young and First Sergeant Jones faced was to bid farewell to soldiers ending their service.

The process of reorganization began while I Troop still lived under canvas in the Infantry Cantonment. As was the case after previous wars, the army offered soldiers who had served their terms honorably the option of ending their enlistments early. Under War Department General Order 108, which required the army to reduce its wartime numbers, the following members of I Troop were discharged from the army in November 1902: Sgt. James L. Drew and Privates Abner Jones, Jefferson Parker, Joseph Taylor, Jesse Jones, Robert Lenox, Ed Simpson, Oscar Redmond, William Coleman, Lewis W. Wilson, William Burr, Alfred W. Wright, and Silas Scott. Of these thirteen, only Taylor, a cook, enlisted for another term. This twelve-man loss constituted a significant cut for a cavalry troop authorized sixty-five enlisted men, though I Troop arrived in San Francisco the previous month overstrength with an aggregate total of ninety-five enlisted men.[9]

Some in I Troop were too sick to continue performing regular duties in the army. Soldiers had been exposed to various diseases in the Philippines, including cholera, dengue, malaria, and beriberi. Pvt. William H. Lloyd, a laborer from Tennessee who enlisted in 1900, was among twenty-five enlisted members of the Ninth Cavalry who were still hospitalized for illnesses. Captain Young discharged Lloyd "for the good of the service" in November 1902. Two others, Privates Samuel White and James Daniel, had also been hospitalized and were discharged on disability in November. One other, Pvt. William Hamilton, was sent to Fort Bayard, New Mexico Territory, to recuperate from his illness. Fort Bayard housed the army general hospital dedicated to treating officers and soldiers for tuberculosis.[10]

### *Deserters*

In addition to this organized reduction of manpower in I Troop, four men deserted soon after they set foot on U.S. soil. Cpl. Schuyler C. Black and Pvt. Charles Price deserted on November 9, Pvt. Eugene F. Lane on

November 10, and Pvt. Edward A. Williams on November 15, 1902. Young dropped all four soldiers from the rolls at the end of the month. Since only two other soldiers from the entire regiment deserted in November 1902, this was especially embarrassing for Captain Young. Thereafter, the Ninth had one man desert in October and one in December 1902.[11]

Why did these soldiers desert? Soldiers going absent without leave (AWOL), or "French leave" in soldier slang, was a growing problem in the army in 1902. The desertion rate in the year ending in 1900 was 3.2 percent; in 1901, 7.5 percent; and in 1902, 11 percent. One department commander named two principal causes for the increase in desertions: "first, resentment to unaccustomed limitation and restrictions felt by men returning from field service [i.e., Philippine-American War] to the monotony of routine work of garrison life; second, the abolition of the canteen feature of the post exchange."[12]

Reacting to pressure by the Woman's Christian Temperance Union, congressional legislation in 1901 forced the War Department to eliminate post canteens, where soldiers previously could enjoy a few glasses of beer or wine in a controlled environment. According to the department commander, this led the soldiers outside the boundaries of the reservations to seek saloons that were run by "unprincipled scoundrels who leave nothing undone to debauch the soldiers and obtain their money." Prior to deploying to the Philippines in 1901, the Ninth Cavalry had allowed a post canteen to operate at Fort Duchene, Utah, that First Sergeant Jones and his noncommissioned officers had supervised.[13]

The specific reasons for the men's desertions are not known. Nearly two years of continuous guerrilla war against the Filipinos was almost certainly a contributor, and the sudden freedom from the combat zone was perhaps too tempting to resist. The allure of the dance halls and saloons of the city's infamous Barbary Coast was likely the spark that caused the soldiers to go absent on French leave. According to First Sergeant Jones, the soldiers of I Troop were "paid off" on November 5, 1902, collecting their monthly pay. Liquored-up soldiers with money in their pockets do not always make good decisions after a night of carousing.[14]

Who were the deserting soldiers? The first was Cpl. Schuyler Black, a thirty-three-year-old, third-term soldier from Alabama who was initially assigned to I Troop in 1898. After the Spanish-American War, he was discharged in 1899 as a private with a good character rating. Following a three-week break in service, he reenlisted and was assigned to the Twenty-Fifth Infantry, serving in the Philippines until 1902. He enlisted a third time the same year and was assigned again to I Troop, which he joined in the Philippines. That a third-term soldier who had been awarded corporal stripes by Captain Young would go AWOL is puzzling.[15]

Since Pvt. Charles Price went AWOL the same day as Corporal Black, they may have deserted together. Price was a thirty-two-year-old, second-term soldier born in Franklin County, Virginia. He, like Black, enlisted in 1898 and was assigned to I Troop. Given that he and Black both trained at the recruitment center, joined I Troop at the same time, spent their initial tours as bunkmates, and served the closing actions in the Philippine War side by side, it is not surprising that these two, for reasons known only to themselves, likely left together.[16]

The motives for Private Lane's desertion on November 10 seem clear. Lane, a twenty-four-year-old from Mobile, Alabama, enlisted in March 1901 and joined I Troop in the Philippines. Soon after his arrival in the combat zone, he spent four months hospitalized on two occasions and received a general court-martial between those stays. The nature of his illness and the reason for his court-martial are unknown, yet he was likely an unhappy and unhealthy soldier when he arrived in San Francisco. That he deserted at the first opportunity is not surprising.[17]

The final soldier to take French leave, Pvt. Edward A. Williams, had been in the army less than nine months. Williams, a thirty-year-old born in Warrington, Florida, enlisted in Houston, Texas, in early 1900, listing his occupation as cook. He joined I Troop in the Philippines and took the first chance to desert once he reached U.S. soil. Perhaps he was one of many soldiers who joined the army to get away from home, travel west, and desert at the first opportunity.[18]

Added to the twelve men who ended their enlistments and the four who left due to sickness, the four deserters brought the total losses in I Troop to twenty enlisted men. The reduction in manpower constituted a substantial shortfall for Captain Young, First Sergeant Jones, and the noncommissioned officers of the troop. These leaders faced the task of reorganizing to fill the gaps in the ranks to maintain the reputation of I Troop in the Ninth Cavalry. More losses were in the offing.

*Shooting Incident*

November was an exceptionally challenging month for the leadership of I Troop. Two days before Corporal Black and Private Price deserted, one of Young's soldiers shot his tentmate. The shooting and its aftermath played out during the rest of the month and was headline news in the San Francisco newspapers.

The *San Francisco Examiner* on Saturday, November 8, 1902, headlined, "Cavalryman Is Shot in His Tent." A reporter described the scene:

> Sleeping soldiers of I Troop, colored, Ninth Cavalry, at the Presidio, were awakened yesterday morning by the report of a rifle shot fired by a member of the troop at his comrade. At that early hour some of the troopers were astir, and they quickly caught Corporal Walter Lockett, rifle in hand, standing over the crouching form of [Cpl.] George W. Fearington, who was gasping for breath and clutching spasmodically at a wound in his left breast.
>
> As told later by a tentmate of the two men, Lockett made a cowardly attack upon Fearington.
>
> "Wake Up!" he growled at his comrade, at the same time dropping a cartridge into his rifle. He then raised the weapon to his shoulder and held the muzzle close to Fearington, who still lay upon his back upon the tent floor bed.
>
> An inarticulate sound escaped from the drowsy trooper, who failed to move in response to the demand.
>
> Hardly were the words spoken by Lockett when he pulled the trigger, and a Krag-Jorgensen bullet pierced the breast of the prostrate soldier, entering at the apex of the lung and penetrating the shoulder blade. The projectile came out in the soldier's back, cut a clean hole through the tent floor, and embedded itself in the earth beneath.
>
> There were five other troopers in the tent, two of whom—Privates Silas Scott and Edward Simpson—witnessed the shooting. First Sergeant Jones happened to be passing the tent when the shot was fired and he looked in, thinking that a rifle had been discharged accidentally while the men were dressing. He saw Lockett with the rifle and Fearington shot on the floor. Scott and Simpson made a statement of the crime, and upon it Lockett was placed under arrest.[19]

First Sergeant Jones told the reporter there had been a fight between Lockett and Fearington over a gambling dispute the night before and that the former had been drunk. He said the troop had been "paid off Wednesday, and the boys had their back pay." All the witnesses agreed that Lockett shot his tentmate while he was asleep. Fearington told the first sergeant, "Lockett fouled me," meaning he was "not given a chance to stand up and fight for his life."[20]

According to one newspaper account, Fearington and Lockett had visited the Barbary Coast district and "liberally patronized the saloons" in that section of the city. The two "found their way back to camp at about 4:30 o'clock in the morning." The shooting, according to this account, occurred just after the first call for reveille.[21]

Another newspaper noted that I Troop was commanded by Captain Young, "the only colored graduate of West Point." He observed "his troop has always enjoyed a splendid reputation for discipline and good behavior." The article stated that both Farrington and Lockett had ten years of service and excellent records. It added the two had served in Cuba and the Philippines, and "were tentmates for many years." Lockett and Fearington had been corporals together at Fort Duchesne before their deployment to the Philippines.[22]

First Lt. Samuel Pearson was the first officer on the scene. Pearson reported that both Fearington and Lockett were good soldiers, and "there was not a mark against them." He refused to give any details, pending an official investigation, but admitted he heard the shot and was the first officer to arrive. Pearson recounted Lockett's story that "his carbine accidentally discharged while he was lying under his blankets." When Pearson arrived, soldiers were dragging Lockett out of the tent, and Fearington lay on the floor, bleeding from his chest wound.[23]

Fearington survived the grievous wound and was back to full duty the following month. After Lockett was arrested and locked in the guard house, Captain Young forwarded charges to the post commander, who convened a general court-martial. A proceeding a month later found Lockett guilty of the charge of assault with the intent to kill and sentenced him to a dishonorable discharge and ten years' imprisonment at Alcatraz Island, a military prison that would not host civilian convicts for another thirty-two years. No motive for the shooting came out in the trial, but First Sergeant Jones was probably right to blame an argument over gambling fueled by alcohol.[24]

*Criminal Incidents*

Several other crimes involving Black soldiers and ex-soldiers made headlines in the newspapers in the months following the Fearington shooting. Newspapers in this era were inclined to run negative stories about African Americans committing crimes and rarely ran stories with a positive slant. Captain Young and the entire command at the Presidio did their best to offset negative publicity with constructive outreach to the local community and cooperation in law enforcement matters.

Just two days after the I Troop shooting, a newspaper reported on a former Black soldier who stabbed a man during a quarrel. The reporter noted that "James Fleming, who once shot a comrade and escaped punishment, is again in trouble." Fleming and another Black man named George Saddler "engaged in a quarrel over a woman," and during the argument, the latter received a minor cut to the abdomen. Fleming was a former member of the Black Forty-Eighth U.S. Volunteer Infantry who had been court-martialed in the Philippines for drunkenness on duty and threatening to shoot a noncommissioned officer. Sentenced to discharge and five years' hard labor, his conviction had been later overturned on a technicality, and he had been released from Alcatraz in May 1902.[25]

In mid-November, a tabloid reported that a Black porter named Arthur Oliver slashed a Black trooper of the Ninth on the arm. Oliver, employed by a barber named Charles Doherty on Fourth Street, was enjoying the company of two women in a saloon on Pacific Street when two troopers "dropped in and tried to 'cop' his sweethearts. This aroused the porter's ire so that he drew a razor and slashed at the soldiers, cutting one of them severely on the arm." The authorities locked Oliver in the city prison and charged him with assault with a deadly weapon. The soldiers were not named.[26]

Finally, in December 1902, a paper reported that a former Black soldier named Ernest Best was arrested for purse snatching. Miss Madge Rust, described as a graduate of the University of California, was walking down Sutter Street when Best snatched her purse and ran. Rust's screams attracted the attention of two soldiers and a civilian who gave chase. Best was caught, arrested, and later sentenced to one year at San Quentin Prison. Ernest Best was a former member of M Troop, Ninth Cavalry, and had been discharged in November 1902.[27]

The headlines covering these incidents proved an embarrassment for Captain Young and the leadership of the Ninth Cavalry at the Presidio. Newly arrived in San Francisco, they were keen to make a positive impression on the citizens of their new host city. The negative publicity surrounding these cases was detrimental, especially when they involved Black soldiers and former soldiers preying on white citizens.

### *New Barracks*

Most of the members of the Third Squadron, Ninth Cavalry stayed out of trouble and were happy to trade the soggy tents of the Infantry Cantonment for the new brick barracks on the main post. The three troops of the Third Squadron—K, L, and M Troops, which arrived on the first ship from the Philippines—moved from the tent camp to the main post of the Presidio at the end of October 1902. Since I Troop arrived on the second ship on October 31, they did not move into the new barracks until mid-November.[28]

The four troops of the Ninth, about three hundred officers and enlisted troopers, shared the main post with five companies of coast artillery and four batteries of field artillery. Coast artillery manned the big, fixed guns at the Presidio, and the field artillery crewed the smaller guns pulled by horses. The twelve companies of the Tenth Infantry Regiment occupied the Infantry Cantonment on the eastern side of the military reservation. The terms "troop," "battery," and "company" refer to roughly equal-size units consisting of cavalry, artillery, and infantry, respectively.[29]

A great deal of time-honored competition existed between the members of the cavalry, infantry, and artillery. In the soldier slang of the time, cavalrymen were known as "bowlegs" from riding horses or "yellow legs" because of the yellow stripe on their uniform trousers. Field artillerymen were called "wagon soldiers" for their horse-drawn caissons or "red legs" because of the red stripe on their uniform trousers. And infantrymen were already referred to as "doughboys," which came into more common use during World War I, though few can agree why.[30] Occasionally, this branch rivalry led to unhealthy altercations on the Barbary Coast.

The enlisted members of the artillery and the cavalry enjoyed living in the new brick barracks on the main post, built from 1895 to 1897, complete with reading rooms, mess facilities, coal heating, plumbing, and bath accommodations. The lodgings must have seemed luxurious to soldiers who had spent the previous two years in temporary camps in the Philippines and the past two weeks in a tent camp. The Buffalo Soldiers were fortunate with respect to their new living conditions.[31]

The Third Squadron benefited from congressional appropriations in the 1880s and 1890s to concentrate army units in brigade-size formations at larger posts selected for retention. These new living conditions were a welcome change for I Troop, and it was not lost on the Black troopers that they lived in barracks identical to those of their white artillery brethren. The army achieved this equality of housing not by design but by practical circumstance. Military planners had no idea whether members of a Black or white regiment would eventually occupy the barracks or stables they designed and constructed.

### *Black Officer*

While the soldiers lived in barracks, the army assigned officers individual quarters, either government housing on post or leased accommodations in San Francisco. Young was a senior captain at a time when seniority in the army counted for everything from promotions to housing privileges. It was not unusual for a senior officer to arrive at a post and decide he wanted a desirable set of quarters that was already occupied. He would bump that officer and his family out of the residence; they, in turn, would bump another officer and family out of the next most-desired set of housing and so on until the most junior officer had to move off post.[32]

Young knew the bureaucratic system of the army by this time in his career and did not, on this occasion, hesitate to take advantage of his privileges. Young exercised this prerogative, as detailed by the *San Francisco Call* in November 1902. Sally Sharp, the writer of the gossipy column, complained:

> The injustice of some of the prevailing rules in Uncle Sam's great army can be no better illustrated than that which gives the superior officer the claim upon the quarters of the inferior, no matter how long the

> latter may have occupied the same and how cozy his hands may have made it. Lieutenant [Jesse G.] Lowenberg and his bride (who was Ruth Dunham) were nicely settled in a pretty vine-covered cottage at the Presidio, kindly offered to them by Captain [Frederick E.] Johnston, who had occupied it. But along came a colored officer, Captain Young, who desired the cottage, and lo! The lieutenant and his bride have now rented a house on Scott Street, where they will be undisturbed. A darker bride may soon grace the interesting cottage.[33]

Young had previously occupied officers' housing on frontier posts such as Fort Robinson, Nebraska, and Fort Duchesne, Utah, as a lieutenant, yet this was the first time he exercised his prerogative as a captain to bump a white lieutenant from his quarters. In all things social, Young was forced to stay on his side of the color line that prevailed in a white officer corps. In all things official, however, Young was treated in accordance with U.S. Army regulations and guidelines, and he never hesitated to exercise his privileges.[34]

Though Sally Sharp did not give the exact location of the "pretty vine-covered cottage," a later description placed it at the intersection of Presidio Boulevard and Funston Avenue (Quarters 11). Young's house was one of twelve such officers' quarters built during the Civil War and right next to the old Alameda, a formal entrance to the parade ground that led to a bandstand. Each house was described as "being built of rough boards set upright and clapboarded." The first floor featured a parlor, one bedroom, a hall, a dining room, a kitchen, closets, and a bathroom. The upper floor had two bedrooms and a garret (attic room). Both the front and the back had a covered veranda (see figure 9).[35]

Young's official responsibilities occasionally included military community events that all officers were obligated to attend. One such affair was reported in late 1902 in the *Seattle Republican*, a Black newspaper, under the title "Tillman's Son." The article described a dinner that was mandatory attendance for all officers at the Presidio, including Young. Also present was an officer named Lt. Benjamin J. Tillman, who was at the Presidio with his regiment, the Seventh Infantry, after its return from the Philippines. His father, Sen. Benjamin R. Tillman (D-SC), was a firebrand white supremacist who opposed civil rights for Black Americans and promoted lynching.[36]

According to the story, knowing his father's views and thinking he might be uncomfortable in the presence of a "colored officer," someone informed Lieutenant Tillman that Young would be attending the dinner. Tillman responded, "Oh yes, I know the captain is colored. I know him well. But color doesn't matter with me. Captain Young is a captain in the Regular Army, and he must be a gentleman." The reporter concluded that the younger Tillman's "manly stand might win him over to decency."[37]

Young took part in all professional activities but did not fully participate in the social affairs at the Presidio with his fellow officers. The post had an officers' club and mess where the officers and their wives could dine and socialize. The post commander hosted dances when dignitaries visited, and the Officers' Club held more informal card parties, dances, and other social gatherings. Young did not dine with his fellow officers at the mess, though he made short appearances for certain obligatory social activities such as the one mentioned in the *Seattle Republican*.[38]

Because of Young's social exclusion from the Officers' Club, he took meals at his home, alone, served by his former cook Abner "Peggy" Jones. In the old army, officers hired soldiers, nicknamed "strikers," as servants in their households; the term comes from the act of striking the officer's tent. These soldier-servants worked for the officer, cooking meals, doing laundry, feeding and grooming horses, and acting as orderlies. Since Peggy Jones left the army after arriving in San Francisco in October, Young was free to hire him as his household servant.[39]

While Young was stationed at the Presidio, the officers of the Ninth Cavalry conducted lyceums, where they gathered periodically at the Officers' Club to hear and discuss papers on pertinent professional topics. The War Department earlier instituted regular lyceums for the officers' professional education as an army-wide practice. Since they were considered official functions to promote the officers' professional development, Young was included in such activities.[40]

Social activities were another matter entirely. According to Young's classmate Alexander Piper, who was one of a small number who befriended him at West Point, "[Young] observed strictly all the social rules and customs. Every officer in the post called upon him as they did upon every new officer who came to the post, and Young returned the call in every instance. At such general social affairs as the hops [dances] and receptions, he always appeared, paid his respects to the hostess and after waiting about a while would retire." This was the pattern of Young's army social conduct, as he kept to his side of the color line: he would fulfill the obligations customary of any army officer on post but bow out quickly to avoid making his fellow officers and their wives uncomfortable. It was his means of surviving in a white officer corps.[41]

Captain Young enjoyed riding and was an excellent horseman. For him, riding was another form of escape from the social isolation of being a Black officer. He learned to love horses while growing up in Ohio, where his father had a livery business, and had excelled at horsemanship at West Point. He honed his equestrian skills during his frontier tours at Fort Robinson and Fort Duchesne. After the Philippines, Young was probably delighted to be stateside, where he could enjoy riding again. He kept his horse down the street from his quarters in one of the stables designated for officers.

The army expected cavalry officers to purchase their horses and paid them a monthly allowance toward the horses' care and feeding. In 1902 the army paid a cavalry captain $167 a month, slightly more than his infantry counterpart who made $150. A good horse could cost more than $150, plus an additional $100 a year in maintenance costs, which was the reason for this difference in salaries. The cavalry officer had to pay the rest out of his own pocket.[42]

### *New Horses*

In contrast to the officers, the army provided horses to the enlisted soldiers of I troop. The most significant event for the enlisted men during the month of November, besides settling into the new barracks, was the issuing of their horses. The Ninth left its worn-out and diseased mounts in the Philippines, so the quartermaster at the Presidio delivered new horses in mid-November. Each troop of the Third Squadron received about fifty government-owned, or "public," horses.[43]

The post quartermaster, Capt. Amos W. Kimball, issued I Troop fifty-one horses on November 15. Captain Young and First Sergeant Jones were likely delighted to have horses for several reasons. First, a cavalry trooper is not complete without his horse, and I Troop had spent much of two years in the Philippines without mounts. Second, training and caring for horses kept the soldiers busy and contented. Many of the horses had to be broken and taught to tolerate a saddle and bridle. It is perhaps no accident that I Troop suffered no more desertions, shootings, or serious trouble after the quartermaster issued their horses.[44]

The records are silent on the quality of I Troop's horses. According to a newspaper article in 1903, cavalry horses had to be less than eight years old, weigh 950 to 1,150 pounds, and stand between fifteen-and-a-quarter and sixteen hands (sixty-two to sixty-four inches) high. The army remount depot system was not established until 1907, so the Presidio quartermaster purchased horses directly from ranchers under contract. The Third Squadron at the Presidio had about 250 public horses, not counting the officers' mounts. The ten Regular Army cavalry regiments were authorized a total of about 17,000 horses in 1902.[45]

The army favored solid-colored horses, and the regiments preferred to assign them by color. When possible, the Ninth Cavalry would have a black troop, a bay troop, a sorrel troop, and so on. The last troop in the alphabet, M Troop, often received leftover roans, piebalds, and pintos, along with the nickname "Calico Troop." The color of the I Troop's horses, if they had a uniform color, is unknown. At least one reference described them as bay colored. Since only four troops of cavalry were at the Presidio, it is possible the squadron commander, Major Garrard, tried to sort out the troop horses by color, leaving the odds and ends to M Troop.[46]

The cavalry drill regulations had been recently amended to read as follows:

> Horses when received at regiment are assigned to troops according to color, under the direction of the commanding officer. They are branded on the hoof of one foot, one and one-half inches below the coronet, with the letter of the troop and the number of the regiment. Captains will make permanent assignments of horses to men. After a horse has been so assigned his rider will not exchange him nor allow him to be used by any other person without the permission of the captain.

Once issued to the troop, each horse was marked. The troop and regiment were branded with a hot iron on the hoof, and since the hoof band grew, it had to be renewed about twice a year. In addition to this hoof marking, "U.S." was branded on the left shoulder of every army horse and mule.[47]

Captain Young selected a horse for each trooper, and that man was saddled with this horse until it died, the regiment moved, or the soldier left the army. Young probably based his selection on the advice of his noncommissioned officers, the skill of the individual soldier, and an assessment of the new horse. Once assigned, the individual soldier had to develop a working relationship with his horse. All this made the selection of horses a momentous occasion for I Troop.[48]

The soldiers of I Troop spent a great deal of each day with their horses. After reveille sounded at 5:30 a.m., followed by breakfast, troopers spent ninety minutes at stable call, when they watered, groomed, and fed their horses. Sergeants and corporals then led the troopers in mounted drill from 8:00 a.m. to 10:30 a.m. before taking the horses to the stables and returning to the barracks for dinner (lunch). Troopers went back to the horses for a second stable call at 4:00 p.m. to water, groom, and feed them again before returning to the barracks for supper. On an average day, according to one source, a cavalryman spent about five hours a day caring for and riding his mount, leading to a close bond between man and horse.[49]

To the disappointment of the Buffalo Soldiers, the post commander assigned the Ninth the new but flimsy shed stables on the flats of the Lower Presidio near the water. The post refused the Ninth's request for stables on top of the bluff because of competition for space with the field artillery units, which also had horses. The cavalry troopers described the flats as boggy lowland that had been filled in and leveled with 125 loads of crushed rock from Angel Island. In wet weather, the roads around the stables were impassable, the flies unbearable, and the long walk from main post tedious.[50]

### *Notable Visitors*

With his soldiers busy breaking and training their horses, Young had time to focus on social matters. In San Francisco, he was able to host Black friends and family he had not seen during his overseas duty in the Philippines. He had last visited his home in Wilberforce, Ohio, in 1899. Captain Young could host guests at his spacious, vine-covered house on

Officers' Row at the intersection of the carriage road running west and the main street running north and south.[51]

According to Sergeant Nicholas, "Captain Young was visited by such notables as Mrs. [Malvina] Mitchell of Wilberforce University; his mother, Mrs. [Arminta] Young; Booker T. Washington; T. Thomas Fortune, of the *New York Age*; Ernest [Hogan of] Hogan's Comedy Company; and many others that knew of him." Nicholas did not mention when these individuals visited, yet it was likely, because of the training schedule, during Young's first months at the Presidio.[52]

First among the visitors was his mother, Arminta Young. Born in enslavement in Kentucky prior to the Civil War, Arminta found a way to educate herself, an exceedingly rare accomplishment at the time. She later escaped with her husband, Gabriel, to freedom in Ohio, and while he went off to fight in the Civil War, she raised and homeschooled their only son. Charles was always close to his mother, who had stressed education and music in his childhood. She was also a very strong-willed woman, never afraid to express her opinions.[53]

After his father's death in 1894, this relationship grew in importance for both Young and his mother. They purchased a house together in Wilberforce, where both resided while Young served as the professor of military science and tactics at Wilberforce University. Their home turned into a meeting place for the Black intelligentsia in the area that included Dayton poet Paul Laurence Dunbar and fellow Wilberforce professor W. E. B. Du Bois. According to author David L. Lewis, "Young's was the first genuine male friendship in Du Bois' life, and one of a handful in which there was genuine affinity." Again, according to Lewis, Young and Dunbar "were as dissimilar physically and professionally as they were similar in terms of artistic temperament and interest." Young formed friendships with both Dunbar and Du Bois that lasted their lifetimes.[54]

Another visitor, Malvina (née Fairfax) Mitchell, was a teacher and dean of students at Wilberforce University and the wife of the Reverend Samuel T. Mitchell, the university president. Her visit indicates Young maintained contact with the leaders of the institution where he had taught from 1894 to 1898 and would serve again in the future. He considered the university and his nearby home to be his refuge throughout a long army career and returned there often to recover from his physical and emotional wounds.[55]

One more on the list was Ernest Hogan, the comedian, singer, dancer, songwriter, producer, and first African American star on Broadway. He began his career, as did many Black vaudevillians, as a performer in the all-Black minstrel companies. Later, in addition to working as a single act, he moved into management, and his troupes toured across America and as far away as Australia. His success—along with that of Bert Williams and his partner, George N. Walker—helped pave the way into mainstream show business for African American actors, musicians, and comedians. Hogan was to the acting profession in the theatrical realm what Young was to the officer corps in the U.S. Army. Hogan died in 1909 of tuberculosis, his career cut short at the height of his success and popularity.[56]

An additional visitor, T. Thomas Fortune was one of the most prominent Black journalists in the late nineteenth and early twentieth centuries. Born Timothy Thomas Fortune, he was eight years older than Young, though they shared the experiences of being born in enslavement, doggedly resolute in continually educating themselves, and determined to excel in their respective professions. In the 1880s, when Young was attending West Point, Fortune was sixty miles down the Hudson River in New York City, establishing himself as a writer and newspaperman. A largely self-taught man and eloquent orator, he achieved fame as the militant and maverick editor of a newspaper named the *Globe*, later the *Freeman*, and finally, at the time he visited Young, the *New York Age*.[57]

In 1900 Fortune had joined Booker T. Washington in organizing the National Negro Business League. This and several other failed equal rights organizations were significant precursors to the Niagara Movement and the establishment of the National Association for the Advancement of Colored People. Fortune was also responsible for coining the term "Afro-American" as a substitute for "Negro" or "colored" in the New York newspapers. He believed it was a more accurate term, arguing that Blacks were "African in origin and American in birth."[58]

Fortune likely asked Young about his wartime experiences, since Fortune was on his way to serve as a special agent to the Philippines from 1902 to 1903. He supported the American colonial enterprise in the Philippines and believed that Black Americans should be offered the chance to immigrate to the Philippine Islands as a "respite from their oppression in the U.S." He also advocated employing African Americans to administer and act as intermediaries between the Black American emigrants and the Filipinos. Fortune thought that combining "Negro labor with American capital" would help make the occupation of the Philippines a success. The idea had currency for a time but faded by the end of 1903.[59]

At least one other local Black California resident likely visited Young at his home—Dr. William W. Purnell. On their way to the Philippines, newly promoted Captain Young and Sgt. Maj. Benjamin O. Davis had met Purnell in 1901 in San Francisco. Purnell had taken them on a tour of the city while the two waited for their embarkation to the Philippines. Davis had already passed his officer commissioning examination and was awaiting his commission promoting him to second lieutenant in the Tenth Cavalry.[60]

Dr. Purnell was a graduate of Howard University College of Medicine and had practiced medicine in Washington DC in the 1890s. He was appointed first lieutenant and assistant surgeon in 1898 of the Black Eighth "Immune" U.S. Volunteer Infantry Regiment, and during the Spanish-American War, he served with Davis in Cuba. Dr. Purnell was later appointed captain and surgeon with the Black Forty-Eighth U.S. Volunteer Infantry and served during the Philippine-American War. After returning from the Philippines in 1901, he decided to stay in the Bay Area and established a practice as the leading Black physician in Oakland.[61]

### *Panama Trouble*

On the other side of the Pacific from the Philippines, trouble was brewing in Central America that would soon involve the Ninth Cavalry in contingency planning. The U.S. Pacific acquisitions after the Spanish-American War, and the Philippine Islands in particular, led the U.S. government to approve the purchase of land from the failed French Panama Canal venture in June 1902. Since this land was part of Colombia, President Theodore Roosevelt began negotiations with that country to obtain the necessary rights. Colombia was not in favor of inviting Uncle Sam to dig a canal and take control of part of the country.

In December 1902, as the Ninth Cavalry was settling into garrison life at the Presidio, newspapers began to sound warnings of military deployments to Panama involving the Ninth Cavalry and other units from the Presidio. Headlines in the *San Francisco Examiner* on December 30, 1902, heralded: "Army Takes Steps to Have Hand in Isthmian Affairs," "Prepares to Send Troops to Panama," and "Western Regiments Chosen for Service in the South." The newspapers in the city identified the Ninth Cavalry as slated to go to Panama and listed all the troop commanders of the Third Squadron, including Captain Young.[62]

In the last weeks of 1902, U.S. secretary of war Elihu Root began negotiations with Gen. Rafael Reyes, the Colombian envoy to Washington. These talks proved inconclusive, so the Ninth Cavalry was not loaded onto ships and sent overseas again. One Presidio army officer, described as a "hardened Philippine veteran," was quoted in the newspaper as saying, "It cannot be any worse than the mountains of Luzon, but I fancy we shall not smell powder." And they did not smell gunpowder in 1902, though the following year would see the crisis over the Panama Canal worsen.[63]

The fall months after their arrival in San Francisco proved far more eventful than Captain Young and the leadership of I Troop would have wished. After a reduction in ranks of those who were unwilling or unable to continue serving in the army, the Ninth Cavalry moved into comfortable brick barracks and Captain Young into a spacious set of quarters. First Sergeant Jones learned early that the temptations of the Barbary Coast would be too much for some of his troopers, though the delivery of their horses proved a partial antidote. A full slate of challenging missions in the new year would do the rest.

# 4

## Presidio Garrison

> Captain Young, the only colored graduate of West Point and colored officer of that rank in the service, was there at the head of his troop and he and his men were heartily cheered.
> —*San Francisco Chronicle*, May 13, 1903

The Third Squadron, Ninth Cavalry composed about one quarter of the Presidio garrison strength in 1903, with the post having slightly larger troop contingents of white infantry soldiers and artillery gunners. The Ninth Cavalry was the first Black Regular Army unit to garrison the Presidio, so the men garnered a great deal of interest from San Franciscans. The first half of the year gave the soldiers a chance to shine as they planned to host several high-level visitors and prepared for duty in the national parks.[1]

### *Booker T. Washington Visit*

The year 1903 was unique to the Presidio because several VIPs visited, and January featured the first—Booker T. Washington. The civil rights leader addressed an overflow audience, white and Black, at the Mechanics Pavilion during his trip to San Francisco on January 9, 1903. The mayor of San Francisco, Eugene Schmitz, introduced Washington, by far the most prominent Black leader in America at the time (see figure 13).[2]

Washington, the founder of the Tuskegee Institute in Alabama, promoted a philosophy of self-help, practical education, racial solidarity, and accommodation. He believed Blacks should accept discrimination for a time and focus on improving themselves through hard work and material prosperity. He advanced education in the crafts, industrial skills, and farming, as well as the virtues of tolerance, enterprise, and frugality. He believed this philosophy in time would lead to African Americans being fully accepted into American society.[3]

After listening to the address at the pavilion, Captain Young invited Washington to visit the Presidio and meet his soldiers. Washington accepted and returned on January 12 to speak to the soldiers and the post officers and their wives. Washington addressed the mixed gathering of Black troopers, white officers, and family members for an hour at the "Hop Room" adjoining the Officers' Club.[4]

According to a newspaper report, Washington spoke earnestly to the Black troopers of the Ninth, using a "mixture of funny stories to make the men laugh and good advice to make them think." He reminded them they were not only fighters but also role models and cultural ambassadors being watched very closely by San Franciscans. He warned them against drinking and gambling, urged them to save money, and told them to take advantage of the reading room and night school offered at the Presidio.[5]

Washington addressed the soldiers:

> You have in a very large degree the reputation of the colored race in your hands, and you must at all times conduct yourselves as gentlemen. I know that when away from home you are subjected to temptations which do not occur when you are with your families in the South but remember that you are watched in San Francisco to see whether it is possible that the black soldier can lead as clean a life as the white man. You have reflected great credit to your race in the Philippine Islands and in Cuba and we who watched your bravery during the war are proud of you.[6]

Captain Young surely approved of Washington's words and hoped his soldiers followed his guidance. First Sergeant Jones and the sergeants of I Troop likely had a more pessimistic view of whether the soldiers would take these words to heart and resist the temptations of San Francisco for the sake of their reputations. The men of I Troop knew that society did not consider soldiers as gentlemen, with Black soldiers least of all.[7]

Young had visited the Tuskegee Institute in 1899, and he and Washington later exchanged letters about the creation of a military training program there. Young initially showed some interest in leading the program, but this cooled quickly when Booker T. Washington told him he would not arm the cadets in his program, fearing the hostility he might face among whites in Alabama. Young was adamant that Black students training to be military leaders must be supplied with weapons. He wrote that guns are "very valuable things when backed by common sense and very harmless when the student has been educated to know their use and know not to abuse this use."[8]

When serving as a military science instructor years earlier, Young had hosted Washington during a visit to Wilberforce University. Young had disagreements with Washington's ideology as he did with that of his good friend W. E. B. Du Bois, with whom Young developed a close friendship while they were faculty members together at Wilberforce. The year Washington visited the Presidio was coincidentally when Du Bois published an article titled "Of Mr. Booker T. Washington and Others," in which he rejected Washington's willingness to accept the status quo and called instead for political power, civil rights, and higher education for African American youth. This was the opening salvo of the well-publicized dispute between the two Black leaders about the best way to overcome the pervasive racism of the day.[9]

Young felt somewhat comfortable with Washington's philosophy of hard work and accommodation since they were his keys to survival in the white officer corps of the army. On the other hand, he was an activist promoter of higher education, as shown in his efforts as a high school teacher in Ripley, Ohio; a student at West Point; and an instructor at Wilberforce. Young developed a pragmatic middle road of his own out of necessity and would never totally embrace either Du Bois's or Washington's competing philosophies, though a speech he gave later that year at Stanford University sounded more like that of his friend and former colleague Du Bois.[10]

### *Garrison Routine*

After Washington's visit, Young's soldiers returned to their garrison routine: military drills, work details, stable duty, and guard mount. As often as possible, Captain Young and the officers of the Ninth engaged their soldiers in more appealing activities such as target practice, athletic competitions, field days, and military exercises, hoping to keep them occupied and out of trouble. The local papers reported on the special events, mock battles, and sports activities that drew crowds of civilian spectators; their accounts revealed important details on the everyday lives of the members of the Ninth Cavalry.

Not all soldiers stayed out of trouble. On the first day of February, Major General Hughes, commanding the Department of California, issued special orders appointing a general court-martial to convene at the Presidio. Captain Young was appointed to this board, along with 1st Lt. E. Holland Rubottom and 2nd Lt. John H. Howard of the Ninth Cavalry. Seven officers from the artillery on post were also appointed to the board, a duty that was common for company-grade officers. The board convened on February 2 to hear cases brought before it. The only member of the Ninth Cavalry found guilty by general court-martial in this period was Pvt. George L. Vinegar of M Troop, who was dishonorably discharged on March 7, 1903.[11]

There were occasions that brought the Black members of the Ninth Cavalry into contact with white San Franciscans. The only known civilian event in which Young mixed with white society in San Francisco was the annual Mardi Gras Ball in 1903. Young received an artfully engraved invitation from the Mark Hopkins Institute of Art as well as a letter signed by Willis E. Davis of the San Francisco Art Association for the gala event held on February 24, 1903 (see figure 14). The invitation specified that Young attend in uniform or costume in accordance with the rules of the ball restricting spectators. Wives and lady members of the family were also invited and asked to appear in costume. Since Young was not married, he attended stag and in uniform.[12]

In another event in early April, troopers of the Ninth Cavalry took part in a charity exhibition that raised $1,500 for the California Training Home for Girls. An audience of four hundred white citizens watched young women demonstrate their prowess at double tandem driving, jumping, and other horseback-riding skills. The article noted that "Sergeant Brice of Uncle Sam's cavalry, who has taught many recruits how to bestride and ride horses in peacetime and war," commented that the "ladies ride gayly, and they know jest how to handle hosses." Edward F. Brice was from K Troop, Ninth Cavalry.[13]

The Buffalo Soldiers put on quite a show for the white audience. According to the *Examiner*, "Twelve members of the third squadron, Ninth Cavalry, who won fame at San Juan Hill, showed society what soldiers and their horses will do." Lt. Beauford R. Camp directed the cavalry demonstration, which included "platoon drill, sabre exercises, a sham battle, unsaddling of horses, bareback riding, throwing of horses to the ground by riders, resaddling, and skillful Cossack riding."[14]

Later in April, the *San Francisco Chronicle* reported on the field event competitions between the artillery units on post and the cavalry troops of the Third Squadron that drew large crowds of mostly white citizens. The overall competition, which included both athletic and tent-pitching and striking competitions, was won by the artillery, which had nine batteries competing against four troops from the cavalry. Every troop or battery had two entries for each event for a total of twenty-six. From the Ninth Cavalry, K Troop won the competition for shelter tent pitching, and I Troop won the 10×100-yard relay. Individual winners from the Ninth Cavalry included Pvt. Samuel W. Dillahunty of K Troop in the 100-yard dash and 220-yard run, and Pvt. Thomas Mosely of K Troop in the standing broad jump. Dillahunty was a twenty-four-year-old former preacher from Columbia, Tennessee, and Mosely was a twenty-five-year-old first-term soldier from Brandenburg, Kentucky, who transferred to I Troop later in 1903.[15]

### *Conflict and Fights*

When not involved in official activities, a soldier's life included a dose of San Francisco culture, which was not always a positive measure for African Americans. For nightlife, off-duty cavalry troopers commonly frequented the dance halls and saloons along Pacific Avenue, the epicenter of the city's notorious Barbary Coast, where they often came into contact with civilians and white soldiers from the Presidio's artillery and infantry units. Even in the popular Black nightclubs of the Barbary Coast, Buffalo Soldiers got into trouble, and fights were a nightly phenomenon.

The troopers were not picky about whom they brawled with, and the newspapers carried many articles covering violent altercations between Black troopers of the Ninth and African American inhabitants of the Barbary Coast. For example, in May 1903, authorities arrested Sgt. Josh Boose of the Ninth Cavalry for assault with the intention to commit murder as well as a Black saloonkeeper named Henry Randall from Pacific Avenue for assault with a deadly weapon. When the two got into an argument,

Randall produced a hatchet and used the flat side to pummel Boose about the back and head. Boose later returned with his pistol and tried unsuccessfully to shoot Randall. Sergeant Boose, of K Troop, must not have been charged, since he ended his enlistment with a good character rating ten days after the incident.[16]

On occasion, white criminals committed crimes against Black soldiers. In March 1903, a soldier named William Haslett met a man at a Pacific Avenue saloon who introduced him to a white woman. After the two left the saloon, the woman, acting as a decoy, lured the Black soldier to a room. Soon after, the man reappeared and robbed the soldier of a valuable watch and a large sum of money. After the two thieves escaped, Haslett went to the Hall of Justice and "secured John Doe warrants for the pair," who could not be found.[17]

Three months later, Haslett spotted a man on Pacific Avenue he thought was the one who had robbed him, and the soldier notified a policeman, who arrested the suspect. After a visit to the police station, the accused identified himself and proved his innocence. Haslett was then asked to repeat his description of the robber, whom the police recognized as someone already in their custody. The thief was a man named Victor Walkirez, "the heartless and self-confessed murderer" of an older woman.[18]

Victor Walkirez, described as a "light-colored negro," was convicted of killing a Black woman named Elizabeth Leroy at her cabin in Golden Gate in May 1903 and was given a life sentence at San Quentin. His accomplice, a white woman named Anna Ross, was charged with complicity in the murder and likewise sentenced to life at San Quentin. She was described in the newspaper reports as "the consort of Victor Walkirez." Haslett was probably fortunate that he only lost his valuables in his brush with this dangerous pair.[19]

On rare occasions, former Black soldiers also committed crimes against white citizens. One evening in May 1903, Albert Daspit, an ex-member of C Troop, Ninth Cavalry, snatched Mrs. Jane Sanford's purse and ran. The victim's screams brought a policeman, who gave chase and captured Daspit with the purse containing ninety-five cents. Daspit, who had been discharged in Monterey, California, six months earlier with a good character rating, pleaded guilty to petty larceny and was sentenced to six months in the county jail.[20]

*Yosemite Mission*

Military duties soon took half the members of the Ninth at the Presidio far from the temptations of the Barbary Coast. Part of the Third Squadron, consisting of K and L Troops, mounted their horses in late April 1903 for the long road march to Yosemite National Park. Pursuant to General Order 15, Department of California, the army charged this detachment with patrolling Yosemite National Park for the summer season.[21]

U.S. Army cavalry units had been patrolling California's three national parks—General Grant, Sequoia, and Yosemite—since they were established by Congress in 1890. The secretary of the interior turned to the War Department for cavalry troopers to patrol and protect the new parks just as they had done previously in Yellowstone National Park, Wyoming. Initially, two troops from the Fourth U.S. Cavalry were sent to the Presidio of San Francisco with orders to patrol the parks in 1891. This force increased to four troops in 1894 and succeeding years, though the Spanish-American War disrupted this rotation in 1898.[22]

Col. Charles Morris, an artillery officer assigned to command the garrison at the Presidio of San Francisco in 1903, had other tasks besides park duty in mind for the Buffalo Soldiers on post. He wrote to the War Department soon after his arrival "about the need for more cavalry to control dogs running loose, automobiles speeding, fires, and incidents of robbery on the reservation." Colonel Morris wrote to the Automobile Club of California about the new problem of "autos utterly disregarding the posted speed limits." The two troops assigned to park duty in April were likely happy to be relieved of duties as dogcatchers and traffic enforcers.[23]

The departure of the two troops of the Ninth for the parks in 1903 was probably much like that described in 1899 by a cavalry officer assigned to the Presidio. At the trumpet call of boots and saddles, followed by assembly, the mounted cavalrymen mustered in front of the brick barracks. While the post band played "The Girl I Left Behind Me," the troopers swung into the saddle and marched up the hill to the Presidio Boulevard gate. The cavalry was trailed by four-mule army wagons with white canvas covers, the troublesome pack mules bringing up the rear. After the troops cleared the gate, the troop dogs began to slink after the column in small groups, "avoiding arrest and the pound and the other bugbears of dogdom."[24]

The detachment sent to Yosemite in 1903 was led by 1st Lt. James E.

Fechét ,who commanded L Troop, and assisted by 2nd Lt. Joseph V. Kuznik, commanding K Troop. Maj. Joseph Garrard, the Third Squadron commander, who was named the acting superintendent of Yosemite National Park for the summer of 1903, joined the detachment the following month.[25]

The two lieutenants leading this force had very different backgrounds. First Lieutenant Fechét, born in 1877 at Fort Ringgold, Texas, had been commissioned from the ranks in 1900 after serving as a private, corporal, and sergeant in the Sixth U.S. Cavalry. He had joined the Ninth in the Philippines in the summer of 1900 and had commanded L Troop since October 1902. The other, Second Lieutenant Kuznik, was born in Breslau, Germany, in 1880. He had served in the Eleventh Volunteer Cavalry as a private, corporal, and sergeant before winning his commission in the Ninth Cavalry in 1901. He commanded K Troop because the assigned captain, John F. Nance, was on leave, and the first lieutenant, E. Holland Rubottom, was serving court-martial duty at the Presidio.[26]

The total distance of the march to Camp A. E. Wood at Wawona, California, outside Yosemite National Park, was 285 miles. The two troops made the trip in thirteen days, arriving on May 7, 1903. The officers and troopers of this detachment settled into camp life in the High Sierra, which must have seemed exceedingly foreign to soldiers who had spent the last six months at the Presidio of San Francisco. They also busied themselves preparing for the arrival of a very important visitor, who, for the first month of their stay, took priority over their normal park patrolling duties.[27]

### *Officer Reassignments*

The Third Squadron's dispatching the Yosemite detachment led by two junior lieutenants revealed how shorthanded in officers the unit operated in 1903. Cavalry units in this period rarely rode with their full complement of commissioned officers, yet to send a detachment of eighty men under two lieutenants on such an important mission nearly 300 miles seems unusual. Captain Young led a similar-size detachment the following month to Sequoia with twice that number of officers.

The Ninth Cavalry reassigned several officers in both the Third Squadron at the Presidio and the First Squadron at Monterey to resolve some of these officer shortages. The reasons for these transfers revolved around seniority and leadership. Seniority was still supreme, but effective leaders were needed at the Monterey Military Reservation, where the squadron had the thankless task of helping build a new post while living in temporary tent camps.[28]

The First Squadron in Monterey had only two captains present: Capt. George W. Read of B Troop and Capt. George W. Moses of C Troop. A Troop was commanded in Monterey by 1st Lt. Winston Pilcher and D Troop by 1st Lt. Frederick J. Herman, who like Kuznik, was born in Germany. Both Pilcher and Herman had served as volunteer officers during the Spanish-American and Philippine-American Wars before accepting Regular Army commissions in 1901.[29]

In March 1903, 1st Lt. Samuel Pearson was transferred from I Troop at the Presidio to A Troop in Monterey to assume command. The man he replaced, First Lieutenant Pilcher, was sent to I Troop as Young's new first lieutenant. Pearson was the senior of the two and perhaps a more effective leader. This must have disappointed Captain Young as much as it did Lieutenant Pearson, since his move to Monterey meant he would miss I Troop's upcoming deployment to Sequoia. Pearson also had to trade his comfortable officer's quarters at the Presidio of San Francisco for the temporary quarters at the Monterey Military Reservation, since the new post housing was not yet complete.[30]

The situation was even worse in the Third Squadron in San Francisco, with only five of twelve officers available for duty. Only Capt. Lester W. Cornish of M Troop and Capt. Charles Young of I Troop were present for duty. Cornish was the senior of the two, though he had been hospitalized since March due to a lingering illness acquired in the Philippines. Aside from Fechét in L Troop, the only first lieutenant available for duty was the newly reassigned Winston Pilcher in I Troop. In Captain Cornish's absence, 2nd Lt. John H. Howard of L Troop temporarily commanded M Troop, and 2nd Lt. Joseph V. Kuznik commanded K Troop.[31]

The officer situation improved for the Third Squadron in the following months when Lieutenant Rubottom and Captain Nance returned to K Troop, Lieutenant Howard returned to L Troop, and M Troop received a new second lieutenant in May. Yet Captain Cornish remained hospitalized or on convalescent leave until October, making Young the senior cavalry captain available for duty at the Presidio. By May when all four elements of the Third Squadron were busy with national park missions, each troop had at least two officers present for duty.

### *Enlisted Turnover*

There were also changes in the enlisted ranks of the Ninth Cavalry. In spite of the reductions experienced by the squadron after its arrival at the Presidio, the ebb and flow of soldiers ending their enlistments or reenlisting continued. Certain long-term soldiers ended their term of service on one day and enlisted the following day, with no break in service. Others took some time off in San Francisco and then marched back into the Presidio recruiting office to enlist again. Still others chose to end their enlistments, travel back to their place of enrollment at army expense, visit family, and then reenlist within three months to retain their pay for consecutive terms. Finally, some chose to hang up their uniforms and return to civilian mufti.

I Troop's losses in the second quarter of 1903 are representative of those of the other troops in the squadron. In April, I Troop lost Pvt. William B. Clinton, a twenty-six-year-old former barber from Washington DC, at the end of his three-year enlistment. Also in April, the troop dropped Pvt. William Hamilton, a thirty-year-old, two-term soldier from Macon, Georgia, after a disability discharge. In December 1902, Captain Young had sent Hamilton for treatment of tuberculosis at Fort Bayard, New Mexico Territory, where the army discharged him four months later. Another member of I Troop sent for tubercular treatment to Fort Bayard was not so lucky. Saddler Alfred Major, who had served with I Troop nearly twenty years, died at Fort Bayard in September 1903.[32]

In May 1903, I Troop had four soldiers reach the end of their enlistments. Pvt. James Green, a twenty-seven-year-old, two-term soldier and former cook from Yorkville, South Carolina, ended his enlistment and returned home. However, Green reenlisted in Charlotte, North Carolina ten days later, and the army assigned him again to I Troop. The second soldier, Cpl. Cornelius Mitchell, a twenty-eight-year-old, two-term soldier from Prescott, Arkansas, ended his enlistment and returned to civilian life. The third, Pvt. Robert Dennison, a twenty-two-year-old, first-term soldier from Frankfort, Kentucky, ended his enlistment, returned home, and reenlisted two months later to be assigned to L Troop, Ninth Cavalry. The fourth,

Pvt. Isaac Pitman, a first-term former waiter from Frankfort, Kentucky, ended his enlistment and returned home to the Bluegrass State.[33]

In addition to the loss of troopers, the men faced shortages of horses to ride. Despite the issuance of horses earlier, both the cavalry and artillery units at the Presidio needed more horses. The Department of California called for bids to secure 120 horses by special purchase in May 1903. The department appointed Capt. George W. Read, the B Troop commander in Monterey—along with an artillery captain, a veterinarian, and a civilian inspector—to visit ranches in Nevada, Utah, Oregon, and California to secure horses.[34]

The loss of enlisted men and the shortage of horses added to the leadership challenges of Captain Young and First Sergeant Jones. The loss of seven soldiers effectively reduced I Troop's strength by one squad of seven troopers, or about 10 percent of its enlisted strength. And I Troop did not begin to receive replacements for these men for several months. This meant Young faced a busy month of May shorthanded, as did the rest of the troops in the squadron.

### *Theodore Roosevelt Visit*

After the two troops of the Third Squadron departed for Yosemite, President Theodore Roosevelt conducted a tour of the western United States that included a three-day stay in San Francisco in May 1903. The two remaining troops of the Ninth Cavalry, under the command of Captain Young, served as the honor guard for the president. When Roosevelt arrived on Tuesday, May 12, Young and the Ninth greeted him at the train station, where the "soldiers of the Ninth Cavalry presented sabers." Thus began a demanding three-day schedule for Captain Young and his men.[35]

The president participated in a gala parade down Market Street on the first full day of his visit, Wednesday, May 13. A film documenting his ride in a horse-drawn carriage shows Captain Young and the mounted soldiers of the Ninth in the parade just ahead of Roosevelt. An entourage of secret service men in top hats walked on either side of the presidential carriage to supplement the mounted police and the military honor guard. The extraordinary number of security guards was bent on preventing an assassination, which had taken down his predecessor, President William McKinley.[36]

A platoon of mounted police led the marching column and "swept the street from curb to curb." Next came the band of the Thirteenth U.S. Infantry, playing marching music. "Then, having the right of line, and very proud of their position, rode the colored cavalry—the honor guard." According to the reporter, it "was in compliment to their excellent service that they were given first place."[37]

Commanded by Captain Young, I and M Troops of the Ninth Cavalry, followed by the regimental colors, led the president's carriage. The honor guard was shown in the film arrayed in ranks of ten spanning the street, totaling about eighty Black mounted troopers. They rode smartly following the red and white swallowtail flag, or guidon, designating their troops, with Captain Young leading the formation. This was the first time African American soldiers served as an honor guard for the president of the United States.[38]

Despite the poor quality of the film, it is easy to pick out the officers in the mounted formation from the enlisted men. The enlisted troopers wore 1895-pattern forage caps and plain service uniforms in formation, while the officers wore cavalry dress uniforms with braided shoulder boards and sported helmets topped with yellow plumes. The latter also carried light cavalry sabers and rode ahead or to the side of the formation of troops. Two white officers, one of whom was Maj. Gen. Arthur MacArthur, Jr., trailed immediately behind the mounted policemen escorting the president's carriage, completing the honor guard formation. After the parade down Market Street, President Roosevelt reviewed I and M Troops of the Ninth Cavalry at the Presidio Golf Course (see figure 15).[39]

The following day, Young and the Ninth again provided an escort when Roosevelt visited the University of California at Berkeley. The president attended graduation exercises at the new Hearst Amphitheatre and received an honorary degree. This day did not go without incident, and a headline the next day read: "Spectator Run Down by Cavalry Escort." According to the reporter, a Mr. and Mrs. Daly were driving a light buggy on the route assigned the soldiers, "who came at a full gallop. . . . The occupants of the buggy were thrown to the ground by the collision, and they had a narrow escape from being trampled." Mr. Daly was unhurt, but "Mrs. Daly suffered bruises and sustained a severe nervous shock."[40]

Captain Young was asked about the accident afterward. Young explained "that he was forced to keep the cavalry at the gallop that the immense crowd might be cleared away." According to the reporter, "So dense was the throng that no sooner would one space be cleared than it would be immediately filled up again. On this account the soldiers were compelled to keep on the alert during the entire drive of the President to and from the amphitheatre." There were no subsequent reports of the accident.[41]

Roosevelt boarded a night train after his visit to San Francisco and arrived near Yosemite National Park the morning of May 15, where the two other troops of the Ninth Cavalry provided an escort. The cavalry escort met him at the Raymond depot, where the president boarded a stage of the Yosemite Stage and Turnpike Company for the forty-four-mile ride into Yosemite. According to one reporter, the president "seemed glad to greet members of the Ninth Cavalry, who had been detailed to act as his escort, and the sight of their uniforms aroused his interest immediately."[42]

Along with the cavalry escort, naturalist John Muir accompanied Roosevelt and described the geology and flora that lined the mountain road. Muir then rode with Roosevelt on a three-day camping trip into the depths of the High Sierra on horses provided by the Ninth Cavalry. A detachment of troopers from the Ninth accompanied Roosevelt and his party the entire time. Lieutenants Fechét of L Troop and Kuznik of K Troop busied their troopers in setting up camp each night. The detachment of the Ninth was with them until Monday, May 18, when it escorted the president back to the station at Raymond and saluted him in farewell.[43]

President Roosevelt had good reason to be fond of the troopers of the Ninth Cavalry and to appreciate their serving as his honor guard. All four Buffalo Soldier regiments fought in Cuba with then-colonel Roosevelt and the white First U.S. Volunteer Cavalry, better known as the Rough Riders, during the Spanish-American War five years earlier. He and some of the old veterans of the Ninth Cavalry had charged up San Juan Hill together. Many of the veterans of Cuba, referred to as "smoked Yankees" by the Spanish soldiers, still served with the unit.

At the time of the visit, some troopers in the Ninth felt Roosevelt still owed them an apology for disparaging remarks in an 1899 *Scribner's Magazine* article about the charge up San Juan Hill. In that piece, he had accused African American infantrymen of being unreliable without their white officers. Roosevelt praised the conduct of the Ninth and Tenth Cavalries in battle but also intimated that their white officers should receive most of the credit. There were Black noncommissioned officers in the Ninth Cavalry who could have challenged the veracity of Roosevelt's account of the battle.

In the article, Roosevelt stated his belief that Black Regular Army regiments had occasionally produced "non-commissioned officers who can take the initiative and accept responsibility precisely like the best class of whites; but this cannot be expected normally, nor is it fair to expect it." The Black regiments needed their white officers, according to Roosevelt, while with "white regulars, as with my own Rough Riders, experience showed that the non-commissioned officers could usually carry on the fight by themselves if they were once started, no matter whether their officers were killed or not."

Later in the article, Roosevelt wrote that "none of the white regulars or Rough Riders showed the slightest sign of weakening; but under the strain the colored infantrymen (who had none of their officers) began to get a little uneasy and drift to the rear." According to this version, he ended the trouble by threatening to shoot the Black infantrymen, at which point they accepted Roosevelt as one of "their own officers" and "flashed their white teeth at each other." This portion of the article especially galled the members of the Buffalo Soldier infantry regiments.[44]

At the time, African Americans supported the president's Republican Party, hoping it would appoint Blacks to government posts and take steps to end the lynching of Blacks. McKinley lost the support of some Blacks during his first term because of his silence on racial violence and promotion of reconciliation with the South, yet he retained the support of Booker T. Washington and other key Black leaders, who continued to vote for the Republican Party. McKinley won a landslide reelection and was inaugurated for a second term in 1901, appointing Theodore Roosevelt as his vice president.[45]

African Americans found President Roosevelt, McKinley's successor, more to their liking despite his *Scribner's Magazine* piece. A month after he took office, he invited Booker T. Washington to the White House for dinner, the first African American to be so honored. His effort to reach out to the leader of the African American community sparked protest and bitter criticism by some whites, especially in the South, but was lauded by the Black press.

With the presidential visit behind them, Captain Young and the Ninth put away their dress uniforms and packed for field duty. The Buffalo Soldiers had only one day in garrison after Roosevelt's departure to complete preparations for a busy summer of patrolling the Sequoia and General Grant National Parks.

The first five months of 1903 were exceptionally busy for Captain Young and the members of the Ninth Cavalry at the Presidio. The period began with the notable visit of Booker T. Washington and ended with high-profile escort duties for President Theodore Roosevelt. Young also bade farewell to his Philippine-American War colleague Lieutenant Pearson and several veteran enlisted soldiers at the end of their enlistments. The dispatch of two troops of the Third Squadron to Yosemite presaged the upcoming departure of Young and the other two troops to the High Sierra.

# 5

# Park Guardians

> Troops K and L of the Ninth Cavalry have been designated to guard Yosemite Park during the coming season and Troops I and M of the same regiment to guard Sequoia and General Grant parks. Major Garrard has been designated to act as superintendent of Yosemite and Captain Young of the Sequoia and General Grant parks.
> —*San Francisco Chronicle*, April 29, 1903

Hard on the heels of the presidential visit to San Francisco, the Ninth Cavalry dispatched Capt. Charles Young leading I and M Troops to Sequoia and General Grant National Parks. The previous month the other two troops of the squadron departed on a similar mission to Yosemite National Park. The U.S. Army sent these detachments because it was responsible for patrolling and protecting the national parks prior to the creation of the National Park Service in 1916. Captain Young and his soldiers would spend nearly six months in the Sierra Nevada mountain range, an experience that not only would challenge the leadership of officers and noncommissioned officers but also would test the competence and training of enlisted soldiers.

## *Deployment to Sequoia*

Sergeant Nicholas recorded: "On May 15 Troops I and M, Ninth Cavalry, were ordered by the War Department to proceed overland, mounted, from San Francisco to Sequoia National Park, Tulare County, California, a distance of 285 miles, for park guard duty under the Department of Interior, for the protection and preservation of the wild game, during the travel season of tourists and hunters of big game."[1] Who would the army select to accomplish such a mission?

Capt. Lester Cornish, commander of M Troop, was initially slated to lead the two-troop detachment. Command of a detachment devolved to the most senior officer present—in this case, Captain Cornish, commissioned from West Point in 1881, eight years before Young. Yet Nicholas wrote, "The duty became too hard for Captain Cornish and Captain Young, being next in rank, took command." What ailed Cornish and when he relinquished command are unclear, but many in the Ninth were still recovering from various debilitating diseases acquired in the Philippines.[2]

There is an alternate explanation for Cornish's absence. Sergeant Nicholas noted in a letter that during most of the summer of 1903, "Captain Cornish, as usual, was off 'Coffee Cooling'—shunning, of course." "Coffee cooling" was an old army term for "one who seeks easy details away from troops; one who is always looking for an easy job." Nicholas also noted that Cornish was prone to stealing credit for things other officers accomplished. There may be a kernel of truth in what Nicholas wrote, though Cornish was hospitalized in March and on convalescent leave until September 1903.[3]

With Captain Young thus in command, the two troops rode out of San Francisco on May 20, 1903, and headed southeast for Sequoia. Young marched the detachment nearly three hundred miles in sixteen days, averaging about twenty miles a day with one day of rest and cleanup, before entering Visalia. According to army doctrine, the unit started each day at dawn and rode for three hours; then the men dismounted, loosened saddle clinches, and walked while leading their horses for one hour. Then after getting back in the saddle for three hours, the men dismounted and walked their horses again for an hour. This continued all day, alternately riding and walking, and pausing to water the horses. They did not trot or gallop their horses; rather, they walked. A horse can walk faster than a man, traveling about five to six miles per hour verses two to three.[4]

In addition to the horses, Young's detachment traveled well equipped for the work ahead in Sequoia. Trailing the cavalry formation rode four escort wagons (for cargo), one Dougherty wagon (with seats for passengers), twenty draft mules pulling the wagons, two civilian packers, and six civilian teamsters. The wagons carried rations for the men, and they purchased fresh meat when needed. Young bought fuel for fires and forage for the animals along the way in the towns and local markets.[5]

A great deal of equipment was carried in the wagons and on the horses, all supervised by QM Sgt. George Brown: "tentage, tarpaulins, Sibley stoves, field ranges (large and small), axes, picks, shovels, crosscut saws, zinc tubs for washing clothing, water cans, galvanized-iron buckets, horse and mule shoes, blacksmith and farrier outfits, picket lines, ammunition, target material, and records." Each man brought "two pair of shoes, one pair at least being hobnailed. Overcoats, blankets, and bed sacks were taken, and came in handy during the latter part of the season."[6]

### *Road March*

Newspaper reports in the cities where the Buffalo Soldiers made stops on the road march to Sequoia offer some valuable information about Young, his men, and the perceptions of local white citizens outside of San Francisco. The fourteen halts en route to the park included Uncle Tom's Cabin, Mayfield, San Jose, Gilroy, Bell Station, San Luis house, Los Banos, Dos Palos, Firebaugh, Madera, Fresno, the King's River Bridge, Visalia, and Lemon Cove.

The coverage in the *Fresno Morning Republican* on the last day of May 1903 was extensive and largely positive. The novelty of cavalry bivouacking in Fresno each year had long ago ceased, according to the report, but "the first troop of colored soldiers that ever visited Fresno" became the "center of attraction for hundreds of spectators." The Buffalo Soldiers were something new, so crowds flocked to the park to "see enacted the same old camp life scenes by men of black instead of white skin."[7]

According to the report, Captain Young elicited the most interest, "being the only man in the United States army of his color and rank." The reporter noted Young "had hard work attaining his present position, for he has had always to work against the race prejudice of his brother officers." Further, "his strength of character and personality have overcome all prejudice," as evidenced by the three white officers serving under him—"all Southern men with the Southerner's natural antipathy toward the colored man, yet who hold their captain in the highest esteem and speak loudly in his praise."[8]

The journalist described Young as a "tall, slender man, with unusually refined features, a man who shows plainly that he is a finer mold than the average colored man." This is a recurring theme when white reporters came face to face with Young's intellect, character, and charm. Whites often tried to explain this away by saying he was the exception to the average Black American, rationalizing the pervasive racism that permeated society at the time.[9]

Young must have been in a talkative mood since the reporter quoted him extensively. When Young announced he was thirty-nine years old, the reporter told him he did not look over twenty-eight. To this Young responded:

> So I don't look my years! Well, that is because I never worry. I don't claim any personal credit for that because it is one of the colored man's racial traits. The white man worries constantly about conditions and things that may happen. The colored man does the best he can for the present and lets the future take care of itself. In the Philippines I have lain in a trench for hours, with only my head above water. But I never worried about such conditions. When I had done the best I could, I would find a place to rest my head and would sleep soundly for hours, awakened refreshed, with renewed vigor, ready to give the "Forward, march!" command.[10]

The reporter complimented Young as an "interesting and entertaining talker, being well informed on all general topics." Young spent part of the afternoon entertaining "twenty or thirty visitors to the camp with an impromptu lecture on the development of negro minstrelsy in the United States." Later that night, when the local militia companies hosted and entertained the Black enlisted soldiers at the armory hall, several of Young's troopers "proved themselves adept at buck and wing dancing," both staples of minstrel shows. The soldiers also presented a quartet "who made the armory ring with the sweetest melodies heard there in many moons."[11]

The militia officers hosted their counterparts from the Ninth Cavalry separately in the evening after the entertainment at the armory. Yet only the white officers—identified as 1st Lt. Winston Pilcher, 2nd Lt. Edwin Luther Cox, and Dr. James Tevis Arwine—attended. Young did not join them, explaining "that he never leaves camp for any social affairs." As noted previously, this was the Black officer's way of avoiding situations that made his white fellow officers uncomfortable in shared settings. In all things social and not involving official duties, Young stayed on his side of the color line.[12]

Not all of Young's soldiers behaved as well as he would have liked. Under the headline "Troopers Made Trouble," a newspaper noted:

> Several of the colored troopers who camped in the courthouse park yesterday gazed too freely upon Fresno beer last night and occasioned the police department a little trouble. One of them happened along just when Officer Simpson was telling a bicycle rider the law about fast riding, and he proceeded to tell the wheelman to ride just as fast as he pleased. Then he got noisy and made a fool of himself in several ways and the policeman took him to jail. A couple of others made the rounds of the tenderloin, and on the way one threatened to shoot three bullet holes through one of the tainted pigeons. She blew a police whistle, and the soldiers were soon on their way to jail. Officer Nelson was obliged to take in one who got particularly noisy on J Street. The men were held at the jail a little while, but were released at the request of their captain, who promised to see to their good behavior for the rest of the night.[13]

Several conclusions can be drawn based on the reporter's good-natured account. Some troopers of the Ninth Cavalry could not hold their alcohol, and at least four likely paid for their misbehavior with some punishment duty meted out by their sergeants after their release from jail. Some Black soldiers also visited the Fresno tenderloin, or red-light district, where the prostitutes (tainted pigeons) did not take kindly to threats. The soldiers carried their side arms during a road march, and weapons and alcohol do not mix well. Finally, the local constables were happy to let Captain Young deal with his troublesome soldiers himself. Young was keen to maintain good relations with Fresno officials since the city was the county seat of Fresno County, which bordered on the eastern gateway to Grant National Park, of which he was the incoming superintendent.[14]

### *Arrival*

Three-days after leaving Fresno, Young's detachment arrived in Visalia, the Tulare County seat and the nearest sizable town to Sequoia National Park.

Visalia was important to Captain Young during the 1903 summer season since it was the nearest rail and communications hub that connected him with his higher headquarters at the Presidio. The local newspaper reported: "Troops I and M (colored) of the 9th U.S. Cavalry, arrived in Visalia this morning en route to Sequoia National Park, having been selected for duty in the Sierras this year. The two colored troops are under the command of Captain Charles Young, the other officers being Lieutenant Winston Pilcher, Lieutenant E. L. Cox, and Dr. J. T. Arwine."[15]

The *Tulare County Times* described Captain Young as "a colored man, and the only officer in the United States Army of his color and rank. He is a graduate of West Point and is a man of brilliant parts, which those in conversation with him cannot fail to recognize. His career has been one of hard struggle against the prejudice of race, largely so while in attendance at West Point. He has, however, risen above all these difficulties by force of character and inherent ability." The article also described Young physically as "tall and slender," and possessing a "striking countenance."[16]

Young was anxious to convey to the reporters how seriously he took his mission in Sequoia. Knowing Young hailed from Kentucky, the newspaper reporter asked, "Do you know, that all Kentuckians are looked upon here as men who will use a gun?" Young responded, "Just tell them the entire troop are all natives of the Blue Grass state, and they will know that my orders will be made to be observed." The Black officer assured the reporters the "game in the Giant Forest will be protected" and the laws posted "obeyed while I am guarding the park."[17]

The reporter, like the one in Fresno, identified the three other officers who rode with Young as "white Southern men." Yet, according to the article, "such are the personal qualities of Captain Young and the whiteness of everything connected with him but his skin that nothing of the Southern man's antipathy for the colored race is manifested and they have only praise for their superior officer." Essentially the newspaper journalist qualified Captain Young's personal qualities as resulting from his "whiteness" of character that somehow trumped the color of his skin. As absurd as this sounds, such was a common and accepted sentiment at the time.[18]

Who were these officers? The first, Lt. Winston Pilcher, was the officer reassigned to I Troop in place of Lieutenant Pearson in March 1903. Pilcher, from Tennessee, had served as a volunteer officer during the Spanish-American and Philippine-American Wars, and accepted an appointment as a first lieutenant in the Ninth Cavalry in 1901. He did not stay assigned to I Troop long and was transferred to M Troop in mid-June 1903.[19]

The second Southern officer, Lt. Edwin L. Cox from Texas, flunked out of West Point in 1890 after one year. Cox was serving as a mining engineer in Idaho when he joined the army in 1898 and served as a corporal and sergeant for three years. In 1901 he passed his officer's exam and accepted a commission with the Ninth Cavalry as a second lieutenant. He commanded M Troop in Captain Cornish's absence until the transfer of Lieutenant Pilcher in June.[20]

A third cavalry officer assigned to Young for the summer was not mentioned in the article—Lt. John H. Howard. Born in Dayton, Ohio, and commissioned from the ranks, Howard had only been assigned to the Ninth Cavalry two years. However, he had shown leadership potential as an enlisted soldier in the Regular Army from 1899 to 1901, serving as a private, corporal, and sergeant in the Seventh U.S. Artillery in 1898 and as a private, corporal, sergeant, and first sergeant in M Troop, Sixth U.S. Cavalry.[21]

Howard was dispatched early to Mount Whitney with fifteen enlisted members of I and M Troops to guard the eastern approaches of Sequoia against livestock grazers. Assigned to L Troop, Howard was sent on temporary detached duty with M Troop beginning in April 1903. He was listed on detached service at Mount Whitney Military Reservation with fifteen men beginning in mid-May 1903, indicating they departed five days earlier than Captain Young and the rest of the detachment to reach Mount Whitney early. Based on information known about his detachment's return trip, Howard likely traveled from San Francisco by train through to Lone Pine, California, where he unloaded his men, equipment, and horses, and rode to a camp in the meadows below Mount Whitney from the eastern side of the Sierra.[22]

Finally, the third officer mentioned in the newspaper article was Dr. James Arwine, a civilian contract doctor employed by the War Department. He was not a Southerner, contrary to the article, since he was born in Indiana. Dr. Arwine was thirty years old and had served as a contract surgeon for the U.S. Army since his first assignment at Fort Ringgold,

Texas, in 1898. Before moving to San Francisco, his most recent assignment as a contract surgeon had been at Fort Liscum, Alaska, in 1900.[23]

Acting Assistant Surgeon Arwine was the man responsible for keeping the members of the Ninth Cavalry healthy while at Sequoia. He was one of thousands hired to make up for the shortage of commissioned medical doctors to staff army facilities. During the frontier period, these acting assistant surgeons were neither commissioned nor enlisted, never promoted, and habitually underappreciated. One author compared their status to that of "the mule, without pride of ancestry or hope of posterity, neither horse nor ass, unloved and unlovely, the recipient of contumelious language, the Army's standby in time of trouble."[24]

Until 1898, contract surgeons did not wear military uniforms. That changed after the army hired more than 650 civilian surgeons to handle the heavy workload during the Spanish-American War. During this war, the U.S. Army learned important lessons about the causes of vector-borne diseases and the effects of high-velocity bullets. It also gained a new appreciation for the importance of good medical personnel. After the war, the army allowed contract surgeons to wear uniforms with the rank of first lieutenant and medical insignia with the letters *CS*. For these reasons, Young and his troopers treated Dr. Arwine with the customs and courtesies of an officer.[25]

The army had been sending soldiers to patrol Sequoia for many years, but the arrival of African American soldiers commanded by a black officer caused quite a stir among the white citizens of Visalia. Its small minority community paid a great deal of attention to the newcomers as well. The newspaper described Captain Young's reaction to the interest shown by a group of local Black children: "He questioned them kindly as to their opportunities and told them to have high aim and to be industrious." He stood before them as a living role model of what that philosophy could achieve for a Black man in 1903.[26]

The day after leaving Visalia, Young arrived in Lemon Cove, about fifteen miles or one day's ride from his destination at Kaweah in Three Rivers. Chief Ranger Ernest Britten met Young at Lemon Cove on June 3 to tell him where to establish his camp the following day. Britten, who was the chief ranger at Sequoia working for the Interior Department, served as Young's right-hand man during the summer season. Britten was the first park ranger at Sequoia National Park and knew the area like the back of his hand, having homesteaded the South Fork of the Kaweah River with his father in the late 1880s. Young was fortunate to have him as a guide, since neither he nor his men had ever been to the area.[27]

On June 4, Ranger Britten guided Young and his eighty-three troopers into the foothill community of Kaweah, a small ranching and logging settlement on the North Fork of the Kaweah River near the Kaweah Post Office. There Young established his headquarters and supply depot on land offered by Ralph Hopping and prepared for a busy summer of patrolling and roadbuilding. Young maintained this camp throughout the summer as a supply depot and a place where the soldiers could conduct their annual target practice. He also kept his headquarters and soldiers there until moving the camp to the Marble Fork Bridge.[28]

Young immediately dispatched parties of soldiers commanded by officers or noncommissioned officers to various entry points of Sequoia and General Grant National Parks to guard against poaching and livestock grazing. This supplemented Lieutenant Howard and his detachment, which had been sent earlier to Mount Whitney. Then Young set about examining what needed to be done to improve the wagon road into Sequoia National Park, his most important mission for the summer.[29]

### *Roadbuilding*

Young put some of the engineering courses he took at West Point to use during his six months at Sequoia, building roads to make the park more accessible to tourists. He had nearly failed to graduate from West Point thirteen years earlier due to his difficulties mastering military engineering. His instructor, 1st Lt. George W. Goethals, a future major general and builder of the Panama Canal, failed him in the subject during Young's senior year. Goethals then spent two summer months tutoring Cadet Young so he could pass the reexamination in engineering and graduate. In a peculiar twist, the year that Young was blasting his way through the mountains to the Giant Forest, the treaty was ratified for the construction of the Panama Canal, an entity that would influence Young's next assignment.[30]

Young's work on the road into Sequoia built on what had begun three years before. In 1899 members of the Visalia Board of Trade and representatives of the Southern Pacific and Santa Fe Railroads had invited Rep. James C. Needham (R-CA) to conduct a twenty-five-day inspection tour of Sequoia National Park. They impressed upon him the need for funds to repair the existing road and extend it into the Giant Forest. Needham took the message back to Washington, and in 1900 Congress allocated $10,000 for constructing the road. Work began in July 1900 and continued in the summers that followed until Young arrived in 1903 to complete about six miles of roadbed. Young's mission was to finish the partially completed road all the way to the Giant Forest, which was the key attraction of Sequoia National Park.[31]

Some work had already been done on the road, which the local Kaweah Co-Operative Colony began building in 1887. Members of the colony, a utopian socialist group established in 1886, constructed a road from Kaweah to the lower edge of the timber belt. They had filed claims in the conifer zone that included the Sequoia groves and hoped to support their co-operative community by logging the pine and fir forest adjacent to the Giant Forest. The colony's utopian vision ended when Congress established Sequoia and Grant National Parks in 1890, and the members dissolved the cooperative in 1892.[32]

Though the colony dissolved long before Young reached Sequoia, the former members still resided in the area and became valuable partners in several ways. Many of the ex-colonists were educated and had valuable skills that Young employed on the road gangs pushing through to the Giant Forest. They were also eager to work and make a living in the wake of the colony's collapse. A number had recently emigrated from Europe and displayed a racial tolerance that made them more accepting of Young and his Buffalo Soldiers. And Young would find friends among them.

Some improvement work on the road had already begun when Young arrived in June 1903. Ranger Britten had supervised a crew of ten men that began work the second half of May 1903, making general repairs and fixing winter damage on the road from the park line to the Marble Fork Bridge. This allowed the new work above the bridge to start in earnest when Captain Young and the two troops arrived along with the rest of the civilian work force.[33]

Young telegraphed the Interior Department on June 3 from Visalia, asking permission to start on the road to the Giant Forest immediately on reaching Kaweah. He wanted roadbuilding to begin in June while the ground was soft instead of July as in previous years. After his arrival at Kaweah, Captain Young rode with Ranger Britten to the Marble Fork Bridge on June 5 to take his first look at the road and the work required in the coming months.[34]

On June 10, Young forwarded the approved payrolls for May 1903 that Ranger Britten prepared to the Department of the Interior. Young also requested that one check be sent to him for this and all future monthly claims to streamline the process of paying for labor, services, and supplies. This request was approved, thus enabling Young to start work early in June and pay for the work of his civilian crew quicker throughout the summer season.[35]

On June 11, Young supervised the return to road construction starting about a mile above the bridge at Marble Fork. According to Sergeant Nicholas, "Captain Young had the mission to complete the remaining five miles before the threat of snow closed the park for the season." His task was to complete five miles of road in only one summer, nearly matching the six miles that other preceding crews had needed three seasons to build.[36]

For the month of June, Young submitted an approved payroll of $1,730.50 for the labor of sixty men. The highest-paid civilians were the four gang foremen and single powderman, who made $3.00 a day. Then came the assistant foremen, blacksmiths, drillers, rider, stump blasters, timber feller, and plow holder who took home $2.50 a day. Finally, the laborers and cooks were paid $2.00 a day. The highest-paid man was gang foreman Abe B. Burdick, who put in twenty-five days of service and received $75 for the month, while the longest-working man was C. E. Wells, who worked every day, including Sundays, fetching water for the camp.[37]

Though Young served as the acting superintendent of Sequoia National Park, providing leadership, administering pay, and supplying tools, wagons, and horses, civilian workers did most of the actual work on the road from Kaweah. Sergeant Nicholas acknowledged "with the assistance of the regular Civil Engineer Mr. [George] Welch, Chief Ranger Ernest Britten, and Ranger [Lew] Davis as powder man to blast the right-of-way, the workmen and laborers were mustered together and work began with great strides in June, or as soon as the snow cleared away."[38]

*Fourth of July*

With a month of work behind them, Captain Young granted his troopers a break to commemorate Independence Day. The Fourth of July was a federal holiday, so the soldiers would have had the day off to prepare for a special evening show. The event provided Young's Black soldiers, still new to the residents of Kaweah, an opportunity to show off their equestrian skills. And the troopers of the Ninth chose a unique way of celebrating the Fourth—a quadrille.[39]

Young frequently organized shows and musical events to entertain and occupy his troopers. Yet according to a colorful newspaper account:

> The equine quadrille was invented by Sergeant Jones and Trooper Merrell of I Troop and Trooper Aiken of M Troop, and was repeated on different occasions to while away the tedious hours while the two troops were on duty in the reserve. The first performance was due to a sudden inspiration, and was entirely impromptu—planned on the Fourth of July as a fitting celebration of the national holiday. No previous drill had rendered the animals familiar with their steps. Their masters had spent many a merry night dancing to the stirring music of the military band. But it was due to other training that the big troop horses were able to go through the difficult evolutions of the dance with grace and spirit and without a hitch.[40]

The sergeant Jones mentioned by the newspaper reporter was Jasper Jones, Captain Young's trusted first sergeant. Jones had been mastering his equine skills since he joined the Ninth Cavalry more than twenty years earlier. William H. Merrell, a twenty-two-year-old private from Horse Cave, Kentucky, had only been in the army three years and had reenlisted for a second term at Kaweah a week earlier. He must have acquired some of his horsemanship skills in Kentucky before his army service.[41]

Young, a talented musician, encouraged his soldiers to form bands as an escape from the tedium of military life. The reporter noted:

> The music for this equestrian quadrille was furnished by a band of ten men from the two troops—natural musicians, all—who played mandolins and guitars with a skill and spirit which went straight to the hearts and feet of the men and horses. Select ragtime was the order of the

> night—ragtime to which a particular piquancy was given by the unusual tempo, for "Creole Belles" in half time has an effect all its own. The notes chimed sweetly with the rustling of the wind in the tall sequoias and the murmur of Three Rivers below. And the hollow thunder of sixty-four iron-shod hoofs on the wooden bridge made striking contrast with the world-old union of music and moonshine.[42]

The performance lasted fifteen minutes and was staged on the wooden bridge over Marble Fork. There, in the moonlight, the report continued,

> mounted on their handsome cavalry chargers, sixteen dusky soldiers of I and M Troops went through the figures of the quadrille in the presence of their fellow troopers and a goodly number of campers, who saw in the holiday antics of the colored riders something to vary the monotony of camp life and also a unique way of celebrating the Glorious Fourth. It was, at least, a welcome change from the over-prevalent small boy, with his popgun and squib and giant cracker.

Since partners were required in such a dance, half the troopers played the part of women, "since ladies were not available."

> Nothing daunted, the dusky troopers obviated the difficulty and preserved the conventions by assigning the character to the men who best looked the part, adding effect by dressing the "ladies" in flowing feminine draperies. Owing to the scarcity of these garments in the forest reserve, it was found necessary to use shelter tents for two or three of the gentle partners, but it is claimed by the troopers that the snowy canvas against the satin bay of the horses was particularly effective.

According to the reporter, who witnessed the equine quadrille, the campers and spectators from Three Rivers were delighted with the show. The writer credited the ease with which the troopers put their mounts through the movements to long military training and a natural love of horses. "So the high-spirited beasts took the new figures as a matter of course, and were willing to face the music and the audience with the same equanimity with which they had stood fire with their black riders."[43]

This was just the opening salvo of Captain Young's campaign to win the hearts and minds of the local residents and open the park to tourists.

The audience included many of the civilian laborers who worked on the road and were key to the success of opening Sequoia to visitors. Showing the human side of the troopers and demonstrating their discipline would contribute to the success of his mission.

*General Grant National Park and Mount Whitney*

After the Fourth of July, while construction continued at Sequoia on the road to the Giant Forest, work began on improvements to General Grant National Park under the supervision of Ranger Davis. Young had responsibility for improvements in both parks, which were reached by different roads—Sequoia from the southwest and Grant from the west. At Grant National Park, which was accessed from Fresno and Squaw Valley (now Palisades Tahoe) in the west, work commenced in early July and continued throughout the month, employing a smaller crew of eight civilians under foreman J. O. Carter. The July payroll of $383 paid the salaries of a foreman, blacksmith, cook, powderman, teamster, and three laborers.[44]

Guided by Ranger Britten, Captain Young rode to General Grant National Park on July 6 to meet with Ranger Davis and Foreman Carter about the work to be done, the completion of two miles of road, by the civilian crew inside the park. Young also talked to the Fresno County authorities outside the boundaries to the west and received assurances they would improve access to the park.[45]

Once Young saw that the work on the two different roads to Sequoia and General Grant Parks were in good hands, he rode on July 9 with a group that would relieve a fifteen-man detachment of Ninth Cavalry troopers under Lieutenant Howard camped in the meadows below Mount Whitney. The relief force under Young took two days of hard riding on difficult trails to reach the detachment. He took Sgt. Wilson Cary as the senior noncommissioned officer in charge of this body of troopers. Sergeant Nicholas accompanied Captain Young and later returned with him and some of the soldiers who had served at Mount Whitney since May.[46]

Nicholas noted, "Captain Young made several trips mounted to Mount Whitney, by trail 75 miles from the parks to see that the trails to the top were cleared of snow. The soldiers cleared this snow away with shovels, as much as 17 feet deep in many places, 13 miles from Lone Pine in Inyo County,

California." Along with the mission of guarding against illegal grazing, the detachment began work on two new trails between Lone Pine and Mount Whitney, the highest mountain in the United States at the time.[47]

When Young returned from Mount Whitney and his other rounds in the park in early August, most of the construction on the road to the Giant Forest was complete. He sent the following report to the Interior Department in Washington at the end of August: "I submit that more work has been done, and better work through rougher country than has been done in any two years previous to this. I claim no special credit for this, as it is largely due to the department's permission to allow work to begin early in the season when the ground was moist and when good men were available."[48]

The local *Daily Visalia Delta* in early August 1903 described Young's satisfaction with the pace of construction: "Captain Young says that the men who have been working on the road have done fully three months of work in just half that length of time and he thinks they are fully deserving of compliments." On August 15, the *Delta* reported that "the wagon road will be completed clean to the forest today and Captain Young will make his first visit into the forest in a wagon. When he began the work he made a vow not to enter the forest until he could do so in a wagon drawn by four horses. This he will do today."[49]

According to Sergeant Nicholas, "To celebrate the completion of the road, four mule teams were hitched to wagons, and Captain Young, some of the soldiers, and the staff of employees were the first to ride into the Giant Forest on a regular built wagon road." Tourists would soon follow but so might poachers and herders.[50]

### *Park Patrolling*

While the workers built roads and his soldiers cleared trails, Young detailed most of his Ninth Cavalry troopers to guard the park against herders grazing their livestock illegally. This was no easy task since the locals knew every back trail and shortcut into the park. They had been doing this for years before the park property was set aside, and for many, grazing their livestock on the land was their livelihood. It became a cat-and-mouse game repeated each season when the mounted soldiers arrived in Sequoia from San Francisco.

Congress had created Sequoia National Park on September 25, 1890, the first such park in California and only the second national park in the United States after Yellowstone was established in Wyoming in 1872. Another bill in Congress a week later on October 1, 1890, tripled the original size of Sequoia and set aside nearby the smaller General Grant National Park. The chief goal of this legislation was the "preservation of all timber, mineral deposits, natural curiosities, or wonders within said reservation, and their retention in their natural condition." As was the case in Yellowstone, Congress intended that Sequoia National Park be developed into a "public park or pleasuring ground."[51]

Roadbuilding and trail clearing were important first steps in creating a public park, yet tourists would stay home if the trees and animals disappeared and if the alpine meadows of the High Sierra were stripped bare of its natural fauna. By the time Young arrived, logging no longer posed a threat in the park proper, but livestock overgrazing did. Sheepherders were the main enemy. In 1876 John Muir wrote, "Incredible numbers of sheep are driven to the mountain pastures every summer, and their course is ever marked by desolation. Every wild botanic garden is trodden down, the shrubs are stripped of leaves as if devoured by locust, and the woods are burned." An estimated 200,000 sheep entered the park illegally in 1898, when the demand for soldiers to fight in Cuba left Sequoia unprotected. After the war, the troops returned to stem the tide.[52]

One ploy Young used to catch the cattle and sheep grazers off guard was dispatching Lieutenant Howard and his detachment to the Mount Whitney area early to cut off the eastern access to the park. According to the *Delta*, "During the time Captain Young was over there, he had no trouble with the sheep men or with any other stock men. As a result of the guard duty, the meadows have not been fed off and there has been plenty of feed for the stock used this year by the tourists." The only way tourists could reach Sequoia was by horse, and their animals had to graze on grass in the park to survive.[53]

The other threat was poaching. The residents had hunted freely for years in the High Sierra, and many depended on wild game to put food on their tables. Additionally, the locals believed that soldiers were taking advantage of their privileged position to poach themselves. In 1903 Captain Young issued an order to lock up the carbines in camp to reassure the locals and keep his own men honest, since their pistols were not effective hunting weapons. The only times Young had the carbines unboxed was for annual target practice and on two occasions when patrols passed outside of the park's boundaries.[54]

Young reported only one case of illegal hunting in 1903 by a man who fired his pistol at a deer and missed. Granted permission to carry a revolver for self-protection in the park, the man had ridden into the Giant Forest in a stage operated by John Broder and Ralph Hopping, whose company had the contract with the Interior Department to bring tourists into Sequoia National Park. Captain Young had appointed both Hopping and Broder as deputy forest rangers to give them authority over tourists and campers under their supervision in the park. Hopper disarmed and arrested the man who fired his pistol on the spot.[55]

### *Firefighting*

Another important task the soldiers performed as park rangers at Sequoia was firefighting. Every summer, when the brush around the giant Sequoias dried out, fires started as the result of random lightning. Fires were a natural and necessary phenomenon in the High Sierra. In the complicated process of seed germination, Sequoias require fires to trigger the release of seeds. The blast of heat from wildfires opens their cones, sending a shower of seeds to the forest floor, where they establish themselves on the newly cleared ground.

Captain Young and his soldiers likely did not understand this seed germination process, but they did recognize the need to fight fires, especially those set by careless campers. According to one account passed down by Ranger Britton, Young and his troopers had been fighting one such fire at Oriole Lake above Lake Canyon, and it took longer than expected. When they ran out of rations, Young asked Mrs. Eliza Grunigen, whose house there served as a way station, if she would feed his men. Young knew the family, who were also former colony members, since Eliza's son John was on the payroll of the civilian crew building the road into the Giant Forest.[56]

When Mrs. Grunigen agreed to feed his men, Young informed her that his troopers would come in the house, pick up their plates, and eat outside. According to historian Sophie Britten, "Highly indignant, she declared they would either come inside and eat or they would not eat at all." Young agreed, and they enjoyed a hearty meal inside the house. After the meal, Captain Young insisted that his men clean up the kitchen in return for the fine food. Again, Britten: "They did, and when they were through, the kitchen shone from ceiling to floor." In this and many other things Young did at Sequoia, he earned the appreciation and respect of the independent-minded locals. The people eventually referred to him as "our Captain."[57]

*Land Purchases*

Young was farsighted in his thinking about the future of Sequoia even though he was assigned as superintendent for a single season. In addition to building roads, protecting the park from poachers and grazers, fighting fires, and keeping his soldiers out of trouble, he found time to tackle other long-term problems in the park. When the U.S. government acquired the land comprising Sequoia and General Grant National Parks, substantial private tracts remained within its borders. Young found a solution to this thorny problem that would save the U.S. Treasury money and reassure the private landholders.[58]

When Young arrived in 1903, individuals held eighteen legal claims to a total of 3,877 acres of parkland that contained nine thousand giant sequoia trees. In 1902 the secretary of interior instructed Young's predecessor, Capt. Frank Barton, to determine the threat posed by this private land at Sequoia. Barton warned that the very road the U.S. Army was building into the park for tourists would lead to its ruin. He concluded that "there seemed to be no reason for doubting, judging from common report, that when the road is completed into the Giant Forest it was the intention of the owners of patented lands in the forest to cut the timber thereon and to make use of the government road to haul the same to market."[59]

Captain Young cultivated good relations with the local landowners in and around Sequoia. He approached them individually during his rounds of the park and tactfully discussed the situation with the help of Ranger Britten. By the end of the season, Young had convinced all the private landholders within the park boundaries to accept a fair price for their lands. Nicholas wrote: "Captain Young secured names and signatures of all homestead owners of park land and the price they would agree to sell to [the] United States. He recommended to the Department of Interior the repossession of these many claims by purchase by the U.S. Government, for the full benefit of the general touring and camping public." Washington did not follow through quickly, however, and the lands were purchased a decade later for three times the price Young had negotiated.[60]

*Winsers, Britten, and Locals*

Surprisingly, even though Young led an all-Black army unit in a remote area populated by independently minded people, he developed a positive relationship with the local white community in the short time he was the acting superintendent. He established an especially close friendship with a local settler and former Kaweah Colony member named Philip Winser; his wife, Blanche; and their son, Lindley. Young also depended heavily on the advice and goodwill of Chief Ranger Ernest Britten. All of this was unusual by the standards of the day and ran counter to Young's self-imposed regime of social separation from whites that he had long practiced in the army.[61]

Nicholas wrote:

> All the people of this section of the park community were white; not one colored of any races, save the soldiers. They were carried away with him [Young] because of his unusual intelligence, ability, and generosity. Information and cooperation from all and to all was always at hand. Social gatherings in the homes and at the camps were many for Captain Young and his men. In fact, he had no enemies among the civilians or the soldiers in any of the places or locations which he happened to be serving.[62]

Shortly after Young's arrival at Sequoia, he received an invitation from Philip Winser and his wife, Blanche. Winser related Young's initial hesitation to accept the couple's invitation:

> We heard he had come and Blanche, sensing what might be, asked me to call and see if he would visit us. He received me as the courteous gentleman he was, but gently turned aside the invitation. Again, we returned, to at last elicit the admission that he preferred to stay on his own side of the fence. Then we told him, for us there was no fence, and after that the promise that one of his men should share the invitation,

they came and so began a friendship with a rare and cultured soul, which lasted till his death.[63]

Winser mentioned the heartfelt note he received from Young, when the latter replied to the invitation in June 1903. Young had the note delivered to Winser by his trooper Henry Whitfield.

> My very dear Mr. Winser:
>
> It seems tame to tell you in the conventional way how much I appreciate the kind invitation of you and Mrs. Winser. I feel like breaking a rule I have sworn by this many and a year and come—. We will be better acquainted, and I shall speak to you from my heart of the many things that you believe I am able to tell you with respect to myself and my people.[64]

Young grew very fond of the Winsers' young son, Lindley. He always mentioned his name in subsequent letters and asked the parents to pass on his love and hugs. Young's troopers also doted on Lindley and marveled at the young boy's ability to ride his mare, Daisey. According to Philip Winser, when Lindley galloped near the Black soldiers, bareheaded, bare legged, and barefoot, the troopers would come out and shout, "Go it, cowboy!"[65]

Philip Winser noted that Captain Young confessed he went through hell to get his commission and therefore conceded that "I have no fear for the future life." He described Young as "a man of fine physique, well built, active, and powerful. His face had an olive tint from an Arab forebearer and most pleasing expression, with eyes of kindness and intelligence all his own."[66]

Young and the Winsers grew to be close friends and met as often as his duties as superintendent allowed. The strength of the friendship endured after Young left Sequoia in the fall. Afterward Philip Winser and Charles Young carried on an active correspondence for years. In a letter written a year later from the Caribbean, Young reflected fondly on his time at Sequoia and yearned for an "hour's ride up the mountain road."[67]

Captain Young also developed a close working relationship with Chief Ranger Ernest Britten. The ranger maintained a diary to keep track of his work that showed frequent meetings with Young during the period. Britten served as his guide the entire summer, helping him and his troopers navigate the rugged roads and steep trails in and around the park. Though he references meeting with Young often, in his diary Britten mentioned the names of only two other soldiers during the summer in the Giant Forest: "With the assistance of Corporal [James A.] Mosby and Corporal [Dee] Smith counted Redwood [Sequoia] trees."[68]

According to historian Sophie Britten, the cavalry troopers and white road workers played poker to pass the time in the evenings. One of the prizes that was won and passed around to the winner each night was a money belt sewn with many silver dollars. At the end of the summer season, the Black troopers of the Ninth gave the money belt to Ranger Britten for the kindness he showed them. Britten kept this keepsake as a prized possession.[69]

Captain Young's experiences at Sequoia and the relationships he developed with local white residents changed him. Heretofore, Young had "preferred to stay on his side of the fence," his means of survival as a Black army officer in a white officer corps. As Young told Philip and Blanche Winser in later years, "he had come to Kaweah with his heart full of bitterness and left it a different man with a better outlook." Psychologically, Young had been isolated for so many years that his sudden release resulted in a flowing friendship. Human kindness can be found in the most surprising places, and Young found it in Sequoia.[70]

When Captain Young rode into Sequoia at the head of two troops of the Ninth Cavalry in May 1903, he had little idea of the challenges ahead. The complex operation required him to organize his Black soldiers to protect the park from herders, to blaze trails, and to fight fires, while he also managed a force of white workers building roads to open the Sequoia and General Grant National Parks to tourists. By August, after three months of work, his chief tasks were complete, and more progress had been made on the roads and trails into the parks than in the previous three years.

Young accomplished his mission while winning the respect of the independently minded residents and negotiated with landowners within the boundaries of the park to sell their properties at a fair price. In the process, Young established friendships with white civilians that endured long after his time at Sequoia and caused him to change his self-imposed philosophy of staying on his side of the racial divide. He had cause to celebrate.

# 6

## Celebration and Departure

> The party of Visalians who will attend Captain Young's barbecue at the soldiers' camp at Giant Forest Sunday, will leave this city today at about noon and expect to arrive at the destination Sunday morning at 5 o'clock.
> —*Daily Visalia Delta*, August 29, 1903

Captain Young was justifiably pleased with his accomplishments in the summer of 1903. His officers, enlisted troopers, park rangers, and civilian work crews succeeded in completing roads to the Giant Forest of Sequoia as well as to General Grant National Park, opening both to tourist wagon traffic. In addition, by maintaining an outpost at Mount Whitney and aggressively patrolling routes into the parks, the soldiers also prevented sheep and cattle from grazing in the reserve. With cold weather approaching, it was time to celebrate and prepare for the move back to winter quarters at the Presidio.

### *Forest Feast*

Young had reason to celebrate, since he had achieved as much in one season as had been done by earlier military superintendents in the three previous years. He decided his soldiers, rangers, and civilians deserved a party to mark the completion of the wagon road to the Giant Forest from the valley below. And by the time of the commemoration, the wagon road had been extended even farther, from the principal camp at Round Meadow to the popular destination of Moro Rock.

According to Sergeant Nicholas, "After the road was completed, Captain Young decided to hold a picnic dinner [lunch] to celebrate and honor the men for their work on the road. All of the campers were also invited. The guests of honor [were the] governor of the state, Governor [George] Pardee, and party, also the chamber of commerce of Visalia, California."[1] The newspaper noted the local dignitaries from Visalia and railroad officials also attended the picnic. Young was politically savvy and invited the local and state politicians whose support was so important for the work yet to be done.[2]

Before a party could be thrown, Young had to gather the fixings for the feast. According to Nicholas:

> While going to Visalia 52 miles away in a Dougherty wagon, [with] 4 mules, Captain Young accompanied Sergeants [William] Nicholas, [Samuel] Pierce, and [Wirt] Langley, to purchase the materials for the picnic dinner. Captain Young had several hundred dollars in gold coins in his trouser pockets, some of which belonged to the men of his troop, for safekeeping. This was at night. We became sleepy and stretched out on the floor of the wagon in the hay for a little sleep. The next morning when we arrived in Visalia, Captain Young was short of just $105.00. The money had fallen out of his pockets in the hay and that amount had sifted through the cracks in the floor of the wagon along the roadside in the deep dust and could not be recovered by diligent search. No trace of any of it was ever heard from, but Captain Young readily reimbursed the men with every dollar lost from his own private funds.[3]

It was no easy task in 1903 to travel from the valley below to the Giant Forest in Sequoia National Park, even with the wagon road completed. According to the *Daily Visalia Delta*:

> The party of Visalians who will attend Captain Young's barbeque at the soldiers' camp in Giant Forest Sunday, will leave this city today [Saturday] at about noon and expect to arrive at their destination Sunday morning at 5 o'clock. They will travel all night and will go in Broder & Hopping's stage. The return trip will be made Sunday afternoon and night. The trip will be a strenuous one for the guests, but they deem it

worthwhile and will, no doubt, think nothing but the good time they had until Monday morning. Then oh![4]

Captain Young composed a poem for the event which was printed on cards mounted atop Sequoia bark with the following words:

We sat in the Redwood's shade
  After the road was made
And ate our lunch from boxes laid
  On shovel, pick, and spade.[5]

Captain Young had help in preparing the place cards with the poem he wrote. According to Young's friend Philip Winser, who missed the picnic because he was away on a fishing trip, his wife, Blanche, and son, Lindley, were camped in the forest and helped in the preparations. "She and the other camping ladies helped in every way they could and one of the things she did was to prepare place cards in water colors, headed with crossed bar, pick, and shovel." The place cards, written in a beautiful script, were mounted upon sequoia bark, and decorated with a red ribbon, a sequoia cone, and a wreath of Spanish moss (see figure 24).[6]

Nicholas wrote that it was "the stewards and cooks who prepared the picnic," which was held at lunchtime on Sunday, August 30, 1903. "Large logs served as tables covered with bleached cotton tablecloths. Small fruit baskets, filled with fried chicken, ham and cheese sandwiches, and assorted fresh fruits of the season, were [served] on picks, shovels, and spades, and passed along to the guests to help themselves. Beer (pint bottles) [and] hot coffee was served with the food" (see figures 22 and 23).[7]

By all accounts, the picnic was a smashing success. According to Blanche Winser, all "had a great time, all of them, the troopers handed the food round as stated in boxes lashed to shovels and pick." To have such an elaborate feast in the heretofore isolated Giant Forest must have been quite a novelty for the participants.[8]

Reports of the event in the newspaper on Monday praised the "great feast that was given last Sunday at Giant Forest by Captain Young" and commended "the splendid road that has been perfected into the forests through the untiring efforts of him." Maj. George W. Stewart, a land agent from Visalia and an editor of the *Daily Visalia Delta*, was the toastmaster and paid tribute to Young, and these honors were "happily responded to by Captain Young in language more choice than eloquent." Adolf Lewis, A. R. Orr, and George Welch also gave remarks, all of which were well received by Captain Young.[9]

The article noted:

> The ability with which Captain Young has completed the road has caused many favorable remarks to be bestowed upon him, and the manner in which he has accomplished the work has made for him many friends. The road is so made now that a buggy or carriage can be driven into the forest without the accustomed packing of several miles that has been necessary in the past to reach the place of beauty. . . . The road is one of the best if not the best mountain road to be found in the state.[10]

After the picnic lunch, Young organized a program "which consisted of instrumental and vocal music and is said to have been very entertaining. Captain Young then took the party of pleasure seekers through the park and showed them all the points of interest that are most known." The representatives from the Southern Pacific and Santa Fe Railroads were especially impressed with the potential for tourism. W. G. Dozier of the Southern Pacific, commented that the "work accomplished by Young is almost beyond comprehension."[11]

The forest feast was a fitting and memorable ending for a successful season of roadbuilding. At the conclusion of the picnic that Sunday afternoon, the crowd of one hundred men, women, and children loaded into wagons for the long ride down the mountain. The article noted that the soldiers, workers, and campers remained to clean up before retiring to their canvas quarters in the Giant Forest.

### *Booker T. Washington Tree*

The newspaper article covering the celebration in the Giant Forest noted one other significant development. According to the reporter, "So much interest had Captain Young taken in the work, and so appreciative are the leading citizens and representative men of this city that a tree has been selected and in the future Captain Young's name will be inscribed on it never to blot out, and the tree will bear his name."[12]

As a government official, Young could not accept such a tribute. Young declined the honor as soon as he got wind of the idea, yet he agreed to name one of the great trees after Booker T. Washington. This decision was influenced by his respect for the great African American leader and by Washington's recent visit to San Francisco.[13]

Young's friend, Philip Winser, noted, "They wanted to name a tree for our Captain but he refused, saying they could do so if they felt the same way, twenty years hence and they compromised on one for Booker T. Washington." Years later in 1933, Winser raised the issue of naming a tree after Young with park officials to no avail. Sequoia National Park would wait 101 years to name a tree after Young as was originally intended by the "leading citizens and representative men" from the area surrounding Sequoia.[14]

Young also addressed the issue of naming the big sequoias in his annual report to the Interior Department. He recommended that none be given to trees at Sequoia National Park unless they were "acceptable to the entire nation." He stated, "I permitted the naming of three trees in Sequoia Park this season: One 'G.A.R.' tree, in honor of the Grand Army of the Republic; another, from its particular growth of three large trees from one big trunk, was named 'I.O.O.F.,' for the Odd Fellows of the country; and the third, after repeated requests from visitors and the wishes of the workmen who finished the Giant Forest road, was named after that great and good American, Booker T. Washington." These new names reflected Young's respect for his father, his own African American heritage, and his country. His father, Gabriel, having served in the Union Army, belonged to the GAR—a fraternal organization of the northern veterans of the Civil War—after the war and was an active member in the Independent Order of Odd Fellows.[15]

Young did not neglect the other giant sequoia trees that had already been named in the parks. He detailed his men to build fences around the General Grant and General Sherman trees to prevent damage to the giants. According to Young, the fences were "necessary to prevent theft of bark and standing upon their roots by photographic parties." Ironically, they constructed these fences out of lumber cut from sequoia trees.[16]

During his summer stay at Sequoia, Young developed a deep respect for the giant sequoias and other trees in the High Sierra. In his final report, he reasoned: "Indeed, a journey through this park and the Sierra Forest

Reserve to the Mount Whitney country will convince even the least thoughtful man of the needfulness of preserving these mountains just as they are, with their clothing of trees, shrubs, rocks, and vines, and of their importance to the valleys below as reservoirs for storage of water for agricultural and domestic purposes. In this, then, lies the necessity of forest preservation." Young also gave an example in his report of the deforestation of once-wooded regions of Serbia in Europe that resulted in erosion and the silting of the Morava River.[17]

In only one area did Young show a shortcoming recognized by modern environmentalists. He suggested that "permission be given rangers for the extermination of coyotes and mountain lions" to increase the number of deer. In spite of this, his careful study of the ecology of the Sequoia and General Grant National Parks in his final report showed Young's sophisticated thinking about the environment of the region.[18]

### *Doctor Arwine*

One man who shared Young's appreciation for science was also his closest companion at Sequoia—Dr. James T. Arwine, the contract surgeon assigned to the detachment. Dr. Arwine maintained an aid station at Camp Kaweah and later the Marble Fork Bridge camp where soldiers who were sick or injured could report for treatment. Since no enlisted Hospital Corps members deployed with the detachment, Captain Young probably staffed the aid station with his own soldiers, who would have referred to the doctor in army slang as "Saw-Bones."[19]

Dr. Arwine had served with the Buffalo Soldiers before. He was stationed at Fort Ringgold, Texas, as the post surgeon in 1899, a time when the fort was occupied by B Troop, Tenth Cavalry, and a detachment of the Black Seminole Scouts. This garrison was later replaced by D Troop, Ninth Cavalry, so he had previously served with Black cavalrymen.[20]

Arwine must have done his job well at Sequoia since the regimental returns showed the detachment had very few men on the sick list from May to October 1903. None were listed as sick in May, two in June, none in July, one in August, one in September, and two in October. This record was impressive considering the hard riding and long hours of patrolling and trail clearing conducted by the troops. The fresh air and scarcity of alcohol probably contributed in a positive way.[21]

The mission at Sequoia was harder on the horses than on the men, especially while soldiers maintained communications between the detachments at Sequoia and Mount Whitney. Captain Young lamented that he left some "dead horses on the trails, either from exhaustion from fatigue and the elevation or from having eaten poisonous weeds in the meadows." He noted that "when horses were not wholly killed, they were in many cases so completely 'played out' as to render them unfit for cavalry service." Young reported losing five horses during the summer.[22]

Since the squadron's single veterinarian was assigned to Yosemite for the summer, Dr. Arwine probably had the added responsibility of caring for the sick horses. In this he was assisted by the civilian teamsters as well as the troop saddler, farrier, and blacksmith, all of whom shared the duties of caring for the horses.[23]

Arwine's wife, Martha, traveled to Sequoia for an extended visit from San Francisco beginning in late June 1903. The doctor must have had a sense of humor because he sent his wife to Visalia with some mischief in mind. According to a newspaper report in August 1903, "The surgeon proposed to do something in the way of entertaining to assist Captain Young." The group of Visalia businessmen was preparing for the journey to Sequoia for the celebration in the Giant Forest two days later, so Dr. Arwine supplied his wife with some information to pass along to the Visalians as a practical joke on his captain.[24]

The newspaper elaborated on Arwine's mischief:

> The Visalians cannot get into the camp without passing his [Young's] quarters which are located near the river. It is not his intention to invite them to come over and drop in. The Delta [*Daily Visalia*] can furnish the password, which is "Hello! Is there anything cool in the creek?" This will be sufficient evidence and the parties giving it will be cordially received and the best brand of "extra pale" will be passed around.

The record is silent on whether the Visalians had the opportunity to carry out the practical joke and collect their beer.[25]

This incident points to an affable relationship between Young and Arwine. The local newspapers reported that Captain Young rode into town often in the company of the camp doctor on what they referred to as their "regular monthly visit." Since both men were educated and about the same age, that they developed a camaraderie is not surprising. They would have spent a great deal of time together in discussions around a campfire or in Young's command post.[26]

*Reenlistments and Replacements*

Although Young's soldiers remained healthy, the routine business of losses and replacements continued. Some soldiers, whose release from the army was pending, had remained behind at the Presidio to facilitate their transition to civilian life. Others, who voiced their intention to reenlist and remain in the army, had ridden with I Troop to Sequoia National Park. Still others took advantage of the opportunity to take a break in service, travel home to visit family at army expense, and reenlist within three months to keep their retention pay.

In June 1903, four soldiers reached the end of their terms of enlistments. Pvt. Joseph H. Grayson, a first-term soldier from Baltimore, Maryland, ended his three-year term, traveled home, and reenlisted two weeks later to return to I Troop. Pvt. David S. Jackson, a first-term soldier from Falls Church, Virginia, ended his enlistment and returned to civilian life, as did Pvt. James W. Benson, a twenty-six-year-old, first-term soldier from Bridgetown, Missouri. These three had remained behind at the Presidio because of their pending release from the army. The last, Pvt. William H. Merrell, who showed off his equestrian skills on the Fourth of July at the Marble Fork Bridge, ended his enlistment and reenlisted the following day at Camp Kaweah.[27]

In July 1903, I Troop lost twenty-seven-year-old, second-term soldier Pvt. Samuel Turpin, from Chambersburg, Pennsylvania, who died of "aortic regurgitation with acute nephritis." Turpin had been with the party sent to Mount Whitney in May 1903 to guard against sheepherders coming into the park from the east. He served there until late June when he was sent back to the Presidio for treatment at the hospital. Turpin died at the Presidio General Hospital and was buried with military honors at the San Francisco National Cemetery.[28]

Added to earlier losses, I Troop had another three soldiers reach the end of their enlistments at Sequoia in July; two of them left the army. Pvt. Lee Bell, a twenty-two-year-old, first-term soldier and former farmer from Milldale, Kentucky, reenlisted at Sequoia and continued to serve in the troop. Captain Young reenlisted Bell at Camp Kaweah and then took him as part of the relief force to Mount Whitney to replace Turpin. Pvt. William Allen, a twenty-six-year-olds second-term soldier from Grand Rapids, Michigan, ended his service and returned to civilian life, as did Pvt. Emmanuel W. Wicks, a twenty-four-year-old, first-term soldier from Baltimore, Maryland.[29]

Captain Young and First Sergeant Jones learned in July that I Troop finally obtained replacements for earlier losses. The troop received three recent recruits: Privates James Smith, William Terrell, and Wilbur Todd, all second-term soldiers who had previously served in the Twenty-Fourth or Twenty-Fifth Infantry. They also received Private William Stokes, who ended his enlistment with K Troop, Ninth Cavalry in May 1903, reenlisted in July 1903, and was assigned to I Troop, Ninth Cavalry. Yet these soldiers would not reach I Troop at Sequoia National Park for weeks, and the unit would have to continue its missions with the troops on hand.[30]

Quartermaster Sergeant Brown, First Sergeant Jones's right-hand man at Sequoia, ended his enlistment in early August and reenlisted the following day. The quartermaster had the formidable task of keeping track of all the wagons, horses, mules, tents, tarps, stoves, axes, picks, shovels, saws, tubs, water cans, buckets, horseshoes, picket lines, ammunition, target material, and records scattered from Camp Kaweah to Mount Whitney.[31]

Captain Young also temporarily lost the service of two key noncommissioned officers because of a shooting competition. The National Trophy Rifle Team Match was the brainchild of President Roosevelt, who lobbied Congress to make appropriations for it under the Army Appropriations Act of 1903. This legislation resulted in the first year of competition while Young's detachment served at Sequoia.[32]

First Sergeant Jones and Corporal Fearington, the best marksmen in I Troop, traveled to Whipple Barracks, Arizona, and attempted to qualify for the team to represent the U.S. Cavalry from August to September 1903. They did not make the cut, and the U.S. Cavalry team eventually finished ninth of fifteen teams of twelve men each. A team from the New Jersey National Guard won the prestigious competition held in September 1903 at Sea Girt, New Jersey.[33]

While Jones and Fearington were away, the flow of replacements continued in August, with eight new recruits recorded as arriving in the regimental records. The new soldiers remained at the Presidio and awaited the return of I Troop, with the end of its mission at Sequoia so near. I Troop was assigned Privates Samuel W. Edwards, Julius Ferguson, Mack Roberts, June Robinson, Robert B. Scott, Henry M. Merryweather, Cecil Robinson, and James S. Williams. Most of these soldiers enlisted in late July but did not arrive at the Presidio until August.[34]

In September 1903, the last full month of I Troop's service at Sequoia, the number of losses and replacements slowed. The troop lost two men at the end of their enlistments. The first, Pvt. Arthur B. Worthy, a first-term soldier from Jonesboro, Georgia, went home in September but reenlisted three months later in Atlanta, rejoining I Troop at the Presidio in December 1903. The other, Charles Goodloe, a first-term soldier from Columbia, Tennessee, went home and reenlisted a month later for a new assignment in the Tenth Cavalry. I Troop gained one replacement named Henry Shepherd, a former member of the Twenty-Fifth Infantry, who remained at the Presidio.[35]

Only one other soldier reached the end of his tenure in the army before I Troop rode out of Sequoia. Trumpeter Frank McKenzie ended his term at Camp Kaweah, California, in late October 1903, and Captain Young gave him an excellent character rating. McKenzie must have taken the train to San Francisco to enjoy ten days of civilian life out of uniform. He signed up again at the Presidio of San Francisco in early November 1903 and was waiting for the troop in the barracks when it rode into the Presidio ten days later. As a veteran on his fourth term of enrollment, he knew how to take advantage of army rules and regulations.[36]

### *New Superintendent*

As the Ninth Cavalry neared the end of its time at Sequoia, the detachment experienced a leadership change. On September 19, 1903, Maj. Gen. Arthur MacArthur, Jr., the new commander of the Department of California, notified the War Department that Capt. Lester Cornish had returned from sick leave and would resume his duty commanding M Troop. MacArthur informed the Interior Department that Cornish would assume duties as acting superintendent of the parks, since he was senior to Captain Young.[37]

Captain Cornish arrived by train at Visalia on September 1, 1903, then took the stage to Sequoia National Park to assume command from Captain

Young. On September 9, 1903, a letter from the Department of California was forwarded to Captain Cornish at Lone Pine, California, stating: "I have the authority to inform you that the Department has selected you by virtue of your seniority as acting superintendent of Sequoia and General Grant National Parks to relieve Capt. Charles Young, Ninth Cavalry of that duty."[38]

The Visalia newspapers reported that Captain Young, in town on business in early September 1903, told a reporter that he and Cornish intended to ride out to Mount Whitney as soon as the latter arrived at the Giant Forest camp. Sergeant Nicholas accompanied the two captains, probably escorted by a small party of troopers, on the fifty-mile trip from the Giant Forest to Mount Whitney. According to Nicholas, who clearly disliked him, "Captain Cornish showed up from sick leave, made one trip to Mt. Whitney and took command of the troops returning to San Francisco to collect the laurels or credit, to which he was not entitled."[39]

Aside from the fact that his captain was being replaced, Nicholas was galled that Captain Cornish, after making the difficult trek to Mount Whitney, did not make the return trip to Sequoia with Captain Young. Instead, he rode eastward to Lone Pine, California, by the easier fifteen-mile trail and returned by train. On his way through Lone Pine, he picked up the official transfer of authority. Cornish spent a night in the hotel in Visalia before returning to the camp in the Giant Forest, where Young and Nicholas were waiting for him.[40]

Since the work was complete at Sequoia and General Grant National Parks, perhaps Cornish was looking for something to burnish his reputation. According to the newspaper, "Captain Cornish has taken much interest in the construction of trails in the mountains to the various resorts. While over on the other side of the mountain Captain Cornish secured the help of a number of influential citizens who will assist him in getting a trail to the top of Whitney from that side." There was no mention of the hard work Lt. John Howard and his Ninth Cavalry troopers had done all summer on the trails to Sequoia and to Lone Pine.[41]

By the time Captain Cornish arrived, the summer season of work on the roads into the parks was complete. Young approved the September payroll, which was $545.00 for the labor done by just thirty-three men, half the number employed in June. Captain Young sent a letter to the secretary of the interior the last day of September, stating: "I have the honor to inform you that the tourist season is now over in Sequoia and General Grant National Parks and the work will be fairly finished for the year by October 10th." He asked for authority to withdraw his men for the season since they would not be needed after mid-October 1903.[42]

Young sent a telegram to the secretary of the interior in early October 1903, informing him that his annual report was nearly complete. He noted in the telegram that the day prior, he had mailed his "report on private claims and patented land." Young's final report, dated October 15, 1903, was sent to Washington via mail.[43]

Captain Young was still signing letters as the acting superintendent as late as October 20, 1903. Clearly, he and Cornish worked out some agreement that allowed Young to close certain accounts. If Young felt any resentment at being replaced by Cornish, he never showed it. Nor would he. He understood, as a professional and especially as a Black officer in a white officer corps, that sentiment had no place in the Regular Army.[44]

Young's final correspondence as superintendent forwarded a letter to the Interior Department closing out his pay accounts at Sequoia and General Grant National Parks. He had expenses of $206.50 for the month of October 1903. His total expenses for the summer to date had been $1976.15 out of appropriations of $2,000 for the year. He had one freight bill of $23.73 yet to be paid, leaving an available balance of just 12 cents. This would have satisfied even the most punctilious finance officer.[45]

Captain Cornish signed his first official correspondence as acting superintendent of the parks on October 12, 1903, when he forwarded a request from Ranger C. W. Blossom for a leave of absence to have some dental work done in Visalia. Chief Ranger Britten had asked the Interior Department to hire an additional ranger because of the heavy workload at Sequoia, and that request had resulted in the hiring of Blossom that summer.[46]

Chief Ranger Britten noted only two meetings with Captain Cornish near Camp Kaweah in October 1903. He also continued to meet often with Captain Young, and on October 29 he rode with him to the "Barnifee place on the Main [Fork] Kaweah River," which was being considered as a possible location for a permanent military base at Sequoia. Two days later, Britten noted that he "closed and locked gate on Giant Forest Road."[47]

Ranger Britten recorded in his diary that he bade "Capt. Cornish goodbye" on November 2, 1903, when the latter departed on the return trip to the Presidio. Cornish returned to the Presidio of San Francisco, where he assumed temporary command of the Second Squadron the first week of November 1903.[48]

### *Return to the Presidio*

The two troops of the Ninth Cavalry, under the command of Captain Cornish but without Captain Young, departed the second day of November and retraced the route of that spring, conducting a mounted march through Visalia. They arrived in Visalia the following day and spent the evening commemorating the summer's accomplishments with local leaders, who by this time they knew well. The city and county had much to gain by opening the park to tourists. They certainly appreciated Young's hard work and leadership in opening the park to wagon traffic.[49]

Some members of the Ninth Cavalry did not have to make the trip back to the Presidio on horseback. The newspaper reported on November 3: "Fifteen of the colored soldiers [who] have been in the Giant Forest Park all summer passed through Visalia on the Southern Pacific last evening enroute to the Presidio, where they were ordered to prepare the quarters for the rest of the troopers that will arrive later in the month." The detachment was under the command of Sgt. Wilson Cary of I Troop, who was the senior enlisted soldier Captain Young had taken to relieve the soldiers at Mount Whitney in July 1903. This detachment of soldiers from Mount Whitney, having served some of the most difficult duty during the past months, rode home in comfort by train.[50]

Lieutenant Howard, who commanded the detachment at Mount Whitney, likely accompanied the group on its return to the Presidio and was unnoticed by the reporter. The officer would have traveled in a different railcar and class of travel. The records show that Lieutenant Howard was back on duty with L Troop in San Francisco by November 6.[51]

The local Visalia newspaper praised the efforts of the soldiers. The day following their visit, the paper celebrated: "The outing for them has been a most pleasant one and at the same time has been beneficial to the county. The troopers have done excellent work in the way of making roads and enforcing the rules and regulations of the government in regard to the park. The place is now one of interest, and as it has always been, for scenery, but is more accessible than ever."[52]

The *Daily Visalia Delta* reported, "In the evening the members of Company E entertained them at Armory Hall and gave them a spread which consisted of varied refreshments. The officers of the troop were banqueted at the Pablo tamale parlors by Colonel Geo. W. Stewart and Captain M. J. Byrnes of Company E [Sixth Infantry Regiment, California National Guard]. The usual good dishes were sat before those present, after which cigars were passed and storytelling was the order. The troops will leave this morning for the north, camping tonight at Kingsburg."[53]

After the celebration in Visalia, the rest of the trip back to San Francisco was routine. The two troops reversed the route they had taken in May as they trekked the 278 miles back to the Presidio. With winter in the High Sierra approaching, the men were anxious to return to the more temperate climate of the coast.[54]

Yet not everyone was eager to be back in the clean, warm barracks of the Presidio. Pvt. James Norman, a second-term soldier from Henry County, Virginia, deserted I Troop in late October, and Pvt. William Gibson, a third-term soldier from Macon, Georgia, went AWOL in early November 1903. Captain Cornish and the two troops, minus the two soldiers on French leave, arrived in San Francisco on November 15, 1903, the same day as the two troops from Yosemite.[55]

### *Land Changing Hands*

Before Captain Young departed Sequoia National Park, he reportedly purchased several properties in the Three Rivers area. According to local historian Sophia Britten, Young "purchased the house at Pierce Corner from Montgomery Barton and lived there for a while, making it his headquarters." This must have been the place he used as his command center during the 1903 season. It would not have been unusual for Captain Young to rent or purchase a house to live in for the extended period he spent at Sequoia.[56]

At least one other account indicated Young purchased several properties in addition to the Barton house. A November 1903 newspaper report observed, "Land is changing hands rapidly." The writer noted that "Captain Young is reported to have bought several places." In light of the real estate transactions that Young finalized early the following year, he might have been involved in preliminary negotiations for several properties (see chapter 7).[57]

The newspaper writer, who was from Three Rivers, seemed unhappy about the purchases. He lamented the sales and worried that it "begins to look as though we will have a few 'darkies' with us all the time." He noted sarcastically, "They have been some better than the ordinary soldiers but the young men of this vicinity are thinking of getting on a supply of shoe dressing or some such preparations so they can go to oyster suppers, be fed candy, and be presented with bouquets, etc."

Black shoe polish was used to darken the faces of white actors in "blackface" minstrel shows of the era, in which the performers acted out offensive stereotypes of African Americans. With the oyster suppers, candy, and bouquets, the writer must be referring to the banquet that was thrown for the Black troopers in Visalia before their departure. The author ended the article with a flourish: "Three Rivers has had several drunks the past week and they weren't colored either." Clearly, Captain Young and the Buffalo Soldiers had not won over every heart in Three Rivers.[58]

### *Permanent Bases*

Major General MacArthur, the department commander, appointed a board of officers in October 1903 to "select a site for permanent military posts at Yosemite and Sequoia National Parks." This came in response to an attack on the army administration of Yosemite under Lieutenant Colonel Garrard by Howard Shinn, the new director of the Sierra Forest Reserve adjacent to the park. Shinn criticized Garrard for his uninspiring and business-as-usual management of Yosemite in the summer of 1903. A subsequent army inspector general's investigation criticized Garrard's posting of small groups of soldiers with little supervision, and it recommended making improvements in facilities, including housing, barracks, offices, and storage for records. A board of officers was appointed to sort out the details and make recommendations on permanent posts for both locations.[59]

MacArthur appointed four men to the board: Lt. Col. Joseph Garrard, the acting superintendent of Yosemite National Park; Capt. Charles Young, the acting superintendent of Sequoia and General Grant National Parks;

Capt. John B. Christian, commander of L Troop, stationed at Yosemite; and a civilian topographic assistant from the North Pacific Division of the U.S. Army Corps of Engineers named Clement Winstanley. The officers were placed on detached duty collecting information for their report from October 31 to November 20, 1903. So when the troops returned to the Presidio, Young stayed behind to participate in this study.[60]

That Young was appointed to this board and not Cornish is interesting, since the latter was technically the acting superintendent of Sequoia. MacArthur had to know that Young was the man with the knowledge and ability to make the best choices for the army. Perhaps Cornish's late dispatch to Sequoia was made to satisfy the letter of the law involving seniority and his return with the troops a way to clear a path for Young to participate in the important business of the new board.

According to one local newspaper account, Young determined a location for a permanent post at Sequoia even before the board convened. The report noted, "Captain Young, who came down from the mountains Saturday evening . . . brought the news that a military post would be established near the power house shortly and that a body of troops would hereafter be maintained at that point. The post will be installed simultaneously with the one at Yosemite." This information corresponds with the mission of the board of officers.[61]

The newspaper article gave the following details:

> The captain stated that an admirable location for a military post and one that he believes will be selected is located near the old Barnifee place on the middle fork of the Kaweah about three and one half miles from the power house. The place is ten miles from Three Rivers and thirty-eight miles from this city [Visalia]. Captain Young said that the post will be fully equipped. Barracks will be erected to accommodate two troops of 200 soldiers with residences for the officers. There will be stables for an equal number of horses and barns for hay. A supply house and a hospital will also be erected.[62]

The article noted that Visalia was the nearest general supply point and that necessary supplies to support the post would be purchased there. The article concluded by noting the importance of such a decision to establish a permanent post at Sequoia. It also mentioned the considerable commercial advantage Visalia would gain by supporting two hundred men and an equal number of horses.

According to another report, Captain Young traveled to Yosemite the first day of November to meet with the other members of the board. The account noted that he traveled with eight men, though they were not identified. Sergeant Nicholas and a small party of Black troopers probably remained behind to provide him escort. They likely visited the proposed sites for a permanent military base at Yosemite.[63]

Chief Ranger Britten met Captain Young at Kaweah on November 14, 1903, to discuss a site for a permanent post at Sequoia. Two days later, Britten met the entire group of inspecting officers, and they traveled to the entrance of Sequoia National Park where he showed them the Boniface Place. The spot was named after a man—variously named Barnifee, Bonifee, Boniface, or Bonifoy—who squatted on an area around Ash Mountain that later became the main entrance station to Sequoia National Park. The place had sufficient space to build a small military compound and was close to the nearby community and post office at Kaweah. It was also in the foothills of Sequoia National Park and accessible year-round by road. The board of officers recommended it for a permanent post.[64]

After completing his work on the board of officers, Young had one last loose end to tie up. On November 18, Britten again met with Captain Young, who instructed him to take up the matter of securing Tule elk for Sequoia National Park. Tule elk were a subspecies of elk native to California found nowhere outside the state. They had virtually disappeared by 1903, yet small herds were at several locations. Britten later wrote to the Interior Department about Captain Young's request to reintroduce elk to Sequoia. The Interior Department responded that it had no objection so long as they could be "procured without cost to the Government." Eventually, Tule elk were introduced from the Miller and Lux Ranch in the southern valley.[65]

On November 19, Chief Ranger Britten bade Captain Young farewell when he boarded the stage to Visalia for the trip back to San Francisco. Young must have taken the stage as far as the train station in Visalia or Exeter and from there boarded the train to San Francisco. His term of detached service to serve on the board lasted only until November 20, when he had to be back at the Presidio to resume command of his troop.

It is noteworthy that the two white officers and engineer had left on the train on November 19. Young's returning by himself the following day was likely his way of avoiding the uncomfortable situation of having the white officers sit with a Black officer on the return trip to San Francisco.[66]

*Task and Times*

In a final tribute to Young, the Visalia Board of Trade awarded Captain Young a certificate in appreciation for his leadership and accomplishments at Sequoia National Park the summer of 1903. The board met on November 19, 1903, the day before Young's departure, and unanimously adopted the resolution honoring his achievements. The oversize, hand-lettered parchment certificate was signed by the president and secretary of the board. It declared:

> Whereas, this body has observed with pleasure the continued evidence of interest and ability shown by Capt. Charles Young of the 9th U.S. Cavalry, as acting Supt. of the said Parks, and realizing by his energy, enthusiasm, and business qualities displayed, the money set aside for the improvement of the said Parks has been wisely and most economically expended and a great amount of splendid and permanent work accomplished: therefore, be it Resolved: That the thanks of this Board of Trade be extended to Capt. Charles Young for the interest he has shown in the discharge of his official duties, and that copies of this resolution be sent ably engrossed, and that one copy thereof be delivered each to Capt. Young, the Secretary of the Interior, and the Secretary of War.[67]

On the surface, it appears that Captain Young won over the people and politicians of Visalia in the six months he led the enterprise at Sequoia and General Grant National Parks. Unlike the early June 1903 newspaper accounts that greeted his arrival, they did not refer to his "whiteness" of character. They valued Young's accomplishments and made no more mention of his color.

The Visalians also had a chance to compare his character to that of the white officer who might have led the operation, Captain Cornish, and found the latter lacking in vigor. As realistic businessmen, they realized they got more than routine army duty in the summer of 1903. Captain

Young's style of leadership left them wanting more. His accomplishment was impressive given the task and the times.

Young's success in Sequoia National Park illuminated his rapid growth as a professional army officer. The mission at Sequoia and General Grant National Parks demanded both leadership and diplomacy. His accomplishments at Sequoia contrasted starkly with the criticism of the business-as-usual administration at Yosemite. He achieved better results than the officers who had preceded him at Sequoia, and he did so with a leadership style that caused his Black soldiers to honor him, the white workers to respect him, and the local citizens to pay tribute to him. This was no small thing for a Black man in 1903.

# 7

## Return to Garrison Life

> Captain Charles Young of the Ninth United States Cavalry, one of the few colored officers in the army, delivered before the student body this morning one of the most interesting addresses heard since the inauguration of the assemblies.
> —*San Francisco Chronicle*, December 10, 1903

After returning to the Presidio from Sequoia and Yosemite, the last months of 1903 were exceptionally busy ones for Captain Young and the members of the Ninth Cavalry. The Third Squadron welcomed a new commander, who had recently been moved from the First Squadron in Monterey, and the Black troopers also bade farewell to some veteran soldiers at the end of the year. The return to garrison life once more posed leadership challenges to the officers and noncommissioned officers of the Ninth Cavalry given the temptations of the bars and brothels of San Francisco for their men.

### *New Squadron Commander*

The Ninth Cavalry experienced several leadership changes in the last quarter of 1903. Maj. John Bigelow, Jr., transferred from Monterey to San Francisco in early December as the new squadron commander in place of Lt. Col. Joseph Garrard, who moved to his new posting with the Fourteenth Cavalry after completing his assignment at Yosemite.[1]

The Ninth Cavalry likely reassigned Bigelow to San Francisco because the Third Squadron had more prominence serving in the shadow of Major

General MacArthur and the staff of the Department of California, which had its headquarters in San Francisco. Only one other major served with the Ninth Cavalry at the time, Maj. James B. Erwin, the Second Squadron commander at Fort Walla Walla, Washington, the home of the regimental headquarters. After Bigelow's departure, the First Squadron at Monterey was temporarily commanded by Capt. George W. Read, the B Troop commander and senior captain.[2]

Bigelow was an 1877 graduate of West Point who had joined the Tenth Cavalry on the western frontier after graduation and participated in the hard campaigning in Texas against the Comanches and Apaches, including the capture of Geronimo. While in Texas, Bigelow wrote a series of articles titled "After Geronimo" that were published in *Outing* magazine, which was edited by his brother, Poultney Bigelow, and featured one of the first drawings by his friend, the now famous Frederic Remington.[3]

Between frontier cavalry assignments, Bigelow served as a professor of French and tactics at West Point and later as a professor of military science and tactics at the Massachusetts Institute of Technology. He was a brilliant educator in addition to being a superb leader. As a lieutenant at Fort Davis, Texas, Bigelow had honed the skills of his Black noncommissioned officers by scheduling classes twice a week to address specific issues concerning military tactics and field etiquette.[4]

Bigelow returned to the Tenth Cavalry as a captain in 1898 in time to participate in the Spanish-American War's Santiago campaign, where he commanded D Troop. In the charge up San Juan Hill, Bigelow was wounded four times and had to be evacuated for treatment. His first lieutenant, Jules Ord, assumed command and was immediately killed. First Lt. John J. Pershing, the Tenth Cavalry's quartermaster, then took command of D Troop and continued the charge up San Juan Hill. Bigelow was awarded the Silver Star for bravery and cited for gallantry in action, as were several of his enlisted soldiers.[5]

After convalescing three months while recovering from his wounds, Bigelow spent three years in Cuba with the Tenth, using his fluent Spanish to help settle war claims. He declined a position as a lieutenant colonel with a volunteer regiment in the Philippines after the war so he could remain with the Buffalo Soldiers of the Tenth Cavalry. After Cuba, Bigelow was reassigned to the Ninth Cavalry upon promotion to major in December 1902. He joined the Ninth Cavalry in March 1903, where he was initially assigned to Monterey and command of the First Squadron.[6]

Though ten years his senior, Bigelow was a good intellectual match for Captain Young, and Lieutenant Pearson reported they had a mutually supportive relationship. Both valued education, had served as professors of military science at universities, and spoke several foreign languages fluently. Bigelow, having grown up and attended school in Europe, did not exhibit the racism shown by most of his classmates at West Point. Among them were Henry O. Flipper, the academy's first Black graduate, and John Guilfoyle, who had mentored Young as his troop commander at Fort Duchesne, Utah.[7]

### *Ord Barracks*

Major Bigelow left the Monterey Military Reservation, renamed Ord Barracks in August 1903, a few months before the members of the First Squadron, Ninth Cavalry moved into their newly constructed wooden barracks. Since their early November 1902 arrival, the Black troopers of the First Squadron had lived in a canvas cantonment on Pacific Improvement Company's land near Chinatown in Pacific Grove, California.[8]

The U.S. Army had announced the creation of the Monterey Military Reservation the day after Theodore Roosevelt proclaimed the official end of the Philippine-American War on July 4, 1902. It was intended to serve "as a cantonment where troops returning from the Philippines could rest, recuperate, and be trained for future service in the Pacific." The First Squadron, Ninth Cavalry shared the new reservation with two artillery batteries and the Fifteenth U.S. Infantry Regiment, which had returned from the Philippines in September 1902. With the infantry and artillery occupying a canvas cantonment inland at what later was known as Soldier Field, the Ninth pitched their tents two miles away in hayfields near China Point (now the Hopkins Marine Station).[9]

The civilian population of Monterey, which had served as the capital of Alta California under both Spain and Mexico, numbered just 1,748 during the 1900 U.S. Census. Like San Francisco, it boasted a fine bay, and the Spanish erected the Presidio of Monterey to defend the headland. The military reservation encompassing Ord Barracks stretched from the bay eastward and divided the City of Monterey in two. The army population of the reservation in 1903 was about a thousand personnel.[10]

While the Fifteenth Infantry began moving into its newly constructed barracks in June and July 1903, the men of the Ninth had to await the completion of their new accommodations in December 1903. To celebrate the near end of the work on the barracks, the officers and ladies of the Fifteenth Infantry and Ninth Cavalry held an October dance in the "unfinished cavalry barracks building, which was brilliantly lighted with colored lights and decorated with green branches and flags."[11]

Finally, after more than a year under canvas at China Point, the Buffalo Soldiers pulled up stakes and moved the two miles to Ord Barracks. C Troop moved on December 1, and by December 16, 1903, all the troopers of the First Squadron, Ninth Cavalry were comfortably billeted in their four newly completed wooden barracks. The Buffalo Soldiers celebrated Christmas and New Year's Eve in new cavalry barracks with modern plumbing, heating, and mess facilities. Samuel Pearson, Young's former first lieutenant now commanding A Troop, likewise celebrated the holidays with his wife, Margaret, in a new set of officers' quarters.[12]

### *Stanford Speech*

At about the time the First Squadron was moving into its new barracks, Stanford University invited Captain Young to be the principal speaker at its general assembly of students and faculty in December 1903. Young titled his presentation "The Ideals of the Negroes in the United States." The talk was an eloquent plea that Black Americans be given equal opportunity and access to education. Young's oration was not a fiery diatribe against the injustices done to Blacks in America; rather, he patiently and vividly explained to his audience his hopes and views.[13]

Young began his talk:

> I wish to acquaint you with the spirit strivings of the Black race of which I am part and parcel. I fear that the higher interests of my people are going nether ward—and yours with them, for when one part of the body is diseased the whole body is not well, and my people are one-twelfth of the body politic. For the solution of the ill-named "Negro

problem"—for it is your problem as well as mine—you have offered your amalgamation, a hodge-podge of Black and white, deportation, extermination, and finally you have offered your industrialism. I desire to impress upon you the importance of kindliness toward this man who so much needs your good offices.[14]

He belittled the "few thousands of dollars" given "to Booker T. Washington in order to solve this problem" at Tuskegee to train Blacks to work in industry. Young also rejected in his speech the suggestion that the solution was for African Americans to go into business. He did so on the grounds that the Black man's "two centuries of labor have done to build up capital for someone else and he has not money to start with." The real solution, according to Young, was higher education, and he cited the poet Paul Laurence Dunbar and the sculptor Edmonia Lewis as examples of individuals who had excelled in the arts. His speech seemed a clear rejection of the path espoused by Booker T. Washington and an endorsement of the ideas of W. E. B. Du Bois.

Young claimed that Blacks in America were "between the devil, which would bid us give up hope, and the deep blue sea of our ambitions that are surging in our hearts." He cited an African American sculptor who created "a statue of a man eating his own heart" and noted, "Nobody but a Negro would have conceived of such a thing. We know what it is to eat our own hearts." He rejected the white man's efforts to stifle Black aspirations, the pointed "finger of scorn," and attempts to sugarcoat the situation with sycophancy or sweet talk. He maintained the only answer was higher education for African Americans and repeated his call to give Blacks a "white man's chance."[15]

Young ended his speech with some rather raw language and a challenge to the students and faculty:

I do not come today to work up a maudlin sentiment, to make you "nigger lovers." I do come to demand that as you love your country you will not disgrace its escutcheon by oppression of a man most kindly and helpful as God ever made. You are going to have a white man's chance, and that is all I ask for the negro. The time for old "aunties" and "uncles" is past. The "sassy nigger" followed but is now gone. The negro asking for the white man's chance is the one we have now. Will you give it? The nightingale within me soars and sings and says: "Be of good courage, be true to your high ideals, because these are the things on which your salvation depends."[16]

The exact circumstances surrounding the invitation to speak at Stanford are not known. It may have been prompted by Du Bois's publication in 1903 of what became known as his "Talented Tenth" article, which in turn was a response to Booker T. Washington's 1895 "Atlanta Compromise" address. Young and Du Bois had served on the faculty at Wilberforce University together from 1894 to 1896 and had discussed such matters at Young's home. Du Bois, a bachelor, often found refuge at the large house Young shared with his mother at Wilberforce. The visit of Booker T. Washington earlier in 1903 had to have brought the conflict between the two Black leaders to the forefront of Young's thinking in preparing for the Stanford speech.[17]

His talk seems to have been well received, because he was invited after the speech as the guest of the Bachelor Professors' Club at lunch, with Stanford president David Jordan attending. It was not an insignificant gesture in 1903 to sit down at a meal with a Black man. Recall the firestorm of protest elicited by President Roosevelt's invitation to Booker T. Washington to dine at the White House two years earlier. Yet the event must have been somewhat uncomfortable for both Young and Jordan, since the latter was a strong supporter of eugenics and favored "racial unity."[18]

Young mentioned his speech at Stanford University in a letter he wrote a few days later to his Three Rivers friend Blanche Winser:

> I went to Stanford, got scared, spoke, and got my dinner. In fact, had a fine time and found many good people and saw the workings of many departments. I enclose a clipping from the "Call." Believe me, these things interest me very little and I only cut it out to please you. You know I believe that words will do very little good in the case of my people, but acts and more acts and Actions.[19]

These words reveal a great deal about Young's sentiments after giving his presentation. They display his humanity, sense of humor, and humility, admitting he was scared, got his free meal, and remained modest despite the news coverage in the *San Francisco Call*. They also indicate Stanford treated him as a VIP, complete with tours of the faculty departments and an invitation to be the guest of honor at a faculty luncheon. Notwithstanding his luminary treatment, Young was tired of mere words and looked for action on equal opportunity and education.

Stanford professor Max Farrand wrote to Young in February 1904 thanking him for his talk. He acknowledged that it "gave me as much pleasure to learn that you enjoyed your visit to Stanford even a fraction as much as we enjoyed it." In his letter he mentioned that he and Professor Robert Allardice intended to visit Young at the Presidio at the first opportunity. He also thanked Young for a copy of his "report as Superintendent of the National Parks" and stated they were "in sympathy with such recommendation as are made or suggested."[20]

*Sequoia Report*

The report Young submitted to the Interior Department in October 1903 elicited considerable interest in the months following its submission. In a concise and orderly manner, the report covered all the pertinent issues and problems he encountered during his time as the acting superintendent of the parks. *The Report of the Acting Superintendent of the Sequoia and General Grant National Parks in the State of California to the Secretary of the Interior*, eighteen typed pages, was drafted by Captain Young and included a short one-page endorsement by Captain Cornish.[21]

In his report, Young provided an introduction, then he covered the following topics: hunting and trespassing, game, permits, forest fires, roads and trails, forests of the park and adjacent country, the Giant Forest, a penalty for trespassing, park rangers, names of trees in the park, copies of regulations, and an inventory of tools. He included an appendix to assist the officer assigned as the acting superintendent the following year. Another appendix listed the names of the owners of privately held lands within the parks' boundaries, their locations, and the price he negotiated for the U.S. government to purchase them.[22]

The first coverage of his report appeared in the *San Francisco Call* on November 9, 1903, ten days before Young returned from Sequoia. It quoted parts of Young's report and focused mainly on the private tracts owned within the parks' boundaries. The newspaper noted that Young warned the Interior Department the owners of these tracts were "tired of waiting" for the government to purchase their private claims. Some had already cut down some of the big trees near existing roads and sold them as lumber, leaving "devastation and ruin in the shape of stumps and sawdust piles on either side of the high road." Young's completion of the wagon road to the Giant Forest would make it easier to get the lumber to market. The same article commented on Maj. John Pitcher's report on Yellowstone, which focused mainly on steps to take to increase game within the park.[23]

An editorial appearing in the *Call* in December 1903 took on a different issue. The opinion page complained that the government had set aside large tracts of parklands "with little or no consideration of the economic side of the matter." It noted that private owners of land acquired long before the establishment of the parks "had been deprived of all beneficial use of their property." It went on to complain that the secretary of the interior had ignored all the state's requests to tap into the economic potential of resources within the parks' boundaries for reservoirs, hydroelectric power, or mining, among other things.

The last part of this December editorial discussed the role of the U.S. Army in patrolling the parks. It noted the parks were "administered by regular soldiers, an officer being considered its superintendent, and the parks have been protected against grazing, and to a degree from fire." As far as the cost of using the Regular Army to patrol the parks, "the cost is only their pay and subsistence, which would be the same if they were stewed [drunk] in the barracks instead of having the freedom of the mountains."[24]

Detailed extracts of Young's report appeared in the *Tulare County Times* in Visalia, California, in late December 1903. The paper noted that the secretary of the interior had sent the document to the local land office. The *Times* judged the report "an interesting document and would doubtless be read with much interest by all who are interested in the preservation of the grandest natural features to be found in California."[25]

### *Garrison Life*

Major Bigelow arrived in San Francisco a few weeks after the troopers of the Third Squadron returned from six months of forced abstinence in the tent camps of Sequoia and Yosemite. It was only a matter of time before some soldiers were involved in off-post altercations fueled by alcohol. With post canteens closed by congressional mandate in 1901, soldiers from the Presidio had to seek establishments in San Francisco to slake their thirsts. And the saloons and bars near the Presidio were happy to accommodate them.

A November 1903 newspaper article titled "Saloons Cater to Soldiers" reported that military officials were trying to halt the illegal marketing of liquor at the Union Street entrance to the Presidio. The report noted that saloons were "not licensed to retail liquor within a certain distance of the [military] reservation," yet they persisted in selling alcohol to soldiers, both Black and white.[26]

Though police officers were placed at the entrances of various saloons, the violations continued. The newspaper concluded that either "the officers are paid by the proprietors or [they] have received orders to make no arrests." Oddly, when civilians asked for drinks at these establishments, they were refused service. According to the article, "In these cases the police are vigilant, but soldiers are served liquor with impunity."[27]

As mentioned previously, the army could have avoided some of this trouble if Congress had not forced it to abolish the post canteens in 1901. This resulted from the zealous lobbying by the Woman's Christian Temperance Union. According to an official army report, "No moralist can justly claim that it is more injurious to the health or morality of a soldier to drink mild beer in a well-regulated canteen at post, where gambling is prohibited and excesses are not tolerated, than it is to drink bad whiskey in a vile den off the [military] reservation, where drinking and gambling are encouraged without constraint."[28]

As an example of this off-post drinking leading to bad behavior, in November 1903, Black cavalry troopers and white soldiers of the infantry and artillery engaged in a melee in a streetcar on Van Ness Avenue. The newspaper headline read "Soldiers Engage in Fierce Fight on Car" and "Color Line Precipitates a Wordy War which Terminated in Actual Combat." The article noted the Saturday night brawl involved "members of the Ninth Cavalry, a colored regiment that until recently has been doing duty at the national parks of California." The white soldiers involved belonged to the "Artillery Corps and the Tenth Infantry."[29]

The Black and white soldiers were considerate enough to allow the civilians on the streetcar to disembark before the melee began. Evidently the white soldiers already aboard insulted the Black troopers approaching the streetcar, triggering the fight, all lubricated by alcohol. Once the civilians reached a place of safety, "the disputants fought and scrambled and maimed one another." The Black troopers seemed to come away with fewer injuries: Corporal Hodge of Company M, Tenth Infantry was cut across the arm; Private Raymore of Company K, Tenth Infantry had his lips cut open; and Private Robinson of M Troop, Ninth Cavalry had his eyes swollen shut as the result of "terrific blows."[30]

The article promised "a full investigation of the matter by the military authorities," but records showed no formal charges were filed. Pvt. Thomas W. Robinson, the injured member of M Troop, Ninth Cavalry, was one of the handful of soldiers from that unit who stayed behind at the Presidio and did not go to Sequoia. Robinson was on his third enlistment, having joined M Troop after reenlisting in January 1903. He was apparently a troublemaker, since records show he was "in the hands of Civil Authority" in January 1904. Finally, Robinson received a dishonorable discharge following a general court-martial in June 1904.[31]

### *Hospital Attack*

There is only one account of a violent racial confrontation inside the military reservation at the Presidio during this period. In November 1903, the *San Francisco Call* reported an incident under the headline "Big Negro Soldier Tries to Kill Hospital Surgeon." The article was complete with photos of the victim, 1st Lt. Benjamin J. Edger, Jr., and of the assailant, Pvt. Clark McGee; and with a dramatic illustration of the alleged assault.[32]

First Lieutenant Edger was an assistant surgeon assigned to Letterman Army Hospital at the Presidio in November 1902. Private McGee was a former soldier with the Twenty-Fifth Infantry who enlisted in the Hospital Corps, the only branch of the army that was integrated. He was assigned to Letterman in September 1902 as an ambulance driver.[33]

The paper described the circumstances surrounding the incident in detail. McGee was "allowed three all-night passes a week and two midnight passes." After McGee reported from a midnight pass twenty-five minutes late, Lieutenant Edger, the executive officer of the hospital, asked him for an explanation. McGee, per the report, "complained that Edger was prejudiced against him and that he could not get a square deal." Edger then threatened McGee with a summary court-martial, which made him furious, and McGee returned an hour later with a revolver to shoot the surgeon. When the gun failed to fire, McGee hit Edger in the head with the butt of the weapon. Several nearby soldiers rescued the lieutenant and removed McGee to the guardhouse.[34]

McGee made a full confession of his crime at the Presidio in December and expressed regret only that he had failed. He was represented at the general court-martial by a civilian attorney named Walter Gallagher, who hoped a plea of temporary insanity would save the soldier. The court found McGee guilty and sentenced him to a dishonorable discharge and ten years' imprisonment at Alcatraz.[35]

The *San Francisco Call*'s coverage of this case was clearly biased; the other large newspapers in the city did not cover the incident. The *Call*'s description of McGee as a "brawny negro" and previous troublemaker while portraying Lieutenant Edger as the "hero of the hour" says it all. Its inclusion of pictures of the two men and an artist's illustration of the attack was intended to present a negative view of the Black soldier. The story likely would have warranted no coverage at all if McGee had been white.

### *Sports and Athletics*

The leadership of the Ninth Cavalry promoted constructive activities to help the soldiers settle back into garrison life and keep them out of trouble. The army in 1902 had no formal on-duty physical training or testing program as it did in later years, yet enlisted soldiers played sports and held competitions at every opportunity. This included fielding troop and squadron teams and playing against local military and civilian groups. Soldiers enjoyed team sports, which were encouraged by their officers who used troop funds combined with individual donations to purchase uniforms and equipment.[36]

Newspapers reported on soldier teams, which held several competitions in early December. One such Sunday afternoon series attracted a crowd of three thousand soldiers, officers, families, and "town folk." The football game played in the morning between the Twenty-Fourth Field Artillery Battery and the Ninth Cavalry was won by the artillerymen by a score of 20 to 0. The Ninth Cavalry football team beat the squad from Fort Miley several weeks later, 5 to 0. In a baseball game later in the month, the Fifteenth Infantry from Ord Barracks prevailed over the Ninth Cavalry nine by a score of 17 to 5. Both baseball and football were increasingly popular in the United States at the time.[37]

While most of the sports competitions occurred on Sundays, a non-duty day for the soldiers, the garrison sponsored larger field events on normal duty days. These monthly competitions pitted the garrison troops and batteries against each other in track and field events, as well as military-related tasks such as tent pitching. That Black cavalry troopers competed against white artillerymen added an element of racial rivalry to the contests and perhaps provided an alternative to fighting off post. The events also attracted large crowds of San Francisco citizens.[38]

One such field day was held on Tuesday, December 22, the beginning of the military holiday period at the Presidio of San Francisco. By order of the post commander, all duties were suspended until January 2, 1904, except for the necessary guard, stable, and fatigue duties. This time off was customary during the Christmas and New Year's holiday season at all stateside military posts and provided the soldiers with a break in their military duties.[39]

The newspaper noted the Ninth Cavalry, recently returned from park duty, was expected to "make the artillery hustle for prizes" in the day's contests. The events included a 100-yard dash, standing broad jump, running high jump, 220-yard dash, relay race, and Sibley tent pitching. A Sibley tent is a conical canvas shelter that holds a squad of eight soldiers. A team of five soldiers brought the rolled-up tent to the field and worked ardently to erect it according to regulations in the shortest time. Winners of the events received $3 for a first-place finish and $2 for second place, with prize money provided by the post exchange. This was a great deal of money to a private paid $13 a month.[40]

These monthly field days were considered mandatory military duty for the soldiers on post. According to the *Call*, "Failure or neglect therein is the same as any other military neglect or failure. Consequently, all those who take part enter into the different events with as much vigor and earnestness as any of their military duties." The enlisted soldiers either competed in events, helped run the various contests, or cheered on their comrades as spectators. The officers served as officials, judges, timekeepers, and starters, while noncommissioned officers served as clerks and announcers.[41]

According to a lengthy newspaper article after the event, the Presidio field day attracted a "great throng of spectators who applauded the victor in each event." The weather was ideal, according to the paper and confirmed by published photos of the competitions. The four troops of the Ninth competed against ten batteries of artillery, all approximately equal in numbers. The artillerymen claimed bragging rights and "hustled" most of the prize money. Ninth Cavalry members who walked away with cash were Cpl. Dee Smith of I Troop, who finished second in the 100-yard dash; Pvt. Dock Smelly of I Troop, who won the standing broad jump; and the L Troop team, which placed second in the relay race.[42]

### *Departures, Demotions, Death*

About a week after the field day competitions, Captain Young lost the services of his trusted veteran Sgt. William Nicholas. He mustered out of the army at the end of December 1903 with an honorable discharge and an excellent character rating from Young after a span of two three-year enlistments. Nicholas served his entire six years of service with Young in I Troop as a private, troop clerk, supply sergeant, and section sergeant in Utah, the Philippines, and California. Their connection would last well beyond their service together in the Ninth Cavalry since Nicholas would travel to Three Rivers to oversee Young's properties.[43]

Young and Nicholas shared a special bond. As Young's troop clerk, Nicholas spent long hours each day keeping troop records, taking dictation, and writing reports. He and Young shared a literacy that was uncommon among African Americans at the turn of the century. Of his relationship to Captain Young, Nicholas wrote: "To myself, he was a father, brother, teacher, and a *real true* friend at all times under all conditions, good and bad, in all times of *need*. I *really loved him*."[44]

The same month Nicholas departed, another of Young's noncommissioned officers got into trouble. According to the *San Francisco Call*:

> Lee Banks, the colored corporal of the Ninth Cavalry, who assaulted two women on Kearney Street Monday night, was sentenced to pay a fine of $100 or serve fifty days in jail by Judge Morgan yesterday. The Judge told the defendant that the only thing that saved him from getting six months in the county jail on each of the two counts was the fact that

the women admitted being under the influence of liquor and were on the street at an unusually late hour.

What was left unsaid in the article, and probably influenced the decision of the judge, was that the two women were likely prostitutes. In this case, and as in most legal cases in San Francisco, the judge treated the Black soldier without bias.[45]

Banks, who was from Mason County, the same Kentucky county where Captain Young was born, had been a good soldier. Young had given him a very good character rating when he reenlisted in 1901 and had awarded him the two stripes of a corporal. Banks must have paid the court's fine since no soldier was listed on the regimental return as "in confinement" during the month of December 1903; however, he did lose his stripes and the extra pay of a corporal.[46]

Young lost another noncommissioned officer of I Troop that month. Cpl. George W. Fearington, the man shot in the chest by Corporal Lockett in November 1902, ended his enlistment in December 1903, and Young gave him a good character rating. Fearington was an old I Troop hand, having served more than ten years with the unit after first enlisting in 1892. He was also one of the best marksmen in the troop, having represented the Ninth in the Cavalry Rifle Team competition.[47]

Fearington signed up for another term, though he did not reenlist in the cavalry. Instead, after a short visit home, he walked into the Durham, North Carolina, recruiting office in January 1904 and signed up with the Hospital Corps. Unmarried enlisted men like Fearington who had served at least one year were eligible to reenlist in this integrated branch. After passing a rigorous test, Hospital Corps privates received training in nursing, first aid, cooking, pharmaceuticals, clerical work, and the care of animals. They worked at hospitals serving as orderlies, attendants, and nurses, and performed other essential jobs, making more money than privates in other branches.[48]

The remaining noncommissioned officers of the Ninth Cavalry mourned the loss of one of their own in early December 1903. The *San Francisco Call* reported, "The remains of the late Jerome Paton, first sergeant of L Troop, Ninth Cavalry, were buried today at the Presidio with full military honors. Paton was a good soldier and had a splendid record in the service."

First Sergeant Paton, who died of heart disease, seems to have been well known at the Presidio, and it is significant that the newspaper found his passing noteworthy. Paton, a forty-year-old born in Pontiac, Michigan, had joined the army in 1885 and was in his fifth enlistment.[49]

*Replacements*

The losses I Troop suffered in the noncommissioned officer ranks had to be offset from within. To replace Sergeants Nicholas and Corporal Fearington, Captain Young and First Sergeant Jones promoted worthy enlisted soldiers from inside the troop to leadership positions. Long-serving privates who had shown promise as leaders were made corporals and deserving corporals jumped to sergeant.

One such candidate for promotion was Arthur B. Worthy, who had ended his enlistment term at Sequoia in September and traveled home to Georgia. He enlisted again in Atlanta within three months, keeping his retention pay, and rejoined I Troop at the Presidio in December 1902. Worthy had served under Young at Fort Duchesne, Utah, and in the Philippines. He must have shown promise since Captain Young promoted him to corporal after his return, perhaps replacing Fearington.[50]

One other soldier Captain Young promoted to corporal was Dock Smelly, a two-term veteran assigned to his troop since early 1898. He had served with I Troop during the Spanish-American War in Florida, at Fort Duchesne, Utah, and in the Philippines. He was the best horseman in the squadron and won prize money for his athletic prowess at almost every field day at the Presidio. One can imagine, however, more than one recruit got into trouble when they smirked after an introduction to their new squad leader, Corporal Smelly.

Among the soldiers waiting for I Troop when it returned to the Presidio was its newly assigned cook, Robert B. Scott. A twenty-one-year-old former waiter from Houston, Texas, Scott enlisted in July 1903 and joined Joseph R. Taylor as one of I Troop's two cooks. As a cook, Scott wore a leadership stripe on his trousers and received the pay and privileges of a sergeant, as well as special training, perhaps carried out at a consolidated mess facility at the Presidio.[51]

Captain Young and First Sergeant Jones could still rely on a core of long-serving noncommissioned officers to bridge the gap until new leaders emerged. Jones was assisted by the old veteran quartermaster sergeant Brown and Sergeants Cary, Malone, and Smith. These senior sergeants were backed up by the younger but no less capable corporals Banks, Ray, and Whitfield. Their job was to develop a new generation of enlisted leaders. And they would get some help with this task in the coming year.

The Third Squadron closed a successful year in the parks with a return to garrison life at the Presidio. The new squadron commander, Major Bigelow, did his best to keep the troopers of the Ninth Cavalry busy with training and athletics, yet with the elimination of post canteens, where soldiers could enjoy a beer in a controlled setting, some soldiers got into trouble by drinking and fighting in San Francisco.

Young's Sequoia and San Francisco service boosted his self-confidence and leadership skills. Accepting his role as a point man for his race in the army, his speech at Stanford clarified his dissatisfaction with the way his people were treated in the U.S. Army and in America. He wanted Blacks to be afforded the opportunity to be educated and given a fair chance at the benefits of American society.

Fig. 1. Trumpeter Frank McKenzie, I Troop, Ninth Cavalry, 1897. Frank McKenzie Collection, the late Ruby Estes McKenzie, and Gloria C. Richard.

Fig. 2. ABOVE: First Lt. Charles Young, Fort Duchesne, Utah, 1899. Three Rivers Historical Society and Museum (TRHSM).

Fig. 3. RIGHT: Second Lt. Samuel B. Pearson, Fort Duchesne, Utah, 1900. Courtesy of the National Afro-American Museum and Cultural Center (NAAMCC).

Fig. 4. I Troop, Ninth U.S. Cavalry, Presidio of San Francisco, California, 1901. *Front row, seated, center,* 1st Sgt. William Jones; *back row with colors,* Sgt. William Nicholas. Courtesy of the NAAMCC.

Fig. 5. I Troop, Ninth U.S. Cavalry, Philippine Islands, 1902. *Front row, seated on bench (left to right):* Sgt. William Nicholas, Sgt. Samuel Pierce, 1st Sgt. William Jones, Capt. Charles Young, 1st Lt. Samuel Pearson, QM Sgt. George Brown, unknown, unknown. *Seated on the ground, left,* Trumpeter Johnsey Walker; *right,* Trumpeter Frank McKenzie. Courtesy of the NAAMCC.

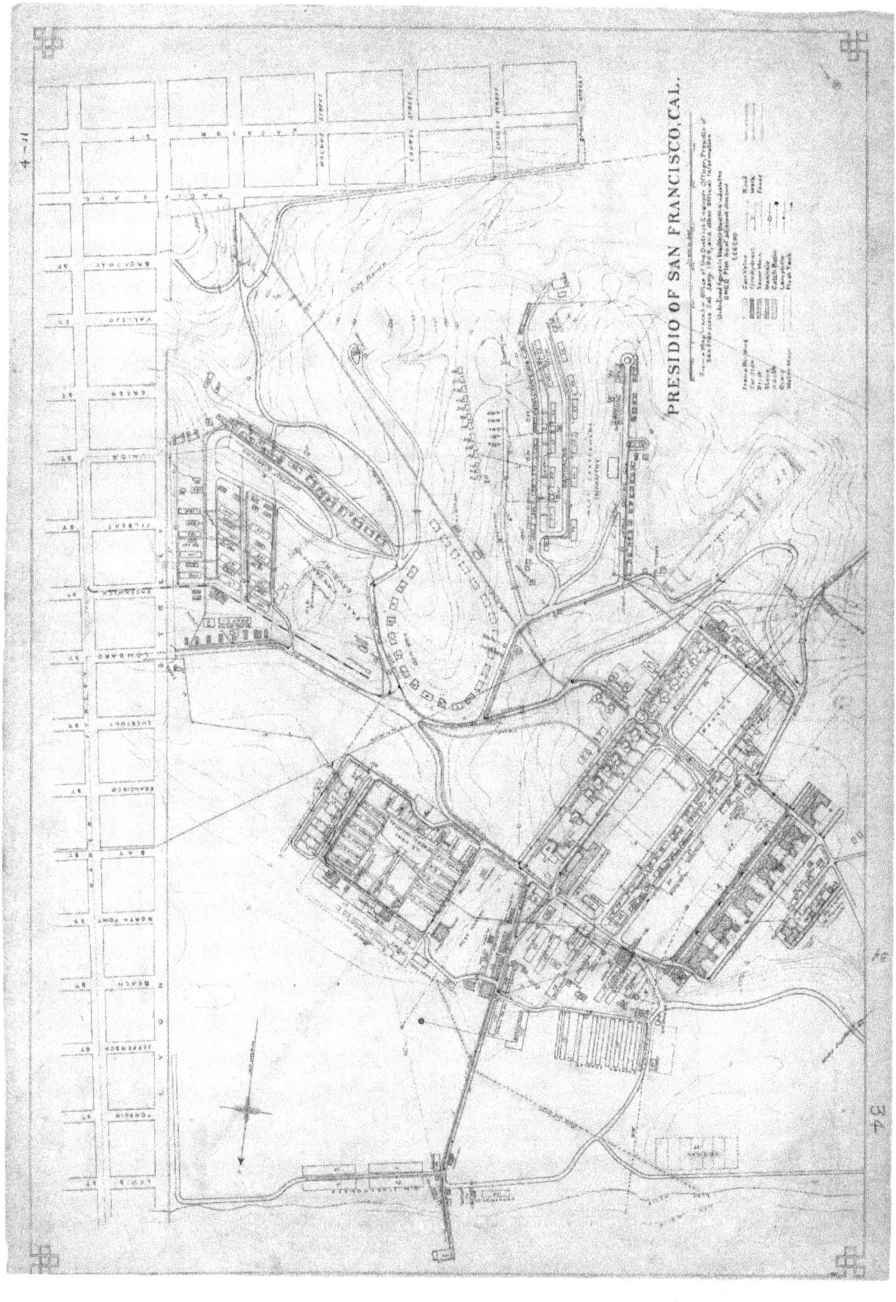


Fig. 6. Map of the Presidio of San Francisco, 1909. Golden Gate National Recreation Area (GOGA), Park Archives, drawer 311, folder 1.

Fig. 7. Main post of the Presidio of San Francisco, circa 1900. GOGA, Park Archives, Presidio Army Museum (PAM) Negative Collection, GOGA 35256.0294.

Fig. 8. TOP: Brick enlisted barracks along Montgomery Street, circa 1898. GOGA, Park Archives, PAM Negative Collection, GOGA 1766.

Fig. 9. BOTTOM: Capt. Charles Young's Quarters 11, circa 1910. GOGA, Park Archives, Post Engineer's Office Historical Records, GOGA 39814.

Fig. 10. ABOVE: Officers' Row, Funston Avenue, circa 1900. GOGA, Park Archives, PAM Negative Collection, GOGA 35256.1357.

Fig. 11. OPPOSITE TOP: First Squadron, Ninth Cavalry training horses, China Point Encampment, Pacific Grove, California, 1902. Historic Preservation Fund (HPF), National Park Service, HPF 3390.

Fig. 12. OPPOSITE BOTTOM: Ninth Cavalry soldiers wearing white utility uniforms grooming horses, Fort Duchesne, Utah, 1899. Colorado Springs Fine Arts Center.

The San Francisco Call.

VOLUME XCIII—NO. 40. SAN FRANCISCO, FRIDAY, JANUARY 9, 1903. PRICE FIVE CENTS.

BOOKER T. WASHINGTON ADDRESSES GREAT AUDIENCE IN THE MECHANICS' PAVILION

DIPLOMAT STIRS IRE OF KAISER

Sensations Behind Von Holleben's Sick Leave.

Ambassador Is Said to Have Been Ordered Home.

CASTRO BOWS TO THE WILL OF NATIONS

Full Acquiescence in All Demands Announced.

Minister Bowen Now Prepared to Leave Venezuela.

Difficulties May Be Settled Out of Hand in America's Capital.

"THE Russian repays oppression with dynamite. The Indian retaliates against wrong with the tomahawk, the Cuban with revolution. The negro, the gentlest, the most long-suffering race in the world, answers his oppression by midnight prayers for deliverance, by faithfulness, by trust in God, and by faith in the righteousness of his cause, knowing that race hatred is no solution for the problem confronting him."—BOOKER T. WASHINGTON.

Famous Colored Educator Is Warmly Received.

Student Cheers for the Black Man's Champion.

Mayor Schmitz Presides Over Big Gathering.

BENJAMIN IDE WHEELER

Distinguished Visitor Talks Eloquently of the Upbuilding of His Race.

RAPID GROWTH OF TUSKEGEE

MUST RIVAL WHITE LABOR

RACE HATRED LESSENING

SALVATION IN EDUCATION

Fig. 13. Booker T. Washington headline, San Francisco, January 9, 1903. *San Francisco Call*.

Fig. 14. TOP: Capt. Charles Young's invitation for the Mardi Gras Ball, February 24, 1903. Courtesy of the NAAMCC.

Fig. 15. BOTTOM: President Theodore Roosevelt at the Presidio of San Francisco Golf Course after the gala parade on May 13, 1903. Two troopers of the Ninth Cavalry flank the president's carriage (*lower left*), and Maj. Gen. Arthur MacArthur, Jr., wearing his Medal of Honor, is the officer with the plumed helmet (*center*). GOGA, Park Archives, PAM Negative Collection, GOGA 1766.

Fig. 16. ABOVE: Ninth Cavalry soldier encampment in a eucalyptus grove, 1903. Sequoia and Kings Canyon National Parks (SEKI) Archive.

Fig. 17. OPPOSITE TOP: Riders on horseback with pack horses on the Colony Mill Road, 1900. SEKI Archive.

Fig. 18. OPPOSITE BOTTOM: Civilian tourists in a wagon on the Colony Mill Road, 1901. SEKI Archive.

Fig. 19. TOP: Soldier Camp at Kaweah, 1903. SEKI Archive.

Fig. 20. BOTTOM: Cavalry patrolling in the Giant Forest, circa 1900. SEKI Archive.

Fig. 21. Sequoia work crew and members of I Troop, Ninth Cavalry, August 30, 1903. *First row seated (left to right):* Sgt. Samuel Pierce, Sgt. William Nicholas, Lew Davis (shovel), Abner Jones, Capt. Charles Young, Phil Alles, Conrad Alles, unknown. *Second row standing (left to right):* unknown, unknown, Abe Burdick, Walter Fry, George W. Stewart, George Welch, J. E. Buckman, Bill Swanson, unknown, QM Sgt. George Brown. *Third row on log (left to right):* 1st Sgt. William S. Jones, William A. McKee, Milo Decker, Noel Britten, Frank Finch, John Grunigen, unknown, Armine Grunigen, unknown, Ernest Britten, unknown. TRHSM.

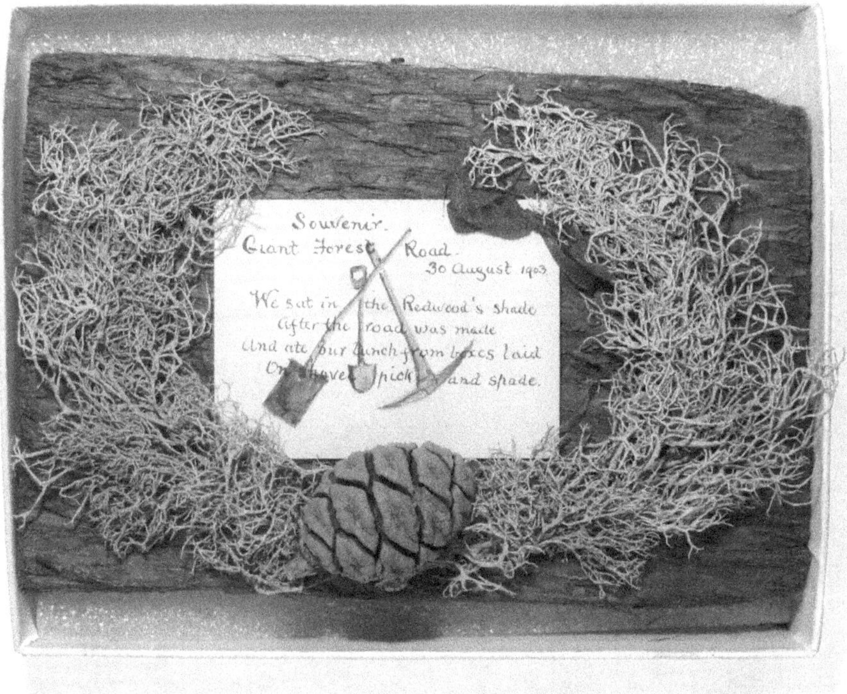


Fig. 22. OPPOSITE TOP: Capt. Charles Young and a soldier serving picnic guests with a decorated shovel in the Giant Forest, August 30, 1903. Courtesy of the NAAMCC.

Fig. 23. OPPOSITE BOTTOM: Fallen sequoia decorated as a table at the picnic feast in the Giant Forest, August 30, 1903. TRHSM.

Fig. 24. ABOVE: Souvenir place card with a poem written by Capt. Charles Young mounted on sequoia bark and decorated with a red ribbon, a sequoia cone, and a wreath of Spanish moss for the picnic on August 30, 1903. SEKI Archive.

Fig. 25. ABOVE: Ada (Mills) Young, 1904. Courtesy of the NAAMCC.

Fig. 26. OPPOSITE: Capt. Charles Young, 1904. Courtesy of the NAAMCC.

Fig. 27. ABOVE: Newspaper photo of sham attack, April 26, 1904. *San Francisco Call.*

Fig. 28. OPPOSITE TOP: Ninth Cavalry riding through Three Rivers, California, May 1904. TRHSM.

Fig. 29. OPPOSITE BOTTOM: Ninth Cavalry riding to Camp Atascadero, San Luis Obispo County, California, July 1904. *Sunset Magazine*, October 1904.

Fig. 30. Ninth Cavalry riding through Templeton, California, July 1904. *Sunset Magazine*, October 1904.

Fig. 31. Ninth Cavalry encampment at Camp Atascadero, San Luis Obispo County, California, August 1904. *Sunset Magazine*, October 1904.

Fig. 32. Samuel Pierce at Sequoia National Park, 1947, standing in front of the Booker T. Washington Tree and holding the 1903 photo of the Sequoia work crew (in figure 21). SEKI Archive.

# 8

# Racism, Routine, Change

> Since Major Bigelow took command, three weeks ago, the troops have been in the field every day, except Saturdays and Sundays, for several hours, and the result of this work is shown by the fine display the squadron made yesterday.
> —*San Francisco Call*, January 28, 1904

The first months of 1904 saw the Ninth Cavalry at the Presidio settle into a routine of training for possible overseas deployment interspersed with inspections, sports, and garrison duties. After spending six months in the High Sierra patrolling the parks in small detachments, Major Bigelow worked his men hard to get the four troops functioning as a squadron again. The troopers of the Ninth had the opportunity to show their skills and horsemanship to civilians who thronged to the Presidio to watch the training. Yet incidents of soldiers getting into trouble in San Francisco continued to receive an inordinate amount of press coverage.

## *Squadron Review*

The Third Squadron held a full military review for its commander the first week in the new year, giving Major Bigelow the initial opportunity to inspect his entire squadron in the six months since it had returned from Sequoia and Yosemite. The newspaper lauded the event and headlined it "Cavalry Makes Splendid Showing during Review." As always for such an event, the command invited the public to watch the spectacle.[1]

The newspaper described the inspection in detail.

> The exercises, which began at 8:30 am, consisted of the usual ceremonies of review, according to drill regulations. The squadron was in fine shape, and the different troops—I, K, L, and M—acquitted themselves in a satisfactory manner. At the close of the inspection as they dashed around the drill grounds at full gallop, with sabers drawn and the bright guidons floating in the breeze, they presented a brilliant appearance.[2]

After the review, Major Bigelow inspected the four troops of the squadron. Then the squadron trumpeters sounded officers' call; the troop commanders, including Captain Young, rode forward; and Major Bigelow made a short speech to his officers. At 10:30 a.m., the trumpeters sounded recall, and the troops rode off the field to the stables on the flats below the Presidio.[3]

For Major Bigelow, this squadron review and inspection had a practical and symbolic importance. Though his official orders assuming authority of the Third Squadron were dated in early December and he had been present at the Presidio for several weeks, it was the first time he had gathered his entire command in one place. As he rode down the line of soldiers, each troop presented sabers, and he returned their salute. Major Bigelow scrutinized each trooper with a practiced eye, noting every detail of their uniforms, horses, and equipment.

### *Scripted Battles*

Following the full military review in early 1904, the Ninth Cavalry at the Presidio busied itself drilling for a possible wartime deployment. The United States had signed a treaty with Colombia in 1903 to facilitate the building of the Panama Canal, but when the Colombian parliament rejected the agreement, Washington moved to support a separatist movement in Panama to enable the project to move forward. A revolutionary junta in Panama took control in November 1903 with support from the U.S. Navy.[4]

When Colombia threatened to attack the revolutionaries, the U.S. Army brass put the Ninth Cavalry on heightened alert for deployment to Central America. Other infantry and artillery units from the West Coast were likewise placed on alert. When it came to overseas deployments for combat operations, the War Department never hesitated to consider the Buffalo Soldier regiments, often moving them to the head of the line.[5]

For much of the first half of 1904, the Third Squadron drilled three times a week and conducted special maneuvers to improve its readiness for combat. This included war games that tested the squadron's ability to conduct various types of combat operations. When participating in war games, one side often wore the older blue uniform and the other the newer khaki ones to differentiate the forces. And the people of San Francisco, who were given free access to watch the exercises, delighted at the spectacle.[6]

The initial practice maneuver attracted civilian audiences in the first week of February 1904. The carefully scripted sham battle featured an attack commanded by Major Bigelow, who led I, L, and M Troops in an assault up a steep incline, where they encountered a battalion of defending artillery reinforced by K Troop. According to the newspaper,

> The three oncoming cavalry troops began the attack and opened the engagement by firing twelve rounds at the entrenched artillery. The artillery replied in lively fashion, and it seemed as if a genuine engagement was on. When the firing had ceased the cavalry advanced in line at a full gallop, and, with drawn sabers, charged the artillery with a tremendous yell.[7]

After the initial success, the assault faltered when it encountered the supporting troop of cavalry. The attacking force then retreated, reformed, and made another charge. This second strike succeeded at first, but when hit in the flank by half of Troop K, it wavered and was forced to retire in the face of a tremendous volley of artillery fire. Both sides fired blank cartridges to create the noise and confusion of combat. The entire sham battle was carefully scripted to teach the officers and men the hard lessons of maneuver warfare in a controlled environment.[8]

Along with mounted maneuvers, the Ninth also exercised on foot. In February 1904, the newspaper reported, "The Ninth cavalry, dismounted, was put through extended orders in the firings. The drilling was done by troop in front of the brick barracks and wound up by the troops being advanced by rushes." As the Ninth had found out in Cuba at San Juan Hill, cavalrymen often fight dismounted, with one troop providing cover as another advanced under fire. Cavalry charges with drawn sabers, though they made a good show for the civilian crowds at the Presidio, were largely a thing of the past.[9]

The second of the mounted sham battles took place in early March 1904. Captain Young's I Troop played the part of the attacking enemy force, which advanced on the McDowell Avenue entrance adjacent to the golf clubhouse. K, L and M Troops, under the command of Major Bigelow, had the mission of defending the grounds of the Presidio and trying to locate where the enemy would strike. The exercise began at 8:30 a.m., and the public was invited to watch what was billed by the newspaper as a "picturesque sight for the onlooker." Forces on both sides fired blank cartridges, making the exercise as realistic as possible. The entire maneuver was again carefully managed, and the American forces defending the post won the day.[10]

The Third Squadron conducted another extensive exercise later in March 1904. The event again won headlines: "Troopers of Ninth Cavalry Theoretically Land on Foreign Shore and Succeed in Annihilating Enemy." The exercise depicted a landing from the sea and an attack on foreign soil by mounted troops from the Ninth Cavalry. Since Major Bigelow was serving on a court-martial board, Captain Cornish directed the exercise.[11]

Early in the morning, I, K, and M Troops, dressed in blue uniforms, made a roundabout detour of the post and stationed themselves on the beach below the waterworks. L Troop, dressed in khaki uniforms, started out from the junction of Avenues A and B, and wound its way up through the woods adjacent to the golf links. After dismounting, the men took up defensive positions in the trees. The attacking forces from the beach dashed up the steep incline and came to a halt under the brow of the bluff, hidden from view by the dense foliage.

The attackers then deployed scouts who located the enemy. Commanded by Captain Young, the attacking troops then dismounted and, leading their horses, climbed up the hill and commenced firing upon the enemy with blanks, taking them by surprise and putting them to flight. Young gave the command to mount and charge the retreating enemy, resulting in a rout where one half of L Troop was annihilated and the rest taken prisoner. Following the battle, field ambulances removed the simulated casualties from the battlefield.

The newspaper reported the weather was fine and that a big crowd from the city watched the demonstration. A photographer named E. A. Rogers was on hand to document the exercise (see figure 27). One of the photos shows the Black soldiers of I Troop dismounted, kneeling in front of their horses, and firing their carbines. The second shows Captain Young, with saber drawn and leveled, leading his mounted troopers in a charge. Young and his troopers were dressed in the older blue uniforms with tan campaign hats and armed with Krag-Jørgenson carbines.[12]

A fourth large exercise was conducted a week later at the end of March. In this scripted skirmish, the Presidio garrison was guarded by the blue force, comprising I, L, and M Troops under the command of Bigelow. The brown (khaki) force, which was Troop K under the command of First Lieutenant Rubottom, entered the south side of the post, probed blue force positions, withdrew, and then reported the situation to the notional invading force.[13]

Bigelow stationed his forces in the heavy woods skirting the north line of the golf links and deployed scouts forward of the main body. Rubottom initially confused the defenders and entered the post behind the Marine Hospital. The invaders were finally chased down by L Troop under Captain Christian, who "poured hot fire after them," resulting in enemy casualties. The wounded were taken to a field hospital and further evacuated by ambulances with simulated injuries. The only real casualty was Trooper W. Hagen of M Troop who suffered slight burn wounds to his cheek when a blank cartridge was fired too close to his face.[14]

Following the sham battle, Major Bigelow reviewed the squadron on the golf links. Bigelow judged the exercise a success, though he commented that "the recent heavy drills had taken up so much time that the troopers were a little bit rusty in ceremonies." As with all such mock battles at the Presidio, large crowds of civilians enjoyed the simulated warfare and rattle of gunfire. The only unhappy San Franciscans were the golfers, who complained about the torn-up turf on the golf course after each cavalry exercise on the links.[15]

A final sham battle in late April 1904 featured Captain Young in a prominent role. As in the previous exercises, all was carefully scripted and controlled. According to one report, "Captain Young with I Troop was supposed to reconnoiter the post and then make his escape. Though he was problematically successful in destroying the barracks, burning up the magazines, and dismantling the disappearing guns, he was supposed to be killed as he was making his escape and with him ten of his troopers were also supposed to lose their lives."

The usual crowds of spectators from San Francisco thronged to see this last in a series of exercises. But since the opposing forces did not fire blank cartridges on this occasion, the crowd voiced disappointment. The newspaper noted the absence of simulated gunfire, "so, much was left to the imagination."[16]

### *Diverse Sports*

When the soldiers were not parading or conducting military exercises, sports were again a popular pastime, and some of the events featured Black teams competing against white squads of civilians or soldiers. White officers never played on the same team with Black enlisted men, but they did occasionally compete against each other. The baseball nines representing the cavalry, artillery, and infantry units competed against each other, and the post teams often played against clubs from San Francisco and surrounding cities.[17]

A baseball team fielded by the Ninth Cavalry at the Presidio, the "San Juans," beat the nine from the Tenth Infantry by a score of 18 to 10 in late January 1904. The following day, the Presidio post squad defeated the visiting Ninth Cavalry nine from Ord Barracks in Monterey. The Ninth Cavalry team from Ord Barracks crossed bats with the officers' "All-Presidio" baseball squad the following day, winning by a score of 11 to 8.[18]

As a diversion from the regular routine at the Presidio, the Ninth Cavalry and other units also enjoyed the monthly track and field sports events, which drew large crowds from the local community. The monthly competition in January 1904 featured mounted athletic events, known in the army as "monkey drills," pitting the troopers of the Ninth against the gunners of the field artillery. The units brought unsaddled horses to the field, and contestants made running jumps onto their backs and then turned somersaults from the backs of the horses onto the ground and did other tricks. During the competition, the horses behaved well except for the one belonging to purportedly the finest horseman and athlete in the regiment—Cpl. Dock Smelly of Young's I Troop. His horse turned fractious and had to be replaced by an unfamiliar horse, which cost Smelly the contest.[19]

The competition in April 1904 took place on the old grounds in front of the commanding officer's headquarters. The eclectic events, pitting the Ninth Cavalry troops against the various artillery batteries, included a relay race, which resulted in a tie in the final heat between the First Field Artillery Battery and L Troop. Pvt. John Lumpkins of L Troop took first and Blacksmith Charles Kyle of K Troop second in the individual fencing event; L Troop captured the team fencing title. L Troop won the competition for speed in setting up a shelter tent, but the First Field Artillery Battery was quicker in striking the canvas. Pvt. Randall Ephraim of K Troop won the running broad jump with 17 feet 7 inches, and Sgt. Dee Smith of I Troop won the 220-yard dash. The prize money for these events was a welcome windfall to the winning soldiers.[20]

### *Slashing Incident*

Amid the squadron's training and sporting activities, the newspapers reported a slashing incident involving a Black soldier in early 1904. The assault occurred off post just a day after the garrison's holiday period ended. Military authorities at the Presidio moved quickly to respond to police inquiries and quiet the negative publicity.[21]

According to the *Call*, the attack on a white woman, Ethel Carney, by a Black soldier took place late on a Sunday night. The initial reports named the victim as Miss Ethel Carney, but subsequent articles gave her married name as Mrs. John M. Carney. She was traveling home in company with Mrs. J. W. Knight on a Union Street trolley near the entrance to the Presidio. That both were married and traveling together suggested that they were respectable women, though subsequent reporting indicated otherwise.[22]

The *San Francisco Chronicle* added details to this initial report: "The two women in the case are both employed in a Pacific Street dance hall patronized by soldiers, and the husband of Mrs. Carney keeps a saloon near the Presidio gate." The article also noted that "angry words were exchanged between the white and colored soldiers" on the trolley and that two of the white soldiers were "friends" of the women and had boarded the car with them. The *Chronicle* reporter criticized the white soldiers for not doing more to defend the two women on the bus and in the subsequent attack.[23]

Seated next to the women, according to the report in the *Call*, were "five negro soldiers, dressed in cavalry uniforms." Also on the trolley were six white soldiers from the Tenth Infantry. The women ignored the Black soldiers when they attempted to engage them in conversation, and the women complained to the conductor, who did nothing. When the two women stepped off the trolley, one of the Black soldiers allegedly followed them. When he approached as they walked home, the women ran. The soldier reportedly overtook Mrs. Carney and slashed her on the neck and cheek with a razor. Cries for help brought a policeman, and the assailant fled.[24]

According to a "well-known citizen" quoted by the newspaper after this incident, "Respectable women who are forced to patronize the cars after 9 o'clock at night are insulted with impunity by drunken and insolent soldiers, who respect neither age nor sex. Conductors and gripmen are powerless, and policemen are never to be found." The incident, stated the newspaper, was the "culmination of a series of insults heaped upon white women by the black troopers of the Ninth Cavalry, and the intense indignation which has been aroused by the attempted murder has goaded the military authorities to great activity in an effort to capture the perpetrator of the latest outrage."[25]

The initial investigation identified the woman's assailant as a member of L Troop, Ninth Cavalry, though the police did not have a name. An article the following day informed readers that Captain Christian, the L Troop commander, was doing his best to identify the suspect and that all his soldiers were present; none had deserted. The detective assigned the case complained that he was handicapped by the apparent apathy of the principals and the witnesses who gave him no leads to work with.[26]

In a final attempt to solve the case, Mrs. Carney visited the Presidio at the request of Major Bigelow. With her head "bound up with bandages and only the front part of her face visible," she was taken to the barracks of all four of the troops of cavalry and shown the men. Accompanying her were those soldiers from the Tenth Infantry who were present in the car before the slashing. Neither she nor the white soldiers were able to identify her attacker, and the case was never resolved.[27]

That the detective investigating the crime complained about the apathy of the principals and witnesses seems odd. This suggests the possibility that the authorities were not serious about the case since it involved dance hall girls who were too friendly with soldiers. It is also possible no Black soldier was involved and that the entire story was made up to cover what really happened.

### *Racist Reporting*

American newspaper stories were full of racist stereotypes at the turn of the century, and those in the major San Francisco tabloids were no exception. A good example appeared in a newspaper in January under the headline "Negro Stabbing Gives Judge Cabaniss Hard Puzzle." The reporter began,

> It was a dark day for Judge [George H.] Cabaniss yesterday. He had on hearing complaints against two negro soldiers, who were accused of stabbing a negro porter named James Parker during a rough house in a dance hall on Pacific [Avenue]. This was conducted by another negro, one Lester Mapps. When all the witnesses had gathered in the courtroom the bailiffs turned on all the available lights in order to brighten up the oppressive darkness.

The newspaper reporter's racist imagery escalated:

> The case was utterly devoid of "sweetness and light." All the participants were negroes, varying in shade from umber to the deep black of a moonless night. One of the defendants was familiarly known as "Pork Chops." Judge Cabaniss did a little christening on his own account, and when the witness of a particularly somber color appeared on the stand, he asked him if his cognomen was "Midnight."[28]

In the end, the case was dismissed when the judge found a lack of evidence to convict the two soldiers, identified as George E. Adams and Charles Heard. The court record noted, "Bottles, chairs, tables, in fact everything in the saloon except the license came into play during the fight, in which forty or fifty negroes participated." Though Cabaniss dismissed the case, he warned every "negro soldier within the sound of his voice" that he would prosecute the first case with sufficient evidence to the fullest extent of the law, especially if they offered "personal violence to a citizen of San Francisco."[29]

Judge Cabaniss gave the two Black soldiers a fair trial, contrasting the blatant racist reporting in the newspaper. Both soldiers were members of

M Troop, Ninth Cavalry. Private Adams was discharged from the army after a general court-martial later in the same year for a different offense, while Private Heard served out his enlistment honorably and received a very good character rating several years later.[30]

*Replacements*

Not reported in the San Francisco newspapers was the large influx of new recruits arriving at the Presidio for the Ninth Cavalry during the first quarter of 1904. These replacements filled the gaps created by soldiers who ended their enlistments or left the army for other reasons. I Troop received the lion's share of the arrivals from the recruiting depots, with two coming in January and eight new troopers in March.[31]

In January 1904, I Troop received two recruits with previous service in the army. The first, Alexander Young, was a soldier from Scioto County, Ohio, who had served his previous three-year tour with M Troop, Ninth U.S. Cavalry. The second, John A. Griffin, from Henry County, Kentucky, had first signed up in 1894 and had served three tours in the army. His first two enlistments were with K Troop, Ninth U.S. Cavalry, during which he was promoted to sergeant; and in his third enlistment, with Company H, Twenty-Fifth U.S. Infantry, he also served as a sergeant and received an excellent rating. These experienced soldiers were welcome additions to I Troop.[32]

Of the eight replacements sent to I Troop in March, five were first-term soldiers with no previous military experience. Alexander Faucett, Don Rice, and John D. Swagerty—all born in Tennessee—were miners from Middlesboro, Kentucky, when they walked into the enlistment office on the same day in March 1904. The fourth new soldier, Major Fish, was born in Fitzpatrick, Georgia, and was working in Nashville, Tennessee, when he enlisted. The fifth, John Enox, was born in Savana, Missouri, and enlisted in San Francisco, where he worked as a butcher. Four of five of these new recruits proved to be good soldiers and served out their three-year terms.[33]

Notably, the three replacements with previous military experience assigned to I Troop in March 1904 proved a mixed bag. The first, Edward F. Brockenborough—a cavalry veteran who had served with I Troop, Ninth U.S. Cavalry from 1898 to 1901 and with G Troop, Tenth U.S. Cavalry from 1901 to 1904—was given a dishonorable discharge a year after joining I

Troop. The second, Walter Garrett, a former member of Company G, Twenty-Fourth U.S. Infantry, also received a dishonorable discharge the next year. With these two men, previous service did not guarantee good soldier potential.[34]

By far the cream of the crop of the soldiers sent to I Troop in March 1904 was Thomas Young. Born in Maury County, Tennessee, in 1872, Young was already an accomplished cavalry leader when he arrived at the Presidio of San Francisco. After initially enlisting in 1892, listing his occupation as teamster, he had completed three enlistments with the Tenth U.S. Cavalry, ending each as a sergeant with an excellent rating. So he arrived in I Troop in 1904 as a proven noncommissioned officer ready to fill one of the open sergeants' positions.[35]

A survey of the places these Buffalo Soldiers were born, worked, and enlisted reveals a remarkable mobility at a time when most Americans never ventured far from the farm or city of their birth. Take Sgt. Thomas Young, for instance. He was born in Tennessee, had his initial cavalry training in Ohio, and served in peacetime in Montana, Wyoming, and California. He had also served in wartime in Cuba during the Spanish-American War and in the Philippines during the Philippine-American War. Sergeant Young had traveled all over the world on horseback, in railcars, and on ships. He would add more miles and modes of transport during his time with the Ninth Cavalry.[36]

### *Back to Sequoia?*

Some more positive news about the Buffalo Soldiers made newspaper headlines from New York to California in early 1904 with Charles Young's *Report of the Acting Superintendent of the Sequoia and General Grant National Parks*. The *Tulare County Times* from Visalia lauded the report as well as Young's efforts to complete the road and open Sequoia to tourists. The *Times* also mentioned a *New York Evening Post* editorial that recommended Captain Young be sent to Sequoia as the superintendent for another year.[37]

The Visalia newspaper complimented "Young's interest, ability, energy, enthusiasm, and business-like qualities." It added: "This fact is of more than passing interest, since Capt. Young is a black man, as well as a graduate of West Point, and accomplished his results with the aid of colored soldiers." The article suggested the army should "avail itself for some years of Capt. Young's interest in the big trees." As a precedent for an army officer spending more than one tour in a national park, the report cited the example of Maj. John Pitcher's serving at Yellowstone for many years to the benefit of that park.[38]

Major Pitcher, Sixth U.S. Cavalry, served as the acting superintendent of Yellowstone National Park from 1901 to 1907. An 1876 graduate of West Point, Pitcher was responsible for instituting many policies to protect the flora and fauna at Yellowstone that had a lasting impact. It is interesting to note that Major Pitcher was on leave from duty at the Presidio of San Francisco for two weeks in February 1904. The records are silent as to whether he shared his experiences at Yellowstone with Captain Young or Major Bigelow.[39]

Apart from Captain Young, most of the officers in the Ninth Cavalry considered park duty a distraction from their mission of maintaining their troops' readiness and training for combat. Many of the army officers who had served as acting superintendents of the national parks in the past did so unenthusiastically, as characterized by Lieutenant Colonel Garrard's term at Yosemite. But Young had a different view of park duty and seemed to genuinely relish the challenge. He took every duty assignment the army detailed to him seriously, knowing he would be under more scrutiny than his white officer colleagues.

It is quite possible the Ninth Cavalry planned to return Young as the superintendent of Sequoia and General Grant National Parks in 1904. The Third Squadron was already anticipating summer park duty at Sequoia and Yosemite since the Ninth Cavalry was scheduled to remain in San Francisco another year. And since 1891 the War Department had routinely delegated responsibility for those two parks to the cavalry squadrons assigned to the Presidio of San Francisco.

### *Local Landowner*

According to letters Captain Young later exchanged with his Three Rivers friends, he was planning to return the following summer season for another tour as the superintendent at Sequoia National Park. To that end, he purchased two parcels of land adjoining the park. One was a ranch close to Three Rivers near the southwestern entrance to Sequoia National Park. He also bought a smaller plot of land in Inyo County near Mount Whitney. Both were ideally situated to be used as his headquarters for another summer as the superintendent of Sequoia.[40]

Sergeant Nicholas described the ranch near Three Rivers as follows: "Captain Young purchased a fruit and stock ranch consisting of 480 acres on which there was 15 acres of apples, and various other fruit trees such as lemons, oranges, nuts, and berries sufficient to market a 10-room house, barn for 8 horses, and a storage house for 40 tons of apples." After Young acquired the house, he "purchased 4 horses (work), one saddle horse, 2 cows, 160 head of hogs, wagons, and sufficient tools to operate the place."[41]

The Tulare County Recorder's Office shows that the 480-acre property, later called the Thorn Ranch, was sold to Charles Young by Marion E. Griffes for ten dollars in gold coin on February 4, 1904. Young registered this purchase four months after his departure from Sequoia, but he must have looked at the ranch and made arrangements for the deal during his summer at the park. The deed stipulated "no portion of said land shall be used directly or indirectly for the manufacture or sale of intoxicating liquors."[42]

The second plot in Inyo County was smaller and probably less developed. Nicholas explained, "Captain Young bought 160 acres in Inyo County, California. Sergeant Pierce and myself homesteaded 160 acres adjacent to this property—all level land, and at the expiration of our term of enlistments, December 1903, Sergeant Pierce and I operated these ranches." Young evidently worked out an arrangement with his two most trusted sergeants who wanted to start their new lives as farmers or ranchers in California. They would keep an eye on his land investments in exchange for managing his farms while he was absent.[43]

Sergeants Nicholas and Pierce were not alone in wanting to settle in this part of California. Another Black army officer and friend of Captain Young's, Lt. Col. Allen Allensworth, founded a Black settlement in Tulare County a few years later. When Allensworth retired from the army as a chaplain in 1906, he was the highest-ranking Black officer in American history, though he was not a line officer like Charles Young. Two years after leaving the army, he established the town of Allensworth in Tulare County.[44]

Before moving to Tulare County, Allensworth and his family had settled in Los Angeles, where he soon championed the idea of establishing a self-sufficient, all-Black community where African Americans could live free of racial discrimination. When he founded the town of Allensworth, a select group of Black settlers constructed homes, laid out streets, and farmed the land. He named one of the roads in the town after Young. But the lack of water and the death of Allensworth in 1914 doomed the community, and after settlers drifted away, it nearly turned into a ghost town.[45]

There was perhaps another reason for Young to contemplate establishing a foothold in California. Young had met a woman in San Francisco named Ada Mills before his departure for Sequoia. He would soon celebrate his fortieth birthday and might have been thinking it was time to settle down and have a family.

### *Three Rivers Visitors*

Some of the best details of Young's life at the Presidio, and the first hints of his courtship of Ada Mills, come from the letters and recollections of the friends he made at Three Rivers. He maintained his friendships with Philip and Blanche Winser and other Three Rivers families, and they visited him at the Presidio. The letters exchanged after these visits provide a valuable window into Young's life as an officer at the post.[46]

All Young's letters begin with "My very dear Mrs. Winser" or "My very dear Mr. Winser." The salutations were customary at a time when society remained rather formal, and first names were rarely used. Yet the language of his letters was striking in its sincerity and frankness, as shown in the following excerpts. And his letters were variously signed "With my highest love and esteem, my dear friends," or "Love to both and a prosperous year," suggesting a genuine friendship.[47]

Young penned an initial letter to Blanche Winser in December 1904, thanking her for her "last kind letter," which indicated a continuing correspondence. Young then wrote: "Your goodness makes me tremble as I so often have told you before. I cannot understand it. It seems so peculiar that in this matter of fact world of ours where so much selfishness exists that the Kingdom of God would come in you. But it has, in spite of your protesting hands." Young, a lifelong bachelor and adherent to his color line, seemed genuinely delighted that he could have a friendship with a white woman unsullied by prejudice.[48]

In the same letter, he mentioned the visit of another family from Three Rivers:

> Mr. [George] and Mrs. [Louise] Ames came and brought their little children, who make it quite lively for us, especially the little girl. She would not make friends with me at first and I felt what it was that prevented it. It was the old leprosy of blackness, which when she found it did not rub off, she became reconciled to. She and I are now the chummiest of chums.[49]

Young's description of a young white girl's aversion to his blackness is striking and his comparison to leprosy evocative. That he would mention the matter to Blanche Winser is remarkable, reflecting a forthright friendship.

In the same letter, Young sent his greetings to other Three Rivers residents whom he clearly knew well. Young was "glad Miss Wright (now Will Purdy's Ida) continues her work of story writing. I think they are bound to be good, give my regards to her." He asked Winser to "hug Lindley and give my regards to Mr. Smith." In a letter the following year, Young passed his good wishes to Sydney Smith. All these people were former Kaweah Colonists or people closely aligned with them. Lindley, the son of Blanche and Philip, was the boy whom the I Troop soldiers grew so fond of in the summer of 1903.[50]

In early January 1904, Young wrote to Philip Winser and apologized for his tardiness in writing. He "was delaying awaiting the coming of the books 'Souls of Black Folk,' one of which I send to you by mail today." Young enclosed a second copy that he asked him "to please deliver to Miss Wright." This refers to Ida Purdy, whom he had previously encouraged in her writing. *The Souls of Black Folk*, a collection of essays and sketches published in 1903 by W. E. B. Du Bois, became a masterpiece of African American literature.[51]

In addition to the books, Young enclosed "some old and some new" music for Blanche Winser, indicating they shared a love of music. He also included some pictures for Lindley and a purple tie "for your Royal Highness, Philip I." This was a reference to Philip Winser's heritage, since he was born in England. Finally, Young included a copy of his superintendent's report. He finished the letter with this thought: "Oh beautiful valley! You are right, Mr. Winser, when you talk of its charms, due in large part to the people living there." Once again, Young reflected on the genuine human kindness and friendship he had discovered in the High Sierra.[52]

In mid-January, Young wrote, "How glad I am that we have you with us next week! We are always ready for you." Philip Winser remarked on that visit to the Presidio in his memoir:

> That winter we visited at the Presidio where the Captain kept bachelor residence with his soldier servant Peggy [Abner Jones]. There we had noble entertainment, such a change from our mountain environment, he spoke French, German, and Spanish, played organ, piano, and violin and sang with the native feeling of a negro, plus his training, also we met his fiancée.[53]

This was the first mention of Young's fiancée, Ada Mills.

Young told the visitors many stories, but one, Philip Winser recalled, was a reminder of the Black officer's enslaved roots. Winser wrote: "Among many anecdotes, we heard how he had met on a train the old family mistress of slave day times. She lamented, 'Oh Charles! Why didn't you stay on with us?' And his reply, I can fancy it, 'Madam, I am not always your obedient servant' and the bow that went with it." This is a remarkable echo of Young's antebellum past tinged with his sense of irony.[54]

One last story Philip Winser related of the family's visit involved Young with his troops on the parade ground. According to Winser, Blanche was watching the parade ground when the commander and a visiting military attaché passed, and she overheard the following conversation. The visitor asked, "Who is that colored man?" The commander, Major Bigelow, replied, loudly enough to be overheard, "That's Young, the smartest officer we have." Major Bigelow's complimentary words about Young commends both officers.[55]

### *White Soldier's Salute*

One other reported incident about Young's time at the Presidio merits mention. The apocryphal story involved white soldiers purposely refusing to salute Young as a Black officer. The dubious tale, which dates to one of his first assignments in the 1890s, followed Young to each of his postings, repeated over and over with a new set of white soldiers refusing to properly acknowledge Young because he was Black.

The narrative was reported again by the Black press in the *Cleveland Gazette* while Young was at the Presidio:

> "The pretty little story" going the round of the race press to the effect that Captain Charles Young of Ohio, now stationed at the Presidio, California, in command of his company [troop], made four white soldiers salute his coat after they had refused to salute him with it on, is doubtless nothing but a story, hardly a "pretty little" one either, from a race viewpoint. We refuse to believe Capt. Young [is] that kind of a "Booker Washington" member of the race. Certainly, the Young we knew was not. Thosc "soldiers" would have saluted him with the coat on or would have been severely dealt with according to the rules of the army, and promptly, too.[56]

This article in a Black newspaper is instructive for several reasons. First, for its reading audience, it refutes the story as the creation of racially biased white newspapers to reinforce racist thinking. It is easy to imagine a white newspaper editor hearing the story secondhand and reporting it as fact. Second, the article indicates Black society had moved on from the accommodationist thinking of Booker T. Washington in favor of the more radical and activist ideology of W. E. B. Du Bois. Finally, it concludes that Young would have never stood for such insubordination by enlisted soldiers.

A more plausible scenario is provided in a firsthand account by Black educator Edwin B. Henderson and reported in 1898 during the Spanish-American War at Camp Alger, Virginia:

> It was there that I first saw Charles Young, then a Major of the 9th Ohio Infantry Battalion. [Young, a first lieutenant in the U.S. Army at the time, was appointed a volunteer major in the Ohio National Guard during the war.] One of the thrilling moments of my life occurred thus: I was seated on the steps of the village feedstore one evening listening to a white Virginia soldier boasting of his experience when Major Young rode past on his return to camp. I heard the white soldier say to his companion, "I'll never salute a damn n——."
>
> I thought Young had not seen the soldier seated on the bench against the wall. In a great cloud of dust, Young whirled his horse around and yelled, "Get up!" "Salute." There stood this soldier listening to as severe

a tongue lashing as ever I had heard one adult give another. Young's final words were: "You're saluting the United States Army."

He returned the salute, spurred his horse round, and was on his way back to Camp Alger. That evening I went across the street to home a proud youngster.[57]

The second version of the story is certainly the accurate account. Captain Young was a proud career officer and would never have let such insubordination go uncorrected. The first story featuring Young having the white soldiers salute his coat is an allegory spawned by racist beliefs. It was a "pretty little story" told by newspaper reporters and gossipers who had not the slightest idea of Regular Army discipline or Young's professionalism.

### *Marriage*

Young was a bachelor when he landed at the Presidio in 1902, but sometime after his arrival, he began courting Ada Mills of San Francisco. Little is known about how they met, yet their romance deepened in the first three months after Young's return to the Presidio from Sequoia. They were certainly engaged by January when the Winsers visited, and Young introduced her as his fiancée.[58]

According to Young's friend Harry Atwood, who served as an officer on his staff during the Spanish-American War, Young "thought men and women were made for companionship." So far as Atwood was able to see, there was never "any suggestion of sex—and yet [Young] thought men and women should naturally drift together—should be stirred to love." Still, as an army officer mastering the profession of arms at isolated frontier posts or overseas in the Philippines, Young had few opportunities to meet women. San Francisco, however, boasted a large Black population with plenty of eligible women of social status.[59]

The newspaper recorded that Captain Young was issued a marriage license on February 17, 1904. The following day, Young married Miss Ada Mills in Oakland, California, scarcely three months after his return to the Presidio from Sequoia. Charles and Ada kept their plans secret until the day they were married in a private ceremony. They had separate wedding photos taken of Charles Young in uniform and Ada Young in a bridal gown (see figures 25 and 26).[60]

Rev. Otho E. Jones of the First A.M.E. Church of Oakland married the couple in a simple ceremony in the home of the bride's aunt, F. P. Henry, in Oakland. According to news reports, there "were no attendants, the whole affair being entirely simple and informal, some of the troopers of the Ninth Cavalry acting as witnesses, and relatives of the bride being present." According to the marriage certificate, Young's former cook Abner Jones and Ada's aunt F. P. Henry stood as witnesses.[61]

The ceremony took place in the evening, and the astonished officers of the Presidio woke up the following day to find Young a married man with a new bride. Young did not invite any of the officers of the regiment to the wedding, since he had no real friends among them. According to one newspaper report, the white officers of the Presidio did gather at the Youngs' home the following day to offer their congratulations. Major Bigelow and the other officers on the post would have stopped by in uniform to pass on their compliments, as military etiquette required.[62]

Even the newspaper captured the surprise of his fellow officers. The first clue they gained of Young's new married status was the sight of "a pretty young woman standing at the door of Captain Young's quarters." The newspaper ran the headline "Presidio Colored Officer Now a Benedict," referring to the newly married man in Shakespeare's *Much Ado about Nothing* who had long been a bachelor. According to the marriage certificate, the thirty-nine-year-old Young, a native of Kentucky, married Ada Mills, twenty-three, who was born in Grass Valley, California.[63]

Ada's parents boasted an ancestry featuring African American, Native American, and white English roots. Her father, Edward Mills, Jr., and mother, Nannie Burrows Mills, had some connection to enslaved people who had been brought to California to work in the Kentucky Ridge gold mine. The owner of the mine, Col. William F. English, brought enslaved laborers to California from family plantations in South Carolina to work the mine and be freed after eighteen months of labor. The mining venture failed, and the Black laborers settled in nearby Grass Valley after gaining their freedom.[64]

According to the newspaper, the day following the Youngs' ceremony, "quite a sensation was caused at the Presidio this morning by the news that Charles Young, who is the senior colored officer in the army, had taken unto himself a bride last night." The article described Young as a "West

Point graduate, an able officer, and a skillful musician." The newspaper reported that Captain and Mrs. Young had "gone into housekeeping in the spacious quarters at the junction of the broad carriage road running west through the Presidio and the main road running north and south," pointing to their residence at the intersection of Presidio Boulevard and Funston Avenue.[65]

### *Hispaniola Bound*

Soon after his marriage, the army selected Young in April 1904 to serve as the military attaché to the island of Hispaniola, comprising Haiti and the Dominican Republic. Military attaché assignments were highly coveted and considered career enhancing, and Young was the first Black officer to be selected for such a position. These assignments were voluntary, and he could have turned it down, yet Young accepted the opportunity. This meant Young did not get the chance to serve another summer at Sequoia.

The request for Young to serve on attaché duty must have come as a surprise and on very short notice. As late as March 1904, Young wrote to the Winsers:

> Dearest Friends:
>
> Greetings. I am so happy and so busy that I cannot write to you like I wish but here goes to show that we are very much alive and you are not forgotten. Ada and I (Ada? That's my wife) talk of you both very often and hope we can come to see you soon, but it all depends upon our going to the parks.[66]

Clearly, he still hoped that he would get another opportunity to serve in the parks and did not yet know of the attaché assignment.

Young recognized there were few if any professional risks posed by serving away from his regiment on detached duty. His previous five years at Fort Duchesne, in the Philippines, in San Francisco, and at Sequoia firmly established his credentials as a successful troop commander and cavalry leader, both in peace and at war. His experience also qualified him to serve on detached duty, since no officer was eligible unless he had served five consecutive years with his regiment. He had to wait for seniority and promotion to advance further in the ranks of positions of responsibility within the regiment, and this took time even in an expanded army. In the meantime, he could contribute to the needs of his country and to the people of his race by serving as a military attaché in Hispaniola.

Captain Young was an ideal choice for the post in Hispaniola for a host of reasons. First, West Pointers nearly always filled these coveted political-military assignments. Second, Young was a seasoned cavalry officer, a gifted linguist, and fluent in both the French and Spanish spoken on the island. Young was also Black, which would enable him to move easily among the Black Creole society of Haiti and the largely Black and mixed population of the Dominican Republic. Additionally, the U.S. minister to Haiti, William F. Powell, was African American, making the assignment of a Black army officer preferable.[67]

Another factor was involved in the decision process. As Young learned in his assignment to Wilberforce University, the War Department was always seeking "safe" postings for its highest-ranking African American line officer. The U.S. Army seized the opportunity to assign Captain Young as an attaché to Hispaniola for this reason: it needed a place to send Young to avoid the awkward situation of having white lieutenants serve under a Black captain and troop commander.

After Young agreed to take the assignment in early April 1904, the War Department requested the State Department's approval for the designation of a military attaché to Haiti and the Dominican Republic. John Hay, the secretary of state, quickly approved the request, and the War Department issued orders assigning Captain Young on detached service as military attaché the following day.[68]

The San Francisco newspapers reported the selection of Captain Young for the attaché assignment on the first day of May 1904. A short article noted, "He is a negro, a graduate of the Military Academy, and possesses a fine record. His ability and fitness for the place led to his designation."[69]

Captain Young turned over command of I Troop to his second in command, First Lieutenant Rubottom, in early May 1904 in preparation for his departure. Rubottom would lead the troop as the acting commander until Young's return from detached duty, though Young retained his slot in the Ninth Cavalry as the captain of I Troop. Captain Young and his wife packed up their belongings and departed the Presidio on May 12, 1904.[70]

After Young's departure for Hispaniola, the Ninth Cavalry remained another five months at the Presidio of San Francisco and at Ord Barracks at Monterey. After a busy first quarter preparing for contingencies in garrison, the Ninth began planning for another busy summer season patrolling Yosemite and Sequoia National Parks. And one of the squadrons of the Ninth Cavalry would soon be assigned a new mission assisting the California National Guard.

# 9

# Park Duty and Encampment

> Major Bigelow, who has been appointed acting superintendent of Yosemite National Park, expects to leave Ord Barracks for that duty in early May.
> —*San Francisco Call*, April 12, 1904

After the departure of Captain Young, the Ninth Cavalry still had another five months in California, and as summer approached, it prepared for one last season patrolling the national parks. Park duty offered the Buffalo Soldiers an opportunity to deploy to the High Sierra and escape the mundane routine of garrison life. Additionally, as noted, park service distanced the troopers from the temptations of the bars and brothels in San Francisco. While this highly desired task went to the Third Squadron at the Presidio the previous summer, 1904 would see the First Squadron at Ord Barracks assigned this duty at Sequoia and Yosemite.

## *Park Duty*

San Francisco newspapers reported in March 1904 that the First Squadron, Ninth Cavalry, stationed at Ord Barracks in Monterey, California, had been selected to patrol the Sequoia and Yosemite National Parks for the summer season. The newspaper noted park duty was "deemed one of the finest details in this department and is much sought after by the different squadrons of troopers on the coast." The decision delighted the members of the First Squadron as much as it disappointed those of the

Third Squadron at the Presidio, many of whom had looked forward to a second summer in the parks.[1]

In a related development in mid-April, the Ninth Cavalry decided it would send Major Bigelow, so recently assigned to the Presidio, back to Ord Barracks in Monterey to resume command of the First Squadron. Bigelow's return to Monterey facilitated his upcoming assignment as the acting superintendent of Yosemite National Park. He would lead C and D Troops of the First Squadron into the High Sierra to take station at Camp A. E. Wood for the summer patrolling season.[2]

The *Tulare County Times* reported in May 1904 that Young would not return to Sequoia, much to the regret of the Visalia Board of Trade, which had hoped to have his services a second year. Instead, Capt. George F. Hamilton, who commanded A Troop at Ord Barracks, was assigned to lead two troops of the Ninth and assume duties as the acting superintendent of the Sequoia and General Grant National Parks. First Lieutenant Pearson, Young's former second in command in I Troop, would assist Captain Hamilton as the commander of B Troop.[3]

Young's ambition in the U.S. Army and his loyalty to his race and country account for his decision not to return to Sequoia. He could have turned down the voluntary assignment to Hispaniola, yet a second tour as a national park superintendent would not have been career enhancing. On the other hand, a military attaché assignment would add a laurel to his earlier service on detached duty as a professor of military science at Wilberforce University. The attaché assignment would position him ahead of his contemporaries when he was considered for promotion to major a few years hence. Young always experienced a tension between what he had already achieved and what he had left to accomplish. As the trailblazer for Black officers in the army, this work could not be done by anyone else.

Additionally, the Hispaniola assignment was one of those rare cases when the ambitions of Young, the needs of the War Department, and the institutional racism of the U.S. Army aligned. Captain Young pursued the promotion to facilitate his continued role as a point man for his race in the U.S. Army. And the army needed a place to temporarily exile its senior Black Regular Army officer to block him from commanding white officers. Young spent the next four years serving away from his regiment on detached duty, making the officer corps of the Ninth Cavalry all white again.

### *Hamilton at Sequoia*

While Young was packing for his new assignment in Hispaniola, Captain Hamilton led two troops of the First Squadron from Ord Barracks for park duty in Sequoia on May 9, 1904. The troops arrived at Three Rivers seventeen days later, having covered 255 miles. The ninety-two-member Sequoia detachment initially went into camp at Kaweah near the entrance to Sequoia National Park as Young had done the previous year.[4]

Captain Hamilton, who graduated from West Point in 1894, five years after Young, was the junior of the two captains then with the First Squadron. After graduating from West Point, he was assigned to the Ninth Cavalry. During the Spanish-American War in 1898, he served as the aide to Maj. Gen. Adna R. Chaffee and later married his daughter. Following a tour as a mathematics instructor at West Point for three years, he returned to the Ninth Cavalry in October 1903 to take command of A Troop, which had been commanded by Lieutenant Pearson in his absence.[5]

Hamilton rode to Sequoia with a modest contingent of officers comparable to Young's the previous year. One of his officers, First Lieutenant Pearson, was moved to command B Troop since its captain was on detached service and its first lieutenant reassigned to serve as Bigelow's adjutant at Yosemite. A Troop's 2nd Lt. Thomas B. Etsy was saddled with the additional duties of quartermaster and commissary while 2nd Lt. Robert R. Love assisted Pearson in B Troop. Finally, 1st. Lt. Ernest G. Bingham served as the medical officer for the Sequoia Detachment with the aid of two Hospital Corps soldiers.[6]

Though the Sequoia Detachment arrived in Three Rivers on May 26, Captain Hamilton seemed in no hurry to get on with his mission inside the park. He tarried more than a week in camp and did not arrive inside Sequoia National Park until the first week of June 1904. In June and every month thereafter, Hamilton recorded simply: "Detachments from the command have been sent out at different times for a period of about 15 days for the purpose of guard duty in the Park." Routine patrolling for half of the month was nothing like the aggressive patrolling Young had demanded of his detachment the previous year. And no soldiers were sent to Mount Whitney as in the previous year to guard the eastern approaches against illegal grazing.[7]

Captain Hamilton seemed more concerned with marksmanship than with park patrolling. B Troop spent the first two weeks of August with pistol practice at Three Rivers; then A Troop also spent two weeks firing at targets. In addition to the soldiers taken away from park patrolling during these pistol practice sessions, officers and noncommissioned officers had to supervise and serve as safety officials for the firing ranges.[8]

Officers were also away from the park most of the summer on other tasks, treating their assignment as if it were garrison duty. Second Lieutenant Love spent all of June and July either on leave or in Yosemite serving as a court-martial witness. First Lieutenant Pearson was on hunting leave and on detached service in Visalia in July. Newly assigned 1st Lt. George H. Winterbottom supervised pistol practice in camp near Three Rivers for the majority of July and August. The officers spent more time outside the park boundaries than inside.[9]

Finally, Captain Hamilton and most of the officers were in the camp near Three Rivers in early September preparing for the arrival of Major General MacArthur. In late September, MacArthur visited Sequoia and General Grant National Parks on an inspection tour for three days. The officers and noncommissioned officers of the Sequoia detachment focused on spit and polish during this time, not park patrolling.[10]

What remained of the detachment left Sequoia National Park on September 24 for camp in Three Rivers. Captain Hamilton withdrew the last soldiers from the park between September 20 and 29. The detachment then spent two weeks packing up, writing reports, and preparing for the road march home. Finally, the entire command left Three Rivers on October 14, arriving in Monterey ten days later.[11]

Visalia's local newspapers in the summer of 1904 covered the work of Captain Hamilton and the Sequoia detachment in just nine short newspaper articles, a fraction of the thirty mentioning Young in 1903. The *Tulare County Times* liked Hamilton's "pleasant manner" but despaired that so little money had been appropriated for repairing the roads, which were in bad shape after the winter. The local press observed Hamilton's accomplishments, which were limited to some repair work on the main road, a few turnouts on the wagon road in the Giant Forest, and a new trail near Alta Peak. The *Tulare County Times* reported that in Captain Hamilton's final report, he repeated Young's recommendation: the government should buy up the private lands within the park's boundaries.[12]

Captain Hamilton, like so many U.S. Army superintendents previously, treated park duty as a distraction from normal military training and routine. Though the Sequoia detachment carried out its assigned mission, it certainly did not match the achievements of Captain Young's troops in the summer of 1903. And Hamilton did not accomplish the allocated tasks with the same imagination and determination as Major Bigelow at Yosemite.

*Bigelow at Yosemite*

Major Bigelow traveled south and assumed command of the First Squadron at Monterey, California, in late April 1904, a month before he was scheduled to assume his duties in Yosemite. Bigelow led the 146 members of the First Squadron out of Ord Barracks on May 9, the same day as Hamilton's detachment, and arrived at Camp A. E. Wood, Wawona, California, fifteen days later, having marched 222 miles.[13]

Bigelow was the ideal choice to serve as the superintendent of Yosemite National Park that summer of 1904. Major General MacArthur, who made the selection, was reacting to the criticism Howard Shinn leveled against the administration of Lieutenant Colonel Garrard the previous summer. Shinn, the civilian director of California's Sierra Forest Reserve adjacent to Yosemite, had criticized the ineffectiveness of Garrard's policy of using small outposts scattered throughout the park with little or no supervision. According to historian Harvey Meyerson, Bigelow "was more than Shinn's match intellectually as well as managerially."[14]

Meyerson, who wrote about the U.S. Army's stewardship of the park, noted that Bigelow "plotted Yosemite's terrain as if it were Gettysburg or Shiloh, preparing special maps that identified principal redoubts of his adversaries (sheepherders, cattlemen), and he consulted extensively with Shinn on coordinating strategies." After spending a summer working in cooperation with Bigelow, Shinn changed his opinion about the effectiveness of the Ninth Cavalry under good leadership at Yosemite.[15]

Though Bigelow provided the overall planning and management, much of the aggressive patrolling and enforcement of park regulations was accomplished by the Buffalo Soldiers of C and D Troops. As was commonplace at the time, these troops operated with just one or two officers. Most of the actual work was done by the 102 noncommissioned officers and enlisted members of the troops.[16]

Commanding C Troop was Capt. Willard H. McCornack, who had transferred from the Eleventh Cavalry in December 1903 and assumed command of C Troop the following April. McCornack had served with the Ninth Cavalry after graduating from West Point in 1892, just three years after Young. Though he spent a four-month stint with the First Cavalry during the Spanish-American War and a two-year tour with the Eleventh Cavalry in the Philippines, the bulk of his twelve years in the army was with the Ninth Cavalry. He was assisted by 2nd Lt. Stephen W. Winfree, who also served as the squadron engineer officer.[17]

First Lt. Frederick J. Herman, a former volunteer officer, commanded D Troop. Lieutenant Herman was a captain in the First Ohio Volunteer Cavalry during the Spanish-American War and a captain in the Forty-Second U.S. Volunteer Infantry in the Philippine-American War. He served briefly as a second lieutenant in the Tenth Cavalry before transferring to the Ninth Cavalry to facilitate his promotion to first lieutenant in 1901. Suited by experience to command, Herman rode to Yosemite as the only officer in the troop until he was joined by 2nd Lt. C. Emery Hathaway in June.[18]

Major Bigelow rode to Yosemite with a full staff of officers to administer duties in the park. He was assisted by his squadron adjutant, 1st Lt. Frederick M. Jones; an assistant surgeon, 1st Lt. Henry F. Pipes; a squadron quartermaster and commissary, 2nd Lt. Edmund A. Buchanan; and a civilian veterinarian, Samuel Glasson, Jr. The surgeon was assisted by two enlisted men from the Hospital Corps, and the quartermaster supervised eight civilian teamsters and muleteers.[19]

The Yosemite detachment took station with seven cavalry officers (one major, one captain, two first lieutenants, and three second lieutenants), compared to Sequoia's four (one captain, one first lieutenant, and two second lieutenants). This level of effort did not match the size of the parks, since the area of Sequoia was 1,351 square miles compared to Yosemite's 1,165. Yosemite received a larger contingent because it was more accessible to tourists and under greater scrutiny after the criticism of Garrard's management the previous year. Sequoia was more remote, less developed, and under no inquiry after Young's successful administration in 1903.[20]

Bigelow's June record of events reflects how seriously he took his mission: "Detachments of troops were on patrol duty at stations designated in Post Orders, to prevent and extinguish forest fires, and to prevent the unauthorized herding of sheep and cattle on park lands, to protect game, to prevent the destruction of timber and unauthorized carrying of firearms." His report then went on to list ten different scouting missions undertaken by C Troop totaling 423 miles and thirteen by D Troop totaling 773 miles. Multiple patrols were out every day of the month led by officers or noncommissioned officers. The following months saw a similar pattern of aggressive patrolling under effective leadership.[21]

In an act of farsightedness, Bigelow created an arboretum at Yosemite, the first of its kind in any national park. According to park historian Meyerson:

> He conceived and constructed this remarkable seventy-five-acre facility in his spare time during the brief summer allotted to him, drawing on his frontier experience and hurried correspondence with horticulturists on the East Coast. His arboretum had "the first marked nature trail in the national park system," with log seats and neatly painted signposts identifying plants by their Latin species names. Bigelow told the interior secretary that he hoped his pioneering facility would serve as a foundation for a full-scale Yosemite "nature museum" and education program such as would in fact eventually be undertaken by the National Park Service nationwide.[22]

Major Bigelow continued his stewardship of Yosemite until the day he retired from active duty in mid-September 1904 after thirty years of service. Captain McCornack assumed duties as the acting superintendent of Yosemite National Park until he received orders to return to Monterey. With the closing of a successful summer of patrolling, McCornack led his two troops of the Ninth Cavalry out of Camp A. E. Wood on October 15 and arrived in Monterey nine days later.[23]

After the troops' departure from Yosemite, San Francisco newspapers praised the work Bigelow had done in the park that season. The newspaper noted that General McArthur was pleased with the park's management after his tour of inspection the previous month. The article commented that a "great many innovations have been made, the most prominent among which are the arboretum, suggested by Major Bigelow, a new bridge spanning the Merced, and the renewal of the Chilnualna Falls trail." The quartermaster, Lieutenant Buchanan, received special credit for the design of the arboretum, as he ensured "every shady nook has a rustic bench, many of fantastic designs artistically arranged."[24]

Also, the article noted that all the park boundaries had been carefully surveyed. The reporter observed:

> A good trail has been built from Sunrise Meadows to Merced Lake and from Rogers Lake through Return Canyon, and Virginia Canyon to Smokey Jack Meadows. More than 75,000 head of sheep have been driven out of the park this year, and Captain McCornack has ably extinguished the numerous forest fires that have occurred during the summer months before more damage could be done to the forests. The method he employed was to make a counter fire.[25]

The acclaim won by the First Squadron under Bigelow and McCornack at Yosemite compared favorably with that of Captain Young at Sequoia the previous summer. The two troops opened new trails for tourists, prevented illegal grazing on parklands, and extinguished forest fires. These accomplishments pleased General MacArthur and silenced the criticism of Howard Shinn. And finally, Major Bigelow's vision and Lieutenant Buchanan's creativity led to the establishment of an arboretum that became a model for the national parks.

### *Murder in Monterey*

Four days before Major Bigelow and the rest of the First Squadron rode into Ord Barracks from park duty, a violent altercation took place involving Black and white soldiers in Monterey. The incident occurred on October 19, 1904, when members of the Ninth Cavalry who had returned from the parks early clashed with white soldiers of the Fourth Cavalry who had arrived to replace them.

As the press reported in Monterey County and in San Francisco the following day, the trouble began soon after the soldiers of the Fourth Cavalry arrived by train in Monterey. According to witnesses at the depot, the soldiers of the Fourth had already been drinking when they disembarked, and the newcomers continued to celebrate in Monterey. Late that night, Black troopers fought with white soldiers at a local brothel, resulting in the death of a sergeant from the Fourth Cavalry. Most of the initial local reporting was factually incorrect, biased, and inflammatory.[26]

Much of the early coverage in the local California newspapers, picked up and used word for word by newspapers throughout the country, led the reader to believe Black soldiers initiated the fight and gunned down the white sergeant in cold blood. The storyline had the Black troopers forcing their way into the "house of ill fame," confronting the white soldiers, and quickly opening fire, killing the sergeant and wounding two others. The Black soldiers reportedly fled, and the enraged white soldiers burned the brothel down.[27]

In the following days, the *San Francisco Examiner* and other nearby newspapers fanned the flames. Under the headline "Race Rioting Terrorizes Monterey," the *Examiner*'s reporter warned that the incident might end in a lynching. He noted, "There has been murder here, then arson, and now there is the thrill of an expected mob and the sudden rule of lynch law." It parroted the previous inaccurate account of the clash and recounted the actions of the angry mob of white soldiers who burned the empty house and prevented local firemen from extinguishing the blaze. The sheriff, who arrested two Black suspects identified as Allen and Butler, had them jailed and placed under guard, worried about the "danger of an attempt to take them out for lynching." Only the intervention of officers and military police from Ord Barracks prevented further violence.[28]

A more accurate account of the shooting was finally reported several days later after charges were filed. The white soldiers started the trouble when they entered the brothel in a drunken state and confronted the Black troopers. Sgt. Arthur E. Tooley asked one of the Black women who worked at the establishment to dance, and she refused. This infuriated the intoxicated Tooley, and when one of the Black troopers came to her defense, a fight ensued. Pvt. Daniel S. Allen drew his gun, and during his struggle with Sergeant Tooley, his gun discharged and caused the fatal wound. Two other white soldiers received minor wounds in the fight.[29]

Why was Private Allen armed with his pistol? The army did not normally allow soldiers to carry weapons when off duty. A report in the *Tacoma (WA)*

*Daily Ledger* provided the answer: while "all weapons are usually kept locked in gun racks, the cavalry gun racks were packed for shipment east Wednesday, and the men being old and presumably reliable members of the regiment, were given their pistols to take care of."[30]

Private Allen was the only soldier arrested and charged in the incident. The newspapers identified the three other troopers of the Ninth involved in the brawl as Sergeant Johnson, Corporal Smith, and Private Brooks. Sergeant Tooley died at the scene, but the other two white soldiers recovered. Three women who worked at the Pear Tree, where the incident took place, were also arrested.[31]

The deceased, a member of K Troop, Fourth Cavalry, was a thirty-four-year-old veteran with a good record. His death was reported in his hometown Columbus, Indiana, newspaper. Tooley was buried at the San Francisco National Cemetery with military honors. The only other white soldier named was Private Moore of K Troop, Fourth Cavalry, who recovered and identified Allen as the man who shot Tooley.[32]

The three "women inmates" of the "notorious house called the Pear Tree" were sentenced to three months in jail for vagrancy, which was a common charge for women who worked in the sex industry at the time. They later served as witnesses in the preliminary examination and trial of Private Allen.[33]

Sgt. Albert Johnson, the senior of the Black enlisted men involved, was a thirty-year-old former tailor from Tennessee on his third enlistment. The other Black noncommissioned officer involved was Cpl. David Smith. Both deployed on park duty during the summer and came back to Ord Barracks early to prepare for the unit's move. They both avoided punishment and continued to serve with the Ninth Cavalry.[34]

The third soldier, Pvt. William H. Brooks, a twenty-two-year-old former laborer from Galveston, Texas, had only been in the army six months at the time of the incident. A member of D Troop, he had been on park duty but returned early also to prepare for the unit's move. Brooks was found guilty at a general court-martial in late October 1904 and dishonorably discharged from the army for his role in the shooting incident.[35]

The accused, Private Allen, a twenty-one-year-old, first-term soldier from Kentucky, had been assigned to C Troop since 1902 and did not deploy to Yosemite with his unit. Why he remained behind is unknown.

His trial for murder began in mid-December 1904, and he was represented by attorneys F. W. Sergeant and J. A. Bardin of Salinas, California. He was found guilty of first-degree murder by a jury after a three-day trial and sentenced to life in prison. In January 1905, Allen was discharged from the army without honor, which was the normal disposition of soldiers who were convicted and sentenced to civilian confinement.[36]

The coverage of the Pear Tree affair in the local and San Francisco newspapers further illustrated the biased reporting and rush to judgment the Black troopers of the Ninth Cavalry had experienced the past two years. The shooting and the subsequent fallout put a damper on the mood of the First Squadron as the men rode into Monterey from a successful summer of park duty.

### *Presidio Garrison*

While the First Squadron patrolled the parks, the Third Squadron initially remained at the Presidio busying itself with garrison duty. The soldiers kept to their barracks routine, which revolved around drills, work details, stable duty, and guard mount. As often as possible, the officers engaged the soldiers in more appealing activities such as target practice, athletic competitions, field days, and military exercises.

With the departure of Major Bigelow in April 1904, Captain Cornish took command of the squadron as its senior officer. In May, however, the Ninth Cavalry moved Lt. Col. Edward A. Godwin, the second-highest ranking officer in the Ninth Cavalry, to command the Third Squadron at the Presidio. Godwin began his career as a private in the Civil War and later attended West Point. He had been assigned to the Ninth since his promotion in February 1903, yet he had not joined his new unit since he was on detached service as the commander of the military guard force for the past year at the Louisiana Purchase Exposition in Saint Louis, Missouri.[37]

Lieutenant Colonel Godwin's arrival at the Presidio caused a stir that was reported in the press. As Captain Young did two years earlier, Godwin exercised his prerogative to select a set of quarters appropriate to his rank. According to one report, his "eyes lighted on the beautiful grounds and commodious home of Major [William] Stephenson, so the major was politely requested to seek other quarters." This, of course, caused the major to bump a captain, resulting "in a grand change all down the line."

Unlike the biased report two years earlier referring to Young as "colored" and mentioning his "darker bride," there was no mention of Godwin's race or wife.[38]

One of Lieutenant Colonel Godwin's first ceremonial duties with the Third Squadron involved the Memorial Day celebration. On the last Monday of May 1904, the Third Squadron joined the other Regular Army units and the California National Guardsmen in a military parade down Van Ness Avenue and McAllister Street, providing an escort of honor for members of the Grand Army of the Republic. Godwin and the four troops of the Ninth Cavalry led the procession, which eventually ended at the San Francisco National Cemetery, where the soldiers of the Tenth Infantry fired volleys over their fallen comrades. Graves of the dead were decorated with American flags and wreaths, and more than five thousand San Franciscans attended the ceremony at the Presidio.[39]

The first week in June 1904, troops at the Presidio conducted their annual pass and review for Major General MacArthur, the department commander. The five coast artillery companies, four battalions of field artillery, two regiments of infantry, and the squadron of the Ninth lined up on the south side of the golf links for the event. After a thirteen-gun salute, customarily given to a general with two stars, the footbound units of coast artillery and infantry marched before the reviewing stand, followed by the mounted troops of the artillery and cavalry at a trot. Troopers of the Ninth then turned about-face and made a final pass before the reviewing stand at a full gallop with sabers drawn. The civilian crowd delighted at the spectacle and cheered wildly.[40]

The Third Squadron also helped San Francisco celebrate the Fourth of July in 1904. According to the *San Francisco Call*:

> Veterans of three wars were in the line of march, some of them too feeble even to totter to the music of the drum to which they once stepped so lightly, rode in carriages. These were the grizzled men of the Mexican and Civil Wars. Before them on well-groomed steeds rode the colored troopers of the Ninth Cavalry, seasoned fighters who saw service in Cuba and the Philippines; and after the veterans of the older wars marched later day heroes, the First Regiment of the [California] National Guard.[41]

*Crimes and Punishment*

As with their first year of garrison duty at the Presidio, some Black troopers of the Ninth found off-duty trouble in San Francisco. The squadron's soldiers continued to frequent the dance halls and saloons of the city's notorious Barbary Coast, and this sometimes resulted in violence and altercations. Such incidents resulted in injuries, arrests, and punishment.

The newspapers reported in April 1904 on a shooting episode involving three Black soldiers. According to the article, "Edward Thomas, a colored soldier, reported to the police last night that two other negro soldiers had taken two shots at him in Pinckney alley, one of the bullets taking effect in his right hand." Thomas had been visiting a woman named Mamie Leyda and was attacked as he left her place. Two police officers heard the shots and responded, but the culprits escaped. Thomas lost his second finger, and the reporter blamed jealousy for the shooting.[42]

In another incident, the newspapers reported in June 1904 that a Black trooper named Robert Powell attacked William Turner, a Black civilian. Powell struck Turner in the head with a Bolo knife, resulting in "a wound several inches in length and cut him to the skull." The soldier probably carried the knife home as a souvenir from the Philippines, where it was used as a cutting tool like a machete. Turner was transported to the hospital for treatment of his serious wound, and Powell was arrested and booked on a charge of assault with a deadly weapon. Private Powell, a member of K Troop, was later hospitalized and discharged in July 1904 from the army on disability.[43]

Also in June, the *Call* reported that "Private James Norman, I Troop, Ninth Cavalry, now in confinement at the Presidio, will be discharged without honor from the army by reason of desertion." Norman had deserted in October 1903 before the return trip from Sequoia to the Presidio. He surrendered from desertion at the Presidio in late April 1904, having been on French leave for six months. Private Norman was discharged from the army and stayed in San Francisco to eke out a living as a civilian.[44]

Since all these events dealt with Black troopers and Black civilians, they received little attention in the newspapers. Reporters wrote brief accounts that were buried in the back folds. This contrasted significantly with the headline news and gaudy illustrations accorded to those stories involving Black soldiers' attacks on white officers, soldiers, or citizens of San Francisco in previous years.

### *Joint Maneuvers*

What did make the headlines in the San Francisco newspapers in June 1904 were reports on the deployment of the Ninth Cavalry to San Luis Obispo County in central California. Details indicated the Buffalo Soldiers would leave the Presidio the first week of July, spend twelve days on the march, and conduct big maneuvers during the month of August with elements of the California National Guard.[45]

This deployment resulted from congressional action the previous year. In 1903 Congress had passed the Dick Act (Militia Act of 1903), which reorganized the various state militias into the universal National Guard and mandated they be trained to U.S. Army standards. The legislation was a reaction to the poor performance in the Spanish-American and Philippine-American Wars of the state militia units, which had degenerated into social clubs after the Civil War. The War Department decided to hold major joint training exercises biennially involving Regular Army and National Guard units, and the governor of California agreed to host one of the first.[46]

Major General MacArthur designated the Third Squadron to proceed to Camp Atascadero for what was to be a two-month temporary deployment. The squadron of the Ninth, along with three of the field artillery batteries from the Presidio, were to arrive early to help set up the camp in preparation for the bulk of the troops slated to arrive in August 1904. This joint maneuver was one of the first of many bringing together units of the Regular Army and the National Guard.[47]

MacArthur personally selected Camp Atascadero for the joint training exercises to take place in August. The Regular Army and the National Guard planned to combine units to form a two-brigade infantry division with supporting cavalry and artillery commanded by MacArthur. This first in a series of exercises on the large Henry Ranch in San Luis Obispo County involved more than five thousand soldiers and a thousand horses.[48]

The 230-mile road march from the Presidio to Camp Atascadero did not go without incident. The San Luis Obispo *Morning Tribune* reported the roads were rough, and the Ninth Cavalry troopers "were so covered with dust that their color was hardly distinguishable." In the cities of Soledad and Gonzales, the Black soldiers wrecked saloons because the proprietors wouldn't sell them "five cent beer." And in Bradley, "the colored cavalrymen got hungry for chickens, and it is reported that there was no crowing in the place the morning after the troops arrived." In San Miguel, per the report, "their behavior was most excellent."[49]

According to the newspaper, "A number of soldiers were placed under arrest for their misdeeds." However, the regimental return reflects that only one soldier, Pvt. Lewis Young of M Troop, was sentenced by general court-martial after the group's arrival at Camp Atascadero for his transgressions during the road march. Young, a former laborer from Louisville, Kentucky, who had been in the army one year, was dishonorably discharged in July 1904.[50]

After the Third Squadron arrived at Camp Atascadero, the men commenced building accommodations and infrastructure to house the roughly five thousand soldiers set to arrive the following month. There was some resentment among the Buffalo Soldiers that they were assigned the thankless task of setting up tents, digging latrines, and building other facilities to house both the Regular Army and California National Guard troops participating in the maneuvers. But as professionals, they completed their task and had the camp set up when the balance of the troops began arriving by train beginning in early August.[51]

The two weeks of field exercises pitted a blue force against a brown force in carefully scripted scenarios controlled by Regular Army officer umpires, who determined winners, losers, and lessons learned. The two opposing forces comprised of a mix of National Guard and Regular Army units to form infantry, cavalry, and artillery components of brigades and detachments. Different exercises allowed the units involved to practice movement, advance guard, rear guard, attack, and defense in all types of terrain, day and night.[52]

Initially organizers encountered a color problem, though it did not involve race. They planned to use blue and khaki uniforms to differentiate the opposing forces and ease the issue of enemy identification, but the California National Guard units, which still operated mostly with the old blue uniforms, did not arrive with a sufficient supply of both uniforms. The army quartermaster saved the day by ordering five hundred khaki jackets to outfit the National Guard troops before the maneuvers commenced.[53]

Lieutenant Colonel Godwin, the commander of the Third Squadron, Ninth Cavalry, praised the cavalry units of the California National Guard. He noted their performance was "very creditable" and that they made "great improvement" during the maneuvers. Further, he observed that the "men have all come from different sections of the State and have never before had an opportunity for squadron training or been assembled as a squadron."[54]

Three troops of the Ninth Cavalry with captains in the field—K Troop with Captain Nance, L Troop with Captain Christian, and M Troop with Captain Cornish—received the most rewarding assignments during the maneuvers. First Lieutenant Rubottom commanded I Troop in the absence of Captain Young, and the troop was given the thankless task of serving as the headquarters guard at Camp Atascadero with a company of the white Thirteenth Infantry. When Rubottom was temporarily assigned to K Troop for the duration of the exercise, I Troop was commanded by a white infantry lieutenant from the Thirteenth Infantry.[55]

The wearisome task of guarding the headquarters led to some misbehavior by members of I Troop at Camp Atascadero. Privates Henry M. Merryweather and Arthur Worthy of I Troop deserted the first three days of August 1904. And Pvt. Albert Smith of M Troop deserted a week later. Both Merryweather and Smith were newly enlisted and apparently decided the army did not suit them. Worthy, on the other hand, was an old I Troop hand who had served under Captain Young at Fort Duchesne and in the Philippines. The first two were never apprehended; Worthy later surrendered to the authorities in his home state of Georgia.[56]

The end of the encampment was marked by a show of military pomp when the troops paraded in review for California governor Pardee on August 25, 1904. The National Guard units departed by train the next day after receiving their pay. Participating Regular Army soldiers were paid off on August 29 and boarded trains for their home stations in the following days. Presidio-based artillery and cavalry units that were the first to arrive were also the last to depart, though a residual quartermaster detachment assisted by a company of infantry remained to close the camp. The four troops of the Third Squadron left Camp Atascadero September 1 and traveled 122 miles to Monterey, arriving a week later. The squadron established a temporary tent camp and conducted annual target practice for the remainder of the month. The squadron left Monterey the second day of October and road-marched 106 miles to the Presidio, arriving six days later.[57]

Major General MacArthur concluded that the encampment was of "incalculable benefit" with valuable lessons learned. The chief umpire, Maj. William P. Duvall, noted important experience was gained in entraining and detraining, camping, messing, marching, outpost duty, advanced guard and rearguard efforts, map reading, and other skills. Due to the positive results, these joint maneuvers continued at Camp Atascadero every two years until the onset of World War I in 1914.[58]

By October, the two squadrons of the Ninth Cavalry had returned to their stations in San Francisco and Monterey from their respective tasks of patrolling the national parks and training the California National Guard. Their return to garrison closed out the missions of the Ninth Cavalry in California for the year 1904.

While training conducted by the Third Squadron with the National Guard under Major General MacArthur won accolades, the accomplishments of the First Squadron in the parks were mixed. Major Bigelow went beyond the pale with his mission's success at Yosemite and won praise from former California critic Howard Shinn. Captain Hamilton, on the other hand, treated the mission at Sequoia with indifference as had so many army officers before him.

# 10

## Rotation Issue

> The Third Squadron, Ninth Cavalry, [Lt.] Colonel E. A. Godwin in command, will depart this morning at 9 o'clock for Jefferson Barracks.
> —*San Francisco Call*, October 22, 1904

When the First Squadron returned from the parks and the Third Squadron from Camp Atascadero, it was time for the Ninth Cavalry to pack up and move to new duty stations. The Buffalo Soldiers served in California for only two years, which was not unusual at a time when the War Department was rotating Regular Army units between stateside bases as well as occupation duty in the Philippines. Periodic movements were routine for the regiments, and the Black troopers of the Ninth had grown accustomed to moving to different posts. Yet the Buffalo Soldier regiments faced resistance in certain areas of the country where these rotations were anything but routine.

### *Regimental Rotation*

Every two to three years, the infantry and cavalry regiments of the U.S. Army rotated to new duty stations. This normal, recurring movement of the U.S. Army's thirty infantry and fifteen cavalry regiments distributed the burden of garrisoning hardship posts and prevented regiments from homesteading. For instance, regiments that saw combat in the Philippines, as the Ninth Cavalry did from 1901 to 1902, shipped back to stations on the West Coast to rest, refit, and retrain. So by late 1904, it was time for a new round of regimental rotations.

When the Third Squadron, Ninth Cavalry returned to the Presidio of San Francisco in early October, it moved into the Infantry Cantonment formerly occupied by the Tenth Infantry. A squadron of the Fourth Cavalry transferred from Fort Leavenworth, Kansas, to replace the Third Squadron, Ninth Cavalry, but the white troopers of the Fourth moved into the Infantry Cantonment on the east portion of the Presidio rather than into the brick barracks on the main post previously occupied by the Ninth.[1]

The Third Squadron then spent the next three weeks turning in equipment to the post quartermaster, transferring its horses to the Fourth Cavalry, packing up gear, and preparing for departure. The squadron pulled up stakes on October 22, 1904, and traveled by train to its new permanent station at Jefferson Barracks, Missouri, arriving five days later. Thus ended the Buffalo Soldiers' two-year stay at the Presidio of San Francisco.[2]

Other components of the Ninth likewise moved to new duty stations. The Second Squadron at Fort Walla Walla, Washington, departed on trains for Fort Leavenworth, Kansas, on October 19, 1904. Before its departure, the unit transferred its horses to the squadron of the Fourth Cavalry that was replacing it. The Second Squadron then traveled to its new post at Fort Leavenworth, arriving four days later. The regimental staff and band, previously stationed at Fort Walla Walla, entrained to Fort Riley, Kansas, the new home of the regimental headquarters.[3]

Finally, the First Squadron, Ninth Cavalry rode into the Presidio of Monterey (Ord Barracks was renamed Presidio of Monterey in August 1904) from Sequoia and Yosemite on October 24, 1904. In preparation for the unit's departure, the troopers transferred their horses to the squadron of the Fourth Cavalry replacing them. The squadron left by special train on the first day of November for the trip to its new home at Fort Riley, Kansas; the regimental staff and band were already there to provide a welcome. The First Squadron was the final element of the Ninth Cavalry to leave, ending the Buffalo Soldiers' remarkable stay in California.[4]

### *Guarded Acceptance*

Despite the competence with which they conducted their military responsibilities, the people of San Francisco treated the troopers of the Ninth with guarded acceptance and cautious tolerance for the two years they were stationed at the Presidio. Large crowds flocked to the post to cheer for the soldiers during mock battles and squadron drills, as well as field days and sporting events. The people lined the streets and admired the military pomp during holiday parades and other special events. Leading citizens also recognized the Black troopers for their service protecting California's national parks, especially when commanded by officers such as Captain Young and Major Bigelow. But this support had limits.

The newspaper coverage of the Third Squadron during its stay in San Francisco reflected the wary but tolerant attitude of the citizens. The press treated the Ninth Cavalry unevenly. On the one hand, the newspapers praised the Buffalo Soldiers' conduct when they escorted President Roosevelt, marched in national holiday parades, entertained them during ceremonies and exercises at the Presidio, and assisted in supporting charitable functions in San Francisco. The press also reported on the Black troopers' important role at Sequoia and Yosemite.

On the other hand, in their reporting on the Buffalo Soldiers, the *San Francisco Call* and other white-owned newspapers employed negative Black stereotypes common in the American press during this era. When African American soldiers got into trouble, especially when violence was directed against white citizens, the newspaper reporting was often blatantly biased and patently prejudicial. White reporters, and citizens, assumed the Black troopers were guilty and judged them harshly. By contrast, the white soldiers of the infantry and field artillery at the Presidio were treated fairly.

To develop an objective comparison of the Ninth Cavalry's treatment in San Francisco, examining the experience of the squadron of the Fourth Cavalry that followed is helpful. The Second Squadron, Fourth Cavalry replaced the Third Squadron, Ninth Cavalry at the Presidio, arriving in mid-October 1904. The Second Squadron's numbers and organization were roughly the same as those of the Third Squadron, Ninth Cavalry.[5]

A review of newspaper articles about enlisted members of the Fourth Cavalry during the year they were stationed at the Presidio indicates the white soldiers were treated differently from the Black troopers of the Ninth. The reporters included greater detail and listed more individual names of white cavalry troopers involved in baseball games, field events, shooting matches, and riding competitions. Also, the newspapers failed to mention a single report of a white Cavalry trooper getting into trouble during the entire year, vastly differing from their coverage of the Ninth. During that time, the Fourth Cavalry Regimental Returns recorded that thirty soldiers deserted, four surrendered from desertion, and three others received general court-martials, all of which merited some mention when the Ninth Cavalry was at the Presidio of San Francisco.[6]

### *Equitable Rotation?*

As was reflected in the newspaper coverage of the Ninth in San Francisco, not every metropolis in the United States wanted Black soldiers stationed in or near its city limits. Salt Lake City had protested in vain the stationing of the Black Twenty-Fourth Infantry at nearby Fort Douglas in 1896. Sen. Frank J. Cannon (R-UT) presented his case to the War Department, noting the undesirability of having "colored" troops stationed next to the University of Utah. Yet the *Salt Lake City Tribune* reported that after the Twenty-Fourth was stationed there for a year, it had "proved to be one of the best regiments ever serving at Douglas." The city welcomed the Black soldiers as heroes on their return from Cuba in 1898 after the Spanish-American War and gave them a heartfelt farewell when they departed for the Philippine Islands a year later.[7]

In contrast, when word reached Minnesota in 1902 that a battalion of the Black Twenty-Fourth Infantry returning from the Philippines would be stationed at Fort Snelling, the people of Minneapolis and Saint Paul complained vociferously. An editorial that ran in the *Saint Paul Globe* in mid-May complained: "Fort Snelling is in great measure a popular resort. It is unfortunately true that its desirability in this regard will be materially lessened by the presence there of a colored regiment."[8]

According to the *Globe*, the Twin Cities were "the object of remarkable discrimination on the part of the War Department in the distribution of its official favors." The editorial criticized Minnesota's Republican congressional representatives, who refused to oppose the posting of the Buffalo Soldiers to Fort Snelling. The protests of white community leaders won out, and the War Department appended its orders in early June, reassigning the Twenty-Fourth to sparsely populated Montana and sending the white Twenty-First U.S. Infantry to Fort Snelling in its place.[9]

The Buffalo Soldiers encountered the same predicament throughout their thirty-five years of faithful service in the Regular Army. When an enemy threatened America, whether they be Native American warriors, Spanish soldiers, or Filipino irregulars, the Black Regular regiments were among the first to be sent to fight. Yet when it came to peacetime service, whites in cities such as Minneapolis, Salt Lake City, and San Francisco were reluctant to have Black soldiers living, working, and socializing among them.

During the frontier period, geographically isolating Black regiments was not difficult. The troopers of the Ninth Cavalry could be stationed at lonely western outposts such as Fort Niobrara in Nebraska and Utah's Fort Duchesne, which the soldiers derided as "Fort DuShame." With the settling of the frontier, the concentration of regiments at bigger posts, and the rise of large metropolitan areas west of the Mississippi River, sequestering Black units was no longer possible, and it led to the posting of the Ninth to San Francisco in 1902.

The white citizens' bias against the Black troops presented an increasingly difficult dilemma for the War Department after the turn of the century. The army partially solved its problem by rotating the Buffalo Soldier regiments through the Philippines on occupation duty as often as possible. But these regiments had to come home at some point, and the rotations to other posts in the United States did not always go as smoothly as it had at the Presidio of San Francisco.

The Brownsville affair in 1906, merely two years after the Ninth departed San Francisco, is an example of how resentment by white residents could lead to tragedy. A battalion of three companies of the Twenty-Fifth U.S. Infantry, another Buffalo Soldier regiment, rotated to Fort Brown, Texas, in July 1906 after the army closed isolated Fort Niobrara, Nebraska. The Black battalion, replacing a white battalion of the Twenty-Sixth U.S. Infantry, was forced to abide by the color line laws mandating separate accommodations in neighboring Brownsville, located on the border with Mexico. The Black infantrymen, who had been treated with respect in Nebraska, resented the blatant segregation as well as other Jim Crow indignities they suffered in Texas.[10]

As in Minnesota, Texas citizens resented the stationing of Black soldiers in their state. Sen. Charles A. Culbertson (D-TX) appealed the decision, but Secretary of War William H. Taft refused to reconsider, insisting Black troops were better behaved and less prone to drunkenness than white soldiers. Taft noted: "It has sometimes happened that communities which objected to the coming of colored soldiers have, on account of their good conduct, entirely changed their view." Taft might have seen attitudes change to the positive in Salt Lake City, but the opposite occurred in Brownsville.[11]

Though the War Department proceeded with plans to station the battalion of the Twenty-Fifth in Brownsville, it canceled the use of Black troops in the Texas National Guard maneuver camp. The white commander of the Twenty-Fifth Infantry Regiment, Col. Ralph W. Hoyt, warned against using his men for the scheduled training. He cited the case of joint training at Fort Riley, Kansas, in 1903, when participating Texas guardsmen threatened and mistreated the Black soldiers of the Twenty-Fifth to the point that open warfare nearly broke out.[12]

In advance of the move to Fort Brown, the white officers of the Twenty-Fifth anticipated trouble in Texas. The only Black officer in the regiment, Chaplain Theophilus Steward, predicted: "Texas, I fear means a quasi-battleground for the Twenty-Fifth Infantry." Indeed, it was. From the moment the soldiers stepped from the train, Brownsville displayed open hostility. One customs inspector pistol-whipped a Black soldier because he allegedly jostled his wife. Another customs officer shoved a Black soldier into the Rio Grande because he did not move out of the way promptly. The final straw came when a Brownsville woman claimed a soldier attempted to attack her.[13]

After midnight on the day following this last incident, shots rang out. An armed mob roamed the streets of Brownsville, killing a white bartender and wounding a police lieutenant. The white citizens of Brownsville immediately cast blame on the Black soldiers at Fort Brown, even though the officers of the battalion confirmed all the Black soldiers were accounted for and the weapons locked in their racks. The army immediately moved the battalion of the Twenty-Fifth Infantry to isolated Fort Reno, Indian Territory, to prevent more trouble.[14]

A local grand jury failed to identify a single person involved in the shooting, so there were no indictments. The army's investigation of the Brownsville affair was badly botched from the beginning. The soldiers maintained their innocence, and the inspector general assigned to the case, pressured by President Theodore Roosevelt, threatened to discharge the soldiers if no one came forward and admitted guilt. In November 1906, the army carried out the threat and discharged "without honor" the 167 Black soldiers present for duty at Fort Brown the night of the event.[15]

The injustice of the army's ruling without a formal trial not only incensed the Black community but also outraged the white press. Even the *Army and Navy Journal*, normally a staunch supporter of the War Department, was offended by the unfairness of the ruling. A court of inquiry in 1910 confirmed the army's decision but allowed fourteen of these soldiers to reenlist; all but one reenlisted and were given back pay. In a final vindication for the Buffalo Soldiers, the army upgraded the discharges of the remaining 153 men to honorable in 1972. Only two of the former Buffalo Soldiers were still alive to appreciate that long-overdue justice.[16]

In view of the Brownsville affair, the Black troopers of the Ninth Cavalry in San Francisco and Monterey were certainly fortunate in their encounters with white citizens from 1902 to 1904. The only violent episode they experienced occurred with the white soldiers in Monterey. And the Black troopers conducted summer training with the California National Guard without incident. Some Buffalo Soldiers who completed their military service even stayed to find their futures in California (see chapter 12).

The departure of the two squadrons of the Ninth Cavalry from California in 1904 concluded the Buffalo Soldiers' memorable stay in San Francisco and Monterey. It was the first time the Ninth Cavalry had been stationed on the West Coast and in a major metropolitan area, and the men had earned that well-deserved rest after their hard fighting in the Philippine War. Major Bigelow, Captain Young, and the cavalry troopers of the Ninth showed that in addition to their past martial achievements in Cuba and the Philippines, they excelled at patrolling and guarding the Sequoia and Yosemite National Parks. Though white cavalry units replacing the Ninth Cavalry carried on the work it had begun in the national parks, the Buffalo Soldiers left an enduring legacy at Sequoia and Yosemite.

During the soldiers' two-year stay in the city by the bay, San Franciscans displayed a guarded acceptance of the Buffalo soldiers. This was reflected in the attitudes of the citizens and took voice in biased coverage by white newspapers. The Black Soldiers won praise for the professional conduct of their official duties but received racially biased and prejudicial treatment when they got into trouble, especially when violence was directed against white citizens. And though this treatment was unjust, it paled in comparison to the attitudes Black soldiers faced in other parts of the country.

# 11

## Postscript

### *Army and the Parks*

> Blessings on Uncle Sam's blue-coats! The quiet, orderly soldiers have done this fine job, without any apparent friction or weak noise, in the still, calm way that the United States troops do their duty.
> —John Muir, 1895

After the departure of the Ninth Cavalry in 1904, the army continued to assign white cavalry squadrons to San Francisco and Monterey to patrol the Sequoia and Yosemite National Parks for another decade. The War Department rotated cavalry regiments between these two California posts and the High Sierra until 1913, when the twin requirements of patrolling the border with Mexico and preparing for war in Europe put a strain on the U.S. Army's ability to carry out this mission. Though the cavalry departed, they left an indelible and lasting mark on the parks.

#### *Fourth Cavalry*

The Fourth Cavalry's stay in California was brief after it replaced the Ninth; the regiment served a single season in the parks. Like the Ninth Cavalry, the Fourth stationed its three squadrons at the Presidio of San Francisco, the Presidio of Monterey, and Fort Walla Walla, Washington. Following the pattern of the Ninth in 1903, the Third Squadron, Fourth

Cavalry sent troops from the Presidio of San Francisco to Sequoia and Yosemite in the summer of 1905.[1]

Capt. Harry C. Benson, the commander of K Troop, served as the acting superintendent of Yosemite National Park in 1905. Benson was well qualified to act as superintendent, having ridden to Sequoia and Yosemite five times previously. He was appointed superintendent in March and reached Camp A. E. Wood at Wawona on the last day of April 1905. His detachment consisted of K Troop; M Troop, commanded by Capt. James B. Hughes; three lieutenants; a medical officer; and eighty enlisted troopers. Captain Benson conducted aggressive park patrolling from May to October 1905.[2]

Capt. John O'Shea, commanding L Troop, served as the acting superintendent of Sequoia National Park in 1905. O'Shea deployed from the Presidio of San Francisco early, arriving at Kaweah in the first week in May and the Giant Forest on June 19, 1905. He, like Benson, conducted active patrolling throughout the summer. O'Shea departed Sequoia in mid-September, anticipating the regiment's upcoming rotation overseas.[3]

By the time Captains Benson and O'Shea returned to the Presidio from the parks, half of the Fourth was already aboard ships bound for the Philippine Islands. The Third Squadron, Fourth Cavalry loaded onto ships in San Francisco and departed for occupation duty in the Philippine Islands with the rest of the regiment in late 1905. Benson, however, newly promoted to major, remained behind for a new assignment with a different regiment involving the national parks.[4]

### *Fourteenth Cavalry*

The army replaced the Fourth Cavalry on the West Coast with the Fourteenth U.S. Cavalry Regiment, which was returning from duty in the Philippine Islands in 1905. The headquarters of the Third Squadron, Fourteenth Cavalry and Troops I, K, and M were stationed at the Presidio of San Francisco for four years, while the Second Squadron took the place of the Fourth at the Presidio of Monterey (formerly Ord Barracks).[5]

Given the rotations, a surprising number of officers who previously had served with the Ninth were on the staff of the Fourteenth Cavalry when it arrived on the West Coast. Col. Edward A. Godwin, commanding the regiment at Fort Walla Walla, formerly led the Third Squadron, Ninth Cavalry at the Presidio of San Francisco. Lt. Col. Joseph Garrard, commanding the Second Squadron at the Presidio of Monterey, had served as the acting superintendent of Yosemite in 1903. Finally, Maj. Harry C. Benson, the new commander of the Third Squadron at the Presidio of San Francisco, had been the acting superintendent of Yosemite in 1905.[6]

The squadron of the Fourteenth Cavalry was at the Presidio of San Francisco when a devastating earthquake struck the coast of Northern California on Wednesday, April 18, 1906. The earthquake was followed by a great fire in San Francisco, and army units at the Presidio turned out to help civil authorities maintain order and extinguish the conflagration. Under the command of Major Benson, the Third Squadron, Fourteenth Cavalry served as the "Provost Guard of the City of San Francisco" to assist city law enforcement until early May 1906.[7]

### *Yosemite*

Despite the devastation of the earthquake, the Third Squadron and Troops K and M rode out of the shattered city of San Francisco for park duty at Yosemite National Park in mid-May 1906. Major Benson, the squadron commander, led the detachment of seven officers and a hundred enlisted men, a very high officer-to-soldier mix. The detachment arrived at Camp A. E. Wood outside Yosemite National Park later in May to commence the summer season of park duty.[8]

As the acting superintendent of Yosemite, Benson was well qualified to lead the effort at the park. A member of the West Point class of 1882, he had served two previous summers seasons at Sequoia and four at Yosemite. Congress had also appointed Benson a member of a commission to report on the conditions at Yosemite in 1899. After his transfer to the Fourteenth Cavalry in 1906, he served as Yosemite National Park's acting superintendent for three summers in succession.[9]

According to historian Harvey Meyerson, Major Benson was the perfect man for the job by aptitude and training. He deftly supervised the incorporation of the state-run Yosemite Valley into Yosemite National Park, noting the place had "come to resemble Coney Island." Benson, who was "incorruptibly committed to Yosemite's protection," dismantled the existing governing state network and rebuilt the administration from scratch with his own brand of "tough love."[10]

Major Benson served as the acting superintendent of Yosemite National Park for four consecutive summers, providing a unique opportunity for continuity in leadership. Moreover, the Third Squadron, Fourteenth Cavalry at the Presidio of San Francisco continued to send the two troops that served in Yosemite, offering an extra measure of stability. Near the end of the 1908 season, the army ordered Major Benson to report to Washington DC for briefings in preparation for his new assignment as acting superintendent of Yellowstone National Park.[11]

A West Point classmate paid this tribute to Major Benson's services in the national parks:

> In the early days of the national parks, it took more than ordinary energy, enthusiasm, and ability to protect them from depredations and misuse. Moreover, it took courage to face the hostility of men, often powerful and influential, whose selfish interests were thwarted by the withdrawal of the park lands from exploitation. If it had not been for the timely protection afforded by the United States Army, our legacy would have come to us seriously impaired. Many officers and men contributed to this valuable service, but Colonel Benson stands pre-eminent among them, not alone because of the long period of his activity in the national parks, but because he also brought to the task his prophetic vision. For more than thirty years he maintained his interest in the parks, and in the later days he beheld the realization of many aspirations.[12]

Maj. William W. Forsyth, a West Point classmate of Benson's, replaced him at Yosemite. Forsyth also had a great deal of experience in the national parks, having served at Fort Yellowstone with the Sixth Cavalry commanding I Troop for seven summer seasons. Forsyth, who was promoted to lieutenant colonel in 1912, remained acting superintendent of Yosemite from 1909 to 1913, adding further stability to the leadership of the park that had begun under Benson.[13]

Two troops from the Third Squadron, Fourteenth Cavalry had continued to patrol the park under Forsyth during the 1909 season, providing a helpful transition. When the Fourteenth Cavalry rotated to a new duty station, two troops of the First Squadron, First Cavalry replaced them at the Presidio of San Francisco and for park duty. When the troops rotated out, it was up to Forsyth, alone, to provide the continuity of leadership for the new cavalry troopers at Yosemite.[14]

Lieutenant Colonel Forsyth and the First Cavalry supervised and patrolled Yosemite National Park until 1913. In early 1914, with cavalry units badly needed on the Mexican border, the War Department decided it would no longer send troops to Yosemite. A rushed and chaotic transition to a civilian administration followed, culminating with the creation of the National Park Service in 1916.[15]

The muddled handover to civilian control would have been worse at Yosemite if not for the steadying presence of a former cavalry trooper. Gabriel Sovulewski, a former sergeant who had served under Major Benson at Sequoia and Yosemite in the 1890s, left the army in 1898 and returned to work at Yosemite as a packer and guide. When Benson assumed the superintendency of Yosemite, he put Sovulewski in charge of the winter management of the park while the army was absent. He retained the title of park supervisor after the appointment of the first civilian superintendent, Washington B. "Dusty" Lewis, in 1916. Sovulewski continued to serve as a deputy to park superintendents until his retirement in 1936.[16]

### *Sequoia*

Sequoia National Park did not get the same dedicated leadership and sizable troop coverage Yosemite received. The Second Squadron, Fourteenth Cavalry dispatched a single troop in May 1906 from the Presidio of Monterey to Sequoia National Park. Capt. Kirby Walker, the F Troop commander, served as the acting superintendent and was assisted by two second lieutenants and a mere thirty-eight cavalry troopers.[17]

Providing a measure of continuity at least, Captain Walker served as the acting superintendent when his F Troop was assigned to Sequoia National Park again during the 1907 patrolling season. He was replaced by Capt. Cornelius C. Smith, who led G Troop into Sequoia for the 1908 and 1909 summer seasons. Both Walker and Smith, operating with one or two assigned officers, employed limited patrolling and posted small parties of enlisted troopers at a handful of locations within the park.[18]

The routine of sending one troop of cavalry to Sequoia continued when the First Cavalry replaced the Fourteenth in 1910 at Sequoia. Troop A,

First Cavalry, commanded by Capt. Edmund S. Wright, set out from the Presidio of San Francisco in May and spent the summer patrolling the park. Captain Wright reported an especially active season of fighting fires before departing Sequoia at the end of the summer.[19]

The First Squadron, First Cavalry assigned Maj. James B. Hughes as the acting superintendent in 1911, and he took his staff, along with A Troop, from the Presidio of San Francisco to Sequoia in May. Hughes continued the previous year's routine of establishing outposts at various points in the park. At the end of the season, Major Hughes departed early to attend a conference of national park superintendents held at Yellowstone in September 1911.[20]

The First Cavalry supplied detachments of troops to three national parks in 1911. Aside from one troop dispatched to Sequoia and two troops to Yosemite, the four troops of the Second Squadron were assigned to Fort Yellowstone, Wyoming. Unlike Sequoia and Yosemite, Yellowstone had a regular army post with facilities to house a squadron of cavalry. The permanent barracks and other facilities recommended by Captain Young and the commission of officers in 1903 were never built.[21]

Because Major Hughes was attending a staff course, the First Cavalry assigned the regimental quartermaster, Capt. Walter M. Whitman, as the acting superintendent in 1912. Whitman took B Troop with him to Sequoia and followed the usual routine of posting noncommissioned officers and small groups of soldiers at key points throughout the park.[22]

Finally, Capt. Douglas McCaskey led C Troop to Sequoia for the 1913 summer patrolling season. When McCaskey was reassigned, his second in command, 1st Lt. Hugh S. Johnson, assumed the duties as acting superintendent. By this time, very little danger was posed by poaching or illegal sheep or cattle grazing. The troopers' duties had devolved to supervising the construction of facilities, counting game, manning entry points, and advising tourists; they acted more like civilian rangers than soldiers.[23]

Lieutenant Johnson's 1913 final report lauded the annual deployment to Sequoia because it "furnishes a very pleasant and desirable detail to any troop of cavalry and one upon which all its members are eager to enter." For the officers, "it provides an independent command, a change from the routine army duties, a pleasant summer outing with fishing and the coolness and enjoyment of a mountain summer." For the enlisted soldier, "there is, in addition to most of these things, a surcease from army discipline, drill, and restraint."[24]

Lieutenant Johnson was the last cavalry officer to serve as the acting superintendent of Sequoia and General Grant National Parks. As with Yosemite, the army ceased sending detachments to Sequoia after 1913. When C Troop rode out of Sequoia National Park on the first day of September 1913, it was the last army unit to serve there. The following year, Sequoia began the somewhat disjointed transition to civilian administration and eventually came under the administration of the National Park Service in 1916.[25]

Walter Fry, who had worked on the road construction crew for Captain Young in the summer of 1903, was appointed the first civilian superintendent of Sequoia National Park in 1914. Fry, who had moved with his family to Tulare County in 1897 and to Three Rivers in 1899, began working on the Sequoia road crews in 1901 and is one of the individuals in the iconic 1903 photo taken in the Giant Forest (see figure 21). Fry became a park ranger in 1905 and was appointed Sequoia's chief ranger in 1910. As such, he assisted the military superintendents each summer and oversaw the parks in the winter when the army was away. Fry served as the superintendent until 1920.[26]

When the last cavalry troopers marched out of Sequoia and Yosemite in 1913, it marked the end of an era. As Muir noted, the officers and soldiers of the Regular Army did their duty in a still, calm manner. Muir knew this better than most, since he had spent four days camped with the Buffalo Soldiers of the Ninth Cavalry at Yosemite during President Roosevelt's visit. If not for the troops' military efficiency, martial discipline, and soldierly professionalism, the legacy of Sequoia and Yosemite Parks would have certainly been seriously diminished. Charles Young and I Troop left their lasting mark at Sequoia National Park, as did John Bigelow and Henry Benson at Yosemite National Park. They laid a foundation on which the National Park Service later built the finest system of national parks in the world.

# 12

## Aftermath

### *Men of the Ninth*

Let's see: there's "Swamp" Pierce, Nicholas, Dee Smith, Malone, Norman, Peggy and Wirt Langley, not to forget Leo Frye, all living and married in San Francisco alone, and getting along.
—Letter from Charles Young, October 15, 1916

Many of the officers and soldiers assigned to I Troop in San Francisco continued to serve with the Ninth Cavalry after it rotated to Jefferson Barracks, Missouri, in 1904 and to Fort Sheridan, Illinois, in 1906. Most enjoyed long and successful careers in the army. Though many of the serving Buffalo Soldiers departed, some old troopers of the Ninth remained in the city by the bay.

*I Troop*

First Sgt. William S. "Jasper" Jones continued as the first sergeant of I Troop for the rest of his military career. He served under Captain Young at Camp McGrath, Philippine Islands, and Fort D. A. Russell, Wyoming, and retired as the I Troop first sergeant in 1913 while the Ninth Cavalry was stationed at Nogales, Arizona, on the Mexican border. Jones spent his entire twenty-seven years in the army as a Buffalo Soldier with the Ninth Cavalry and the last fourteen as the first sergeant of I Troop.[1]

After retirement, Jasper Jones worked for the Union Pacific Railway in Cheyenne, Wyoming, for several years. By 1922 Samuel Pearson recounted that Jones was nearly blind, crippled with rheumatism, and could "barely navigate." His wife, Addie, who had been with him since he had been assigned to Fort Duchesne, Utah, worked two jobs to supplement Jasper's retirement pay. Jones died in 1923 and was buried with a veteran's marker at the Fort D. A. Russell National Cemetery in Wyoming. Addie Jones filed for a widow's pension in 1924, and it was granted in 1926.[2]

Quartermaster Sgt. George Brown, like First Sergeant Jones, served in the Ninth Cavalry for the rest of his long military career. When he retired from the army in 1908, he was a squadron sergeant major and served on the noncommissioned officers' staff of the Third Squadron, Ninth Cavalry. Brown had served eight continuous enlistments totaling nearly thirty years. He returned from the Philippines to retire in January at the Presidio of San Francisco, California.[3]

Trumpeter Frank McKenzie, like his father before him, enjoyed a lengthy career in the U.S. Army and spent most of it with the Ninth Cavalry. He later completed two enlistments with the Twenty-Fifth Infantry before returning to I Troop, Ninth Cavalry in 1913. He remained with the Ninth, serving as a color sergeant at Camp Stotsenburg, Philippine Islands, until he retired in 1920 after more than twenty-nine years in the army as a Buffalo Soldier.[4]

Frank McKenzie returned to the United States and initially settled in Utah. He was fifty-one years old when he married Ruby Estes, twenty-six years old, in 1926 at Salt Lake City, Utah. Five years later, Frank and Ruby McKenzie moved to Los Angeles, California, where Ruby's family resided. McKenzie passed away at the National Military Home, Los Angeles, in April 1936 and was buried beneath a veteran's marker at the Los Angeles National Cemetery. Ruby McKenzie died in 1977 in Los Angeles.[5]

George W. Fearington, the soldier so grievously wounded by his bunkmate at the Presidio of San Francisco in 1902, rejoined I Troop, Ninth Cavalry in 1907 after serving one enlistment in the Hospital Corps. He later served two tours with the Twenty-Fifth Infantry and, after twenty-five years in the army, retired in 1917. Fearington ended his last tour with the Twenty-Fifth in the Territory of Hawaii.[6]

Fearington, forty-four years old, married a seventeen-year-old Portuguese woman named Jessie Silva in 1918 in Honolulu, Hawaii. When they had their first child a year later, the boy was born in the military hospital, and Fearington was a civilian employee of the Quartermaster Corps. He filed for a pension as an invalid in 1925. (A former soldier could file for a higher pension as an invalid on account of disease incurred or injuries received during his military service in the line of duty.) He and his family boarded a ship to San Francisco in 1925, and they settled in Oakland, California, where he died in 1933. He was buried with a veteran's headstone in the San Francisco National Cemetery at the Presidio of San Francisco, the post where he had been shot thirty years earlier.[7]

Herbert Taylor, the member of I Troop whose parents came from Africa, continued to serve with I Troop and was promoted to corporal while stationed at Jefferson Barracks, Missouri. He, like Fearington, was shot by a bunkmate from I Troop but did not survive. The incident occurred after I Troop moved to Fort Sheridan, Illinois. Corporal Taylor was shot on Christmas Eve 1906 in the mess hall by Sgt. John A. Griffin, following a quarrel over a woman. Taylor was buried with a veteran's grave marker at the Fort Sheridan Post Cemetery, and his assailant was convicted of manslaughter and sentenced to nine years imprisonment at Fort Leavenworth, Kansas.[8]

Arthur Worthy, one of the soldiers who went AWOL from I Troop at Camp Atascadero in 1904, surrendered to authorities three years later at Fort McPherson in his home state of Georgia. Why he gave himself up is unknown, but he may have found living on the lam too difficult. Despite being court-martialed and given a dishonorable discharge, he joined the U.S. Navy in 1916 and served as an officer's steward aboard several ships until 1924. The Messman Branch in the navy at the time was composed exclusively of African Americans and Filipino, Chinese, and other foreign nationals recruited overseas. He filed for a pension in 1928 as an invalid based on his service in the Ninth Cavalry and U.S. Navy, and still lived in Los Angeles, California, in 1943.[9]

Jefferson Parker, like Arthur Worthy, served in the U.S. Navy after leaving I Troop. Born in Atlanta, Georgia, Parker joined the army in 1898 and saw combat with the Tenth Cavalry in Cuba during the Spanish-American War. He joined I Troop, Ninth Cavalry on his third enlistment and served under Captain Young in the Philippines. After leaving the army at the

Presidio of San Francisco, Parker served in the navy six years as a fireman first class on seven different ships. He filed for a pension as an invalid in 1926 and lived in Los Angeles in 1943.[10]

John A. S. Blakeney, another former I Troop member, also settled in Los Angeles, California. He had served under Young at Fort Duchesne, Utah, and in the Philippines, and was promoted to the Third Squadron's noncommissioned officers' staff at the Presidio of San Francisco in 1902. After four enlistments, he left the army for the first time in 1906 as a commissary sergeant at Fort Riley, Kansas. After working a few years for the U.S. Post Office in Los Angeles, he joined the army again in 1911 and was assigned once more to I Troop, Ninth Cavalry, serving under Young at Fort D. A. Russell, Wyoming. He left the army in 1914 and filed for a pension the same year as an invalid in New Mexico. He returned to Los Angeles sometime before 1920 and lived there until his death in 1945.[11]

Blakeney carried on an active correspondence with former I Troop members including Captain Young, who regarded him highly. He wrote at least one letter to former Capt. Harry O. Atwood, a Black reserve officer and former Wilberforce cadet who had served with Young during the Spanish-American War and in Liberia. Blakeney later wrote a letter to Wirt Langley, a former I Troop member who settled in Oakland, California, after his army service. Blakeney passed on news to Langley about former members of I Troop who lived in Los Angeles, including Jefferson Parker, Henry Whitfield, and Arthur Worthy.[12]

Several other former I Troop enlisted members also took up residence in California after their military service, with some doing so under rather unusual circumstances. Schuyler C. Black, who deserted from I Troop in November 1902, remained in the San Francisco area and applied for a pension in 1930. Oddly, his pension was approved in spite of his dishonorable discharge. Joseph R. Taylor, a cook from I Troop discharged in May 1904, lived in Vallejo, California, in 1910 and filed for his pension as an invalid in 1922. Taylor worked as a laborer at the Mare Island Naval Shipyard, where his former I Troop bunkmate John Malone was also employed.[13]

One other former I Troop member, not mentioned by Young in his letter (referenced in the epigraph and in chapter 1), lived in Oakland, California, after leaving the service—Lee Bell. Born in Kentucky, Bell enlisted in Ohio and served with I Troop, Ninth Cavalry from 1900 to 1906. After serving two three-year enlistments in the army, he joined the navy and served as a fireman first class aboard five ships. Upon his discharge from the navy in 1910, he settled in Napa, California, where he married Ida M. Bell in 1916. Bell worked in 1919 with former I Troop members John Malone and Joseph Taylor at Mare Island Naval Shipyard as a machine rigger. He filed for a pension based on his service in the army and the navy, and owned a home in the Castlemont neighborhood of Oakland in 1930.[14]

Young's former second in command, Lt. Samuel B. "Sammy" Pearson, continued to serve with the Ninth Cavalry after his time in California. After his promotion to captain, he commanded M Troop, Ninth Cavalry and served under Captain Young again when the latter was the Third Squadron commander at Fort D. A. Russell, Wyoming. Pearson transferred to the Quartermaster Corps during World War I and was promoted to major, lieutenant colonel, and colonel (a temporary wartime rank). He maintained a lifelong friendship with Young through correspondence and visits. After retiring from the army as a lieutenant colonel in 1922, Pearson returned to the High Sierra and, like Young, purchased land in Three Rivers.[15]

Pearson built a house on his land in Three Rivers, where he enjoyed retirement with his wife, Margaret. The two were fond of traveling, a predilection from army service, and never stayed long in one place. They always returned to the High Sierra, however, eventually owning five different houses in Three Rivers. Samuel Pearson died in 1929 after suffering heart problems at his home in Three Rivers and hospitalization in Fresno, California.[16]

John R. White, the second civilian superintendent of Sequoia National Park, wrote about Pearson after his death in 1929:

> Pearson spent a summer under the big trees at Giant Forest and became so enamored of this part of California and the Sierras that on his retirement he built a bungalow on land which he acquired at Three Rivers during his army service. Colonel Pearson had lived here for several years and had endeared himself to the community near the park, and to all of us in the park, by his cheery good nature and his willingness to assist in anything for the good of the community. I believe that the indirect cause of his death was over-strain through lifting a heavy sack for an old man who was a neighbor of his in Three Rivers.[17]

After the death of her husband, Margaret Pearson continued to live in Three Rivers until her death in 1960.[18]

Capt. Charles Young completed his tour as the military attaché to Hispaniola between 1904 and 1907, and rejoined I Troop while it was stationed in the Philippines. Young passed through San Francisco on his way to the Philippines in 1908, but as far as it is known, he never visited Sequoia again. He continued to serve as the I Troop commander at Fort D. A. Russell, Wyoming, until he was assigned as the military attaché to Liberia from 1912 to 1915.[19]

After his promotion to major, Young was reassigned to the Tenth Cavalry and served with Brig. Gen. John J. Pershing as a squadron commander during the Mexican Punitive Expedition from 1916 to 1917, during which he was promoted to lieutenant colonel. After being medically retired and promoted to colonel in 1917, he was recalled to active duty, and during his second assignment in Liberia, he died of chronic nephritis and cardiac failure while on an intelligence mission to Nigeria in 1922. Captain Atwood, to whom Blakeney wrote the same year, was at Young's hospital bedside when he died. Initially buried in Lagos, Nigeria, Young was reinterred with full military honors at Arlington National Cemetery, Virginia, in 1923.[20]

### *Rowdy Gang*

Several of the Buffalo Soldiers Charles Young referred to as that "beloved rowdy gang of mine" remained in California after their enlistments in the army. As Young indicated in his 1916 letter from Mexico, he knew of nine former I Troop soldiers living in or near San Francisco. He noted that most "who have gone out in civil life are doing fine."

The first of this rowdy gang was John L. Malone, a former farmer from North Carolina who enlisted in 1894 and served under Captain Young in I Troop at Fort Duchesne, Utah, and in the Philippines. Malone showed leadership talent, and Young promoted him to sergeant. He spent months hospitalized in 1898 recovering from an illness he acquired during his Spanish-American War service in Florida. In addition, he was admitted to Letterman Hospital at the Presidio of San Francisco between April and July 1903, and missed the deployment to Sequoia.[21]

Poor health probably contributed to his decision to end his service in the army. Malone was discharged from the Ninth Cavalry in February 1904 as a sergeant with an excellent character rating by Young. Two weeks after he left the army, he married Sophia M. Irving in San Francisco. Sophia, originally from Tennessee, was six years older than her husband. Malone continued to suffer poor health and filed for a pension as an invalid in 1907.[22]

After they married, John and Sophia Malone settled in Vallejo City, California, about thirty miles north of San Francisco. By 1910 Malone worked as a wage earner in the Mare Island Naval Shipyard, and the couple owned a house in an otherwise all-white neighborhood just across the Napa River from his workplace. Five years later, Malone worked as a shipfitter helper at Mare Island and in 1920 was a shipfitter. He likely socialized with his former I Troop brothers and fellow Mare Island workmates Joseph Taylor and Lee Bell.[23]

Malone died in 1920 in Vallejo and was buried beneath a veteran's headstone at Sunrise Memorial Cemetery in Vallejo. His wife, Sophia, filed for a widow's pension with the help of an attorney named S. M. Fortier based on John Malone's 1907 invalid pension filing. A widow could file a claim for a soldier's pension, which was increased if the soldier had filed as an invalid.[24]

Another member of Young's rowdy gang was Sgt. Dee Smith. Smith began his army service in 1898 in Nashville, Tennessee, listing his occupation as barber, and served under Young in Utah and the Philippines. Like Malone, he served two tours with I Troop, and Young promoted him to sergeant. And like Malone, he had spent several months hospitalized after service in Florida during the Spanish-American War recovering from an unknown illness.[25]

Sergeant Smith served as one of Captain Young's trusted noncommissioned officers during the summer at Sequoia. Chief Ranger Ernest Britten mentioned him in his diary as counting Sequoia trees in the Giant Forest. Smith was discharged from the army in May 1904 as a sergeant and given an excellent character rating by Captain Young. Poor health probably contributed to the decision to end his army service, since he filed for a pension as an invalid four months after leaving the army in San Francisco.[26]

Dee Smith changed his name to William D. Smith when he married Amelia A. Davis in December 1904. They lived in Oakland, where Smith initially worked as a night watchman at a clothing store and later as a street sweeper, both occupations commonly performed by Blacks at the time. By 1920 Smith owned a house in the predominantly white Wentworth-Holland neighborhood, and the couple had four daughters and two sons.[27]

Smith died in 1925 and was buried with a Spanish-American War headstone at the San Francisco National Cemetery at the Presidio, where he had started his California journey two decades earlier. Amelia Smith filed for his pension with the help of an attorney named L. M. Sherwood. Like Sophia Malone, Amelia Smith could collect an increased amount based on her husband's pension as an invalid. Amelia died in 1940 and was buried with her husband.[28]

Another soldier mentioned in Young's letter, Leo Frye, was a former butler from Dayton, Ohio, who enlisted in the army in 1901 and served three years under Captain Young as a cook. He served with Young in the Philippines, at the Presidio of San Francisco, and at Sequoia. Frye ended his enlistment in 1904 with Young giving him an excellent character rating. He decided like the other members of the rowdy gang to remain in California.[29]

Frye settled in Oakland, working as a waiter on the Southern Pacific Railroad, and by 1910 he and his wife, Sarah, were renting a house in the Emeryville District. Sarah's sister Margaret was married to another member of the rowdy gang, Wirt Langley. Over the years, Frye worked as a waiter, porter, teamster, and laborer. He filed for a pension as an invalid in 1927 and died in 1935. Frye was laid to rest under a veteran's headstone at the San Francisco National Cemetery at the Presidio alongside several of his former fellow troopers.[30]

Another member of Young's beloved gang was Henry Whitfield, a soldier who had served with the Third North Carolina Volunteer Infantry during the Spanish-American War. He was in I Troop at Fort Duchesne, Utah, and in the Philippines, where he earned sergeant's stripes. Yet he lost those stripes and never wore them again, perhaps as the result of the fight he had with Joe Clark that was noted in Young's letter. Whitfield was a corporal under Sergeant Cary with the detachment sent to Mount Whitney, but he lost those stripes, too, by the time he ended his third enlistment at Jefferson Barracks, Missouri.[31]

Henry Whitfield returned to the San Francisco area after he left the army in 1905. Young mentioned in his letter that Whitfield went to the "pen" for fighting, indicating he did time in a penitentiary. Whitfield filed for a pension in California as an invalid in 1922, listing his service with both Company C, Third North Carolina Volunteer Infantry, and I Troop, Ninth Cavalry. In a letter in 1943, John Blakeney wrote that Whitfield was living in Los Angeles, California.[32]

The life of another I Troop member mentioned in Young's letter was difficult to track. James Norman was a former cook from Henry County, Virginia, on his second enlistment when he deserted in October 1903 at Sequoia National Park. Norman surrendered to the Presidio authorities six months later and was discharged without honor. He decided to remain in San Francisco but found making a living difficult with the stigma of such a discharge on his record.[33]

Soon after his discharge from the army, Norman changed his name to George S. Raymond, an alias he used for much of the rest of his life. By 1920 he was married, and he and his wife, Minnie, lived with their son and daughter in the Russian Hill district of San Francisco, where he worked as a hotel cook. He was in the same area in 1930, still working as a cook and living with his wife and three daughters.[34]

Norman was forced to reclaim his old identity when he filed for a pension in November 1930. His paperwork reflects that he filed for his status under the name James S. Norman with the alias George S. Raymond. After he died on New Year's Eve 1930, his wife filed for a widow's pension under the name Minnie A. Raymond. Neither of these applications was approved because of Norman's desertion and discharge without honor.[35]

Another member of the rowdy gang, William Nicholas, moved to Three Rivers to serve as a caretaker of Young's property after leaving the army at the end of December 1903. As mentioned in chapter 8, in 1904 Young purchased property from Marion Griffes that would later become the Thorn Ranch and is situated six miles from the southwestern entrance to Sequoia National Park. Young also bought a smaller plot of land in Inyo County, to the east on the other side of the park near Mount Whitney, where Nicholas also owned land.[36]

Nicholas proved himself a good soldier, and Captain Young had rewarded him with sergeant stripes and an excellent character rating at the end of his first and second enlistments. It is not known how the skills he developed as a soldier transferred to a civilian life as a rancher since his time at Three Rivers was short. Soon after he arrived, Captain Young sold the Griffes property to John M. Wright, and Nicholas returned to the Bay Area.[37]

Nicholas married Edythe B. Hinds of Oakland, California, in April 1905. They settled in Berkeley, where they had two sons named Lester and Marvin. Nicholas first worked at a stable, later as a waiter in a railroad dining car, and finally as a postal clerk in 1920. He filed for his pension as an invalid in 1923. Nicholas was convicted of "stealing U.S. personal property" in 1936 and sentenced to five years at McNeil Island Penitentiary in Washington State. After being paroled in 1937 for good behavior, he returned to California.[38]

Many of the rich details we know about the life of Charles Young, as well as those of his rowdy gang from I Troop, come from letters Nicholas wrote. When Ada Young chose to compile notes on the military career of Charles Young in the 1940s, she wrote letters to former members of I Troop, including Samuel Pearson, John A. S. Blakeney, and others. Nicholas was her most reliable source of information and related many of the fascinating stories used in this narrative. Nicholas died in 1949 and was buried with a veteran's marker at the Golden Gate National Cemetery in San Bruno, California.[39]

Another troop mate mentioned in Young's letter was Wirt L. Langley, a former butcher from Richmond, Virginia, who enlisted in the army in 1898. Langley first served with the Twenty-Fourth Infantry and later with I Troop, Ninth Cavalry at Fort Duchesne, Utah. He completed his second enlistment in the Philippines under Captain Young in May 1902 and was discharged from the army at Angel Island, California. (At the time, the U.S. Army sent soldiers to Angel Island for discharge when they ended their enlistments overseas in the Philippines.)[40]

Langley married his wife, Margaret, in 1905, and they lived in the Golden Gate District of Oakland, California, in a predominantly white neighborhood. He worked in 1910 as a government meat inspector and in the 1920s and 1930s as a clerk for the U.S. Post Office. By 1940 he had retired and owned a house, and his sister-in-law, the widow of former comrade Leo Frye, lived with his family. Langley died in 1962 and was buried beneath a Spanish-American War veteran's marker at the Golden Gate National

Cemetery in San Bruno, California, not far from his former cohort William Nicholas.[41]

One more I Troop member and part of Young's beloved rowdy gang, Samuel "Swamp" Pierce, left the army in mid-January 1904, about two weeks after Nicholas, and accompanied him to Griffes's former ranch in Three Rivers. Like Nicholas, Pierce had proven himself a good soldier, earning his sergeant stripes and an excellent character rating after two enlistments. It is unclear how this training prepared him for the life of a rancher since he also did not stay long in Three Rivers. After Young sold the ranch, Pierce returned to the Bay Area with his former I Troop bunkmate Nicholas.[42]

In April 1906, Pierce married Joanna A. Hinds of Oakland, California, who was a sister to Edythe, the wife of William Nicholas. They settled in Berkeley and lived on the same street as William and Edythe in an otherwise all-white neighborhood. After Joanna died in 1910, he married Georgia L. Hendricks in 1914. They had two children together and were still living in the same house in 1920.[43]

Pierce worked as a Pullman porter, known as a Red Cap, for the Southern Pacific Railroad for about thirty years. (Pullman porters were exclusively Black and wore red caps to differentiate them from other workers on the railroad.) Pierce filed for a pension as an invalid in 1922 but continued to work as a Pullman porter into the mid-1930s. By 1940 Pierce had left the railroad and worked as a maintenance man at a factory. He still owned the same house on the same street, but the neighborhood had more Black residents in 1940.[44]

In 1947 Pierce returned to Sequoia National Park for a nostalgic visit. Still fit and sharp at the age of sixty-six, he brought with him the iconic photo of Charles Young and his work crew taken the summer of 1903. Pierce appears in that photo as a twenty-two-year-old sergeant. During his 1947 visit, Pierce posed for a picture while holding the photo in front of the Booker T. Washington Tree (see figure 32).[45]

Samuel Pierce was the second-to-last member of Charles Young's rowdy gang from I Troop to pass on to Fiddlers' Green.[46] He had been married six times and lived through the Spanish-American War, the Philippine-American War, World War I, World War II, the Korean War, and the Vietnam War. He died in March 1970 at the age of eighty-eight and was buried beneath a Spanish-American War veteran's grave marker at the Chapel of the Chimes Memorial Park in Hayward, California.[47]

The final member of Young's rowdy gang and his former cook, Abner "Peggy" Jones, left the army in 1902. After working as Captain Young's servant for eighteen months, he settled in Oakland, California, employed as a porter and waiter for the railroad. He, like Pierce, worked as a Red Cap for the Southern Pacific Railroad and rented a room with other Black railroad employees in the Prescott District, which was within walking distance of the train station. During his first fifteen years with the railroad, he remained single and moved often. He worked briefly as a stenographer in downtown Oakland in 1918 and as a janitor in San Francisco in 1920.[48]

Jones married Octavia Wilson in 1926 at the age of forty-three. It was his first marriage and her second, and she already had a daughter named Valerie. A year later the couple had a son in Tulare, California, whom they named Abner Young Jones in honor of Jones's former captain, a sign of his enduring devotion. Jones filed for an invalid's pension in 1928 based on his army service, indicating some health problems. By 1930 he worked at Stanford University as a cook at a fraternity house, while his wife, Octavia, did the same work at a sorority house.[49]

In 1940 Jones lived in the Crescent Park neighborhood of Palo Alto and was working as a janitor at the Schlage Lock Works. By the early 1950s, he had moved to the Clawson neighborhood of Oakland while his family remained in Palo Alto. Jones died in December 1971, a year after former I Troop member Samuel Pierce, having also lived through every war from the Spanish-American to the Vietnam War. Jones was laid to rest with a veteran's marker at the Chapel of the Chimes Memorial Park in Hayward, California, not far from Pierce's grave.[50]

There is no record that Young's rowdy gang assembled after they left the army, yet these former Buffalo Soldiers surely met occasionally. The former troop mates stayed in touch with each other, as evidenced by Captain Young's 1916, John Blakeney's 1943, and William Nicholas's 1945 letters. They lived for many years near each other, some as next-door neighbors. And several were married to sisters. They likely assembled on occasion to swap war stories as soldiers are apt to do. It is possible some collected on the San Francisco wharf in 1908 to see Captain Young board a ship to Manila and in 1910 when I Troop returned from the Philippines. And when the men passed away over the years, their fellow veterans probably attended the funerals to bid the cavalryman's farewell to Fiddlers' Green.

With the deaths of "Swamp" Pierce in 1970 and "Peggy" Jones in 1971, the last of Captain Young's former I Troop soldiers who had settled in the San Francisco area were gone. They had worked as ranchers, stable hands, street sweepers, janitors, waiters, railway porters, cooks, meat inspectors, night watchmen, maintenance men, shipfitters, and postal clerks. Two spent time in prison, and one had lived under an alias. All of them married, and most of them had children. Finally, nearly all collected pensions for their wartime service and found a resting place beneath a veteran's gravestone in a national cemetery.

The members of I Troop, and particularly of Captain Young's beloved rowdy gang, forged friendships and lasting loyalties under his leadership at the Presidio of San Francisco and Sequoia National Park. Many of them found opportunities and acceptance after their army service in the San Francisco area that were unavailable to Blacks in other parts of the United States. And I Troop's Buffalo Soldiers left their lasting mark in California before passing on to Fiddlers' Green.

# Appendix A

## *"Fiddlers' Green"*

Although less familiar today, many of the veteran troopers of the Ninth Cavalry probably knew the term "Fiddlers' Green" as the mythical place where all good cavalrymen go after they die.

There is a historical tie to the story of Fiddlers' Green and Samuel B. Pearson, Captain Young's first lieutenant who served with I Troop in the Philippines and at the Presidio of San Francisco. The author of an article that appeared in *Cavalry Magazine* in 1923 quoted Pearson as the source of his information on Fiddlers' Green.[1]

Pearson continued to serve with the Ninth Cavalry after it left California, and he was promoted to captain in 1909. When the Ninth Cavalry moved to Fort D. A. Russell, Wyoming, after service in the Philippines, Captain Pearson was the post quartermaster in 1910. It was about this time that the author of the *Cavalry Magazine* article heard Pearson tell the story of Fiddlers' Green around a campfire in the Medicine Bow Mountains west of Fort D. A. Russell.

This is a full and unedited version of the article:

*Fiddlers' Green and Other Cavalry Songs by John H. Stodter*[2]

Fiddlers' Green was inspired by a story told quite some time back by Captain "Sammy" Pearson at a camp-fire in the Medicine Bow Mountains of Wyoming.

Having mentioned Fiddlers' Green and found that no one appeared to have heard of it, Pearson indignantly asserted that every good cavalryman ought to know about Fiddlers' Green, and forthwith told the story.

He said that about halfway down the trail to Hell, there was a broad meadow, dotted with trees and crossed with many streams (comparable, I suppose, to the Elysian Fields), and here all dead cavalrymen were camped, with their tents, horses, picket lines, and camp-fires, around which latter the souls of the dead troopers gathered to exchange reminiscences and tell stories. There was also the old army canteen store (where liquor was sold), long since hounded from this mundane sphere by the zealous efforts of the W.C.T.U. [Woman's Christian Temperance Union].

No other branches of the service might stop at Fiddlers' Green, but must continue to march straight through to Hell. Though it was true that some troopers, feeling the call to damnation, had packed their equipment, mounted, and set out to continue their journey, none had ever reached the gates of hell, but having finished up their liquor and returned to Fiddlers' Green.

I have never heard any explanation of the name of this "bivouac of the dead," but I believe, as Captain "Sammy" Pearson said, that every good cavalryman ought to know about Fiddlers' Green.

FIDDLERS' GREEN

Halfway down the trail to Hell,
In a shady meadow, green,
Are the Souls of all dead troopers camped
Near a good old-time canteen,
And this eternal resting place
Is known as Fiddlers' Green.

Marching past, straight through to Hell,
The Infantry are seen,
Accompanied by the Engineers,
Artillery and Marine,
For none but the shades of Cavalrymen
Dismount at Fiddlers' Green.

Though some go curving down the trail
To seek a warmer scene,

No trooper ever gets to Hell
Ere he's emptied his canteen,
And so rides back to drink again
With friends at Fiddlers' Green.

And so when man and horse go down
Beneath a saber keen,
Or in a roaring charge fierce mèlée
You stop a bullet clean,
And the hostiles come to get your scalp,
Just empty your canteen,
And put your pistol to your head
And go to Fiddlers' Green.[3]

"Fiddlers' Green" seems to borrow from Rudyard Kipling's "The Young British Soldier," which described the conditions British soldiers faced while in Afghanistan in the nineteenth century. The final verses of both are strikingly similar. Kipling's poem ends with this verse:

When you're wounded and left on Afghanistan's plains,
  And the women come out to cut up what remains,
Just roll to your rifle and blow out your brains
  An' go to our Gawd like a soldier.[4]

The origin of "Fiddlers' Green" is certainly older than Pearson's reference. It generally refers to a paradise where the music of the fiddle never stops, the dancing never ceases, and the drinks never run dry. The *Oxford English Dictionary* originally referred to Fiddlers' Green as a sailor's Elysium in the early 1800s. It later became known as both a sailor's and cavalryman's paradise. The earliest documented American account connecting it with the U.S. Cavalry is the one from the 1923 *Cavalry Magazine* recounting the story told by Samuel Pearson in 1910. U.S. Army cavalry units still use "Fiddlers' Green" to memorialize their fallen comrades.[5]

The U.S. Army cavalry troopers who served their country and protected our national parks for so many years certainly deserve a place at this mythical Fiddlers' Green, as do Captain Young and his rowdy gang.

# Appendix B

## *Biographies of Officers and Soldiers*

### *Officers*

ARWINE, JAMES TEVIS: born October 11, 1872, Indiana; married Martha C. Arwine, 1888; appointed 1898, acting assistant surgeon, Fort Ringgold, Texas; appointed 1901, acting assistant surgeon, San Francisco, California; practicing medicine 1910, Los Angeles, California; serving as hospital reconstruction officer, 1930, San Mateo, California; retired, June 8, 1928, Medical Service; serving 1944, major, Medical Service; died August 24, 1944, San Bruno, California; buried Golden Gate National Cemetery, San Bruno, California.

COX, EDWIN LUTHER: born August 15, 1872, Ringgold, Georgia; attended U.S. Military Academy, 1889–90; enlisted June 4, 1898, Boise Barracks, Idaho, mining expert, assigned F Troop, Fourth U.S. Cavalry; discharged June 3, 1901, Manila, Philippine Islands, corporal, excellent; enlisted June 4, 1901, Manila, Philippine Islands, soldier, assigned F Troop, Fourth U.S. Cavalry; discharged July 1, 1901, Manila, Philippine Islands, to accept a commission, sergeant, excellent; accepted commission as second lieutenant, Ninth U.S. Cavalry, July 2, 1901 (effective February 2, 1901); promoted September 23, 1907, to first lieutenant, Eleventh Cavalry; promoted to captain, July 1, 1916; discharged 1920; died April 4, 1938, Bennington, Oklahoma; buried Bonham, Texas.

HOWARD, JOHN H.: born March 2, 1879, Dayton, Ohio; enlisted April 27, 1989, New Brunswick, New Jersey, student, assigned Battery L, Seventh

Artillery; discharged October 12, 1989, Fort Slocum, New York, sergeant, excellent; enlisted February 18, 1899, Dayton, Ohio, soldier, assigned M Troop, Sixth Cavalry; discharged October 11, 1901, first sergeant; commissioned second lieutenant, Ninth Cavalry, February 2, 1901; accepted commission October 12, 1901; promoted first lieutenant, Eighth Cavalry, August 2, 1908; transferred to Ninth Cavalry, January 15, 1910; unassigned December 14, 1914; promoted to captain of cavalry, July 1, 1916; promoted to major, July 1, 1920; died September 10, 1968, San Antonio, Texas; buried Fort Sam Houston National Cemetery, Texas.

PEARSON, SAMUEL BURNETTE "SAMMY": born August 29, 1870, San Diego, California; enlisted April 14, 1897, Albany, New York; civil engineer, assigned I Troop, First U.S. Cavalry, and served as private, corporal, and sergeant; discharged November 17, 1899, to accept commission as second lieutenant in cavalry at Fort Meade, Maryland; commissioned second lieutenant, Ninth U.S. Cavalry, October 1, 1899; married Margaret V. Vermeule, April 23, 1900, Salt Lake City, Utah; promoted first lieutenant, February 2, 1901; graduated Mounted Service School, 1907; promoted to captain, April 18, 1909; promoted to major, July 24, 1917; promoted to lieutenant colonel (temporary), August 5, 1917; promoted to colonel (temporary), October 29, 1918; promoted to lieutenant colonel, July 1, 1920; retired December 15, 1922; died October 18, 1929, Tulare, California.

PILCHER, WINSTON: born March 9, 1868, Knoxville, Tennessee; appointed second lieutenant, First Tennessee Infantry, May 19, 1898; promoted to first lieutenant, First Tennessee Infantry, June 12, 1899; honorably mustered out July 29, 1899; appointed second lieutenant, Thirty-Seventh Volunteer Infantry, July 5, 1899 (accepted July 30, 1899); promoted to first lieutenant, Thirty-Seventh Volunteer Infantry, March 15, 1900; honorably mustered out February 20, 1901; appointed second lieutenant, Fourteenth U.S. Cavalry, February 2, 1901; promoted to first lieutenant, Ninth U.S. Cavalry, February 17, 1901 (accepted November 18, 1901); transferred to Fifth U.S. Cavalry, June 16, 1905; retired January 18, 1906, for disability in the line of duty; died February 26, 1917, Nashville, Tennessee; buried Mount Olivet, Tennessee.

YOUNG, CHARLES: born March 12, 1864, Mays Lick, Kentucky; escaped enslavement and grew up in Ripley, Ohio, 1864–84; attended U.S. Military Academy, 1884–89; commissioned, Regular Army, second lieutenant, Ninth U.S. Cavalry, 1889; served at Fort Robinson, Nebraska, and Fort Duchesne, Utah, 1889–94; served as professor of military science at Wilberforce University, Ohio, 1894–98; promoted to first lieutenant, 1896; appointed volunteer major and commander of Ninth Ohio Infantry Battalion, Spanish-American War, 1898–99; served in Ninth U.S. Cavalry, Fort Duchesne, Utah, 1899–1901; served in Ninth U.S. Cavalry, Philippine-American War, 1901–2; assigned Presidio of San Francisco, California, 1902–4; served as acting superintendent of Sequoia National Park, 1903; served as military attaché to Hispaniola (Dominican Republic and Haiti), 1904–7; served in Ninth U.S. Cavalry, Philippines, and Fort D. A. Russell, Wyoming, 1907–12; served as military attaché to Liberia, 1912–15; awarded National Association for the Advancement of Colored People Spingarn Medal, February 22, 1916; served in Tenth U.S. Cavalry, Fort Huachuca, Arizona, and Mexican Punitive Expedition, 1916–17; medically retired and promoted to colonel, 1917; recalled to active duty for service at Camp Grant, Illinois, 1919; appointed Knight Commander of the Liberian Humane Order of African Redemption, November 15, 1919; served as military attaché to Liberia, 1920–22; died Lagos, Nigeria, January 8, 1922; buried Ikoyi Cemetery, Lagos, Nigeria, January 9, 1922; reinterred Arlington National Cemetery, Virginia, June 1, 1923.

*I Troop, Ninth U.S. Cavalry Enlisted Soldiers*

ALLEN, WILLIAM: born 1876, Pontiac, Michigan; discharged January 27, 1899, from Company A, Twenty-Fourth U.S. Infantry; enlisted July 26, 1900, Grand Rapids, Michigan, cook, assigned I Troop, Ninth U.S. Cavalry; discharged July 25, 1903, Kaweah, California, private, good.

ANDERSON, ALBERT: born February 1851, Howard County, Maryland; lived June 1, 1870, Catonsville, Maryland, farm laborer; enlisted January 21, 1879, Baltimore, Maryland, laborer, assigned I Troop, Ninth U.S. Cavalry; discharged January 20, 1884, Fort Reno, Indian Territory, private, good; enlisted February 13, 1884, Fort Leavenworth, Kansas, soldier, assigned I Troop, Ninth U.S. Cavalry; discharged February 12, 1889, Fort Robinson, Nebraska, private, good; enlisted February 13, 1889, Fort Robinson, Nebraska, soldier, assigned, I Troop, Ninth U.S.

Cavalry; discharged February 12, 1894, Fort Robinson, Nebraska, saddler, very good; enlisted February 13, 1894, Fort Robinson, Nebraska, soldier, assigned I Troop, Ninth U.S. Cavalry; discharged February 12, 1899, Fort Duchesne, Utah, private, excellent; enlisted February 13, 1899, Fort Duchesne, Utah, soldier, assigned I Troop, Ninth U.S. Cavalry; discharged February 12, 1902, Tabaco, Philippines, private, very good; enlisted February 13, 1902, Tabaco, Philippines, soldier, assigned I Troop, Ninth U.S. Cavalry; discharged February 12, 1905, Jefferson Barracks, Missouri, private, excellent; enlisted February 13, 1905, Jefferson Barracks, Missouri, soldier, assigned I Troop, Ninth U.S. Cavalry; retired October 17, 1907, Presidio of San Francisco, California, cook.

ANDERSON, LEE C.: born July 1880, Xenia, Ohio; joined Company C, Ninth Ohio Volunteer Infantry; mustered into federal service, May 18, 1889, Columbus, Ohio; mustered out of federal service January 28, 1899, Summerville, Georgia; enlisted May 22, 1903, Chicago, Illinois, soldier, assigned Troop I, Ninth U.S. Cavalry; joined June 6, 1903, Troop I, Ninth U.S. Cavalry, Presidio of San Francisco, California; discharged December 8, 1904, Jefferson Barracks, Missouri, saddler, very good.

BANKS, LEE: born July 22, 1879, Maysville, Kentucky; enlisted November 4, 1898, Cincinnati, Ohio, laborer, assigned I Troop, Ninth U.S. Cavalry; discharged November 3, 1901, Tabaco, Philippines, private, very good; enlisted December 24, 1901, Presidio of San Francisco, California, soldier, assigned I Troop, Ninth U.S. Cavalry; discharged December 23, 1904, Jefferson Barracks, Missouri, private, very good; employed July 1, 1905, civilian hostler, Jefferson Barracks, Missouri; died June 6, 1924, New Richmond, Ohio; buried Samarian Cemetery, New Richmond, Ohio.

BELL, LEE: born June 1, 1881, Milldale, Kentucky; enlisted July 2, 1900, Cincinnati, Ohio, farmer, assigned I Troop, Ninth U.S. Cavalry; discharged, July 1, 1903, Kaweah, California, private, good; enlisted July 2, 1903, Kaweah, California, soldier, assigned I Troop, Ninth U.S. Cavalry; discharged July 1, 1906, Arcadia, Missouri, private, very good; 1906–10, U.S. Navy, fireman first class, aboard USS *Franklin*, USS *Puritan*, USS *Newark*, USS *Washington*, USS *Philadelphia*; married 1916 to Ida M. Bell; registered September 12, 1918, for World War I draft, living in Napa, California, working as a machine rigger at Mare Island Naval Shipyard,

California; living April 7, 1930, in Oakland, California, working as a railroad pipefitter; applied July 7, 1930, for pension, Oakland, California.

BENSON, JAMES W.: born June 1877, Bridgetown, Missouri; enlisted June 3, 1900, Fort Leavenworth, Kansas, laborer, assigned I Troop, Ninth U.S. Cavalry; discharged June 2, 1903, Presidio, California, private, very good.

BLACK, SCHUYLER C.: born September 1868, LaFayette, Alabama; enlisted June 2, 1898, Montgomery, Alabama, barber, assigned I Troop, Ninth U.S. Cavalry; discharged January 31, 1899, Fort Duchesne, Utah, private, good; enlisted February 17, 1899, Saint Louis, Missouri, barber, assigned Company D, Twenty-Fifth U.S. Infantry; transferred to Company M, Twenty-Fifth U.S. Infantry; discharged March 2, 1902, Angel Island, California, private, good; enlisted March 19, 1902, Atlanta, Georgia, soldier, assigned I Troop, Ninth U.S. Cavalry; deserted November 9, 1902, San Francisco, California; dropped from rolls, November 19, 1902; applied August 12, 1930, for pension, California.

BLAKENEY, JOHN A. S.: born January 25, 1878, Los Angeles, California; mustered in April 1898 to the Eighth Illinois Volunteer Infantry; mustered out April 8, 1899; enlisted April 27, 1899, Chicago, Illinois, waiter, assigned I Troop, Ninth U.S. Cavalry; discharged April 26, 1902, Legaspi, Philippines, squadron sergeant major, excellent; enlisted April 27, 1902, Legaspi, Philippines, soldier, assigned Noncommissioned Officers' Staff, Third Squadron, Ninth U.S. Cavalry; married August 6, 1902, Azalea E. Simpson, Riverside, California; discharged April 26, 1905, Fort Riley, Kansas, commissary sergeant, excellent; enlisted, April 27, 1905, Fort Riley, Kansas, soldier, assigned Noncommissioned Officers' Staff, Third Squadron, Ninth U.S. Cavalry; discharged May 27, 1906, Fort Riley, Kansas, commissary sergeant, excellent; living April 20, 1910, Los Angeles, California, working as post office mail clerk; enlisted September 9, 1911, Fort McDowell, California, clerk, assigned I Troop, Ninth U.S. Cavalry; honorably discharged September 8, 1914, hail and fit; applied November 27, 1914, for pension as invalid, New Mexico; living January 20, 1920, Los Angeles, California, working as a cleaner; living April 17, 1930, Los Angeles, California; living May 2, 1940, Los Angeles, California; registered for draft, 1942, Los Angeles, California; died January 27, 1945, Los Angeles, California; buried Evergreen Cemetery, Los Angeles, California.

BROCKENBOROUGH, EDWARD F.: born March 1876, Washington DC; enlisted January 26, 1898, Washington Barracks, District of Columbia, druggist, assigned I Troop, Ninth U.S. Cavalry; discharged January 25, 1901, Fort Duchesne, Utah, private, excellent; enlisted February 11, 1901, Denver, Colorado, soldier, assigned G Troop, Tenth U.S. Cavalry; discharged February 10, 1904, Fort Mackenzie, Wyoming, private, good; enlisted February 11, 1904, Fort Mackenzie, Wyoming, soldier, assigned I Troop, Ninth Cavalry; discharged July 9, 1905, private, dishonorable.

BROWN, GEORGE: born February 1856, Rutherford County, Tennessee; enlisted July 22, 1879, Nashville, Tennessee, hostler, assigned Company F, Twenty-Fourth U.S. Infantry; discharged July 21, 1884, Fort Elliott, Texas, private, good; enlisted August 2, 1884, Fort Leavenworth, Kansas, soldier, assigned I Troop, Ninth U.S. Cavalry; discharged August 1, 1889, Fort Robinson, Nebraska, private, good; enlisted August 6, 1889, Fort Robinson, Nebraska, soldier, assigned I Troop, Ninth U.S. Cavalry; discharged August 5, 1894, Fort Robinson, Nebraska, trumpeter, very good; enlisted August 8, 1894, Fort Robinson, Nebraska, soldier, assigned I Troop, Ninth U.S. Cavalry; discharged August 7, 1897, Fort Washakie, Wyoming, farrier, excellent; enlisted August 8, 1897, Fort Washakie, Wyoming, soldier, assigned I Troop, Ninth U.S. Cavalry; discharged August 7, 1900, Fort Duchesne, Utah, sergeant, excellent; enlisted August 8, 1900, Fort Duchesne, Utah, soldier, assigned I Troop, Ninth U.S. Cavalry; discharged August 7, 1903, Kaweah, California, quartermaster sergeant, excellent; enlisted August 8, 1903, Kaweah, California, soldier, assigned I Troop, Ninth U.S. Cavalry; discharged August 7, 1906, Jefferson Barracks, Missouri, sergeant, excellent; enlisted August 8, 1906, Jefferson Barracks, Missouri, soldier, assigned I Troop, Ninth U.S. Cavalry, reassigned Noncommissioned Officers' Staff, Ninth U.S. Cavalry; retired January 22, 1908, Presidio of San Francisco, California, squadron sergeant major.

BURR, WILLIAM: born December 1873, State Line, Tennessee; enlisted September 29, 1900, Memphis, Tennessee, musician, assigned I Troop, Ninth U.S. Cavalry; discharged November 24, 1902, Presidio of San Francisco, private, good; filed December 10, 1902, for pension as invalid, California.

CARY, WILSON: born April 11, 1876, Orange, Virginia; enlisted May 9, 1898, Baltimore, Maryland, laborer, assigned K Troop, Tenth U.S. Cavalry; discharged February 22, 1899, Fort Brown, Texas, private, very good; enlisted May 12, 1899, Cincinnati, Ohio, soldier, assigned I Troop, Ninth U.S. Cavalry; discharged May 11, 1902, Rosario, Philippines, sergeant, excellent; enlisted May 12, 1902, Rosario, Philippines, soldier, assigned I Troop, Ninth U.S. Cavalry; discharged May 11, 1905, Jefferson Barracks, Missouri, private, excellent; enlisted September 29, 1905, San Francisco, California, laborer, assigned Company B, Twenty-Fourth U.S. Infantry; discharged September 26, 1908, Madison Barracks, New York, corporal, excellent; enlisted October 14, 1908, Fort McDowell, California, assigned I Troop, Ninth U.S. Cavalry; discharged October 13, 1911, Fort D. A. Russell, Wyoming, first sergeant, excellent; enlisted October 14, 1911, Fort D. A. Russell, Wyoming, soldier, assigned I Troop, Ninth U.S. Cavalry; honorably discharged October 13, 1914; died August 27, 1951, Fort Riley, Kansas.

CLINTON, WILLIAM B.: born January 1877, Washington DC; enlisted March 19, 1900, Washington DC, barber, assigned I Troop, Ninth U.S. Cavalry; discharged April 18, 1903, Presidio of San Francisco, California, private, good.

COLEMAN, WILLIAM: born January 1875, Maysville, Kentucky; enlisted July 26, 1900, Dayton, Ohio, laborer, assigned I Troop, Ninth U.S. Cavalry; discharged November 24, 1902, Presidio of San Francisco, California, private, good.

DANIEL, JAMES: born December 1876, Madison, Georgia; enlisted June 14, 1898, Macon, Georgia, laborer, assigned I Troop, Ninth U.S. Cavalry; discharged February 1, 1899, Fort Duchesne, Utah; enlisted March 2, 1901, Macon, Georgia, laborer, assigned I Troop, Ninth U.S. Cavalry; discharged November 30, 1902, Presidio of San Francisco, California, disability, private, fair; filed December 8, 1902, for pension as invalid, Georgia.

DAVIS, WALTER R.: born 1877, Corpus Christi, Texas; enlisted May 9, 1898, Indianapolis, Indiana, waiter, assigned I Troop, Ninth U.S. Cavalry; discharged May 8, 1901, Loo, Philippines, private, excellent; enlisted July 2, 1901, San Francisco, California, soldier, assigned I Troop, Ninth U.S. Cavalry; discharged July 1, 1904, Presidio of San Francisco, California, private, very good; enlisted October 1, 1904, Presidio of San Francisco, California, soldier, assigned D Troop, Ninth U.S. Cavalry; discharged February 12, 1907, Fort Riley, Kansas, private, excellent; enlisted February 13, 1907, Fort Riley, Kansas, soldier, assigned D Troop, Ninth U.S. Cavalry; discharged February 12, 1910, Fort D. A. Russell, Wyoming, private, excellent; enlisted February 13, 1910, Fort D. A. Russell, Wyoming, soldier, assigned Troop D, Ninth U.S. Cavalry; discharged February 12, 1913, Douglas, Arizona, sergeant, excellent.

DENNISON, ROBERT: born 1879, Frankfort, Kentucky; enlisted May 19, 1900, Frankfort, Kentucky, waiter, assigned I Troop, Ninth U.S. Cavalry; discharged May 18, 1903, Presidio of San Francisco, California, private, good; enlisted July 3, 1903, Frankfort, Kentucky, soldier, assigned L Troop, Ninth U.S. Cavalry; discharged July 14, 1905, Jefferson Barracks, Missouri, private, dishonorable.

DIXON, DUB: born May 1875, Columbus, Georgia; enlisted March 6, 1902, Phenix City, Alabama, blacksmith, assigned I Troop, Ninth U.S. Cavalry; discharged March 5, 1905, Jefferson Barracks, Missouri, blacksmith, very good; enlisted March 11, 1905, Jefferson Barracks, Missouri, soldier, assigned I Troop, Ninth U.S. Cavalry; discharged March 25, 1908, Presidio of San Francisco, California, private, good; enlisted March 26, 1908, Presidio of San Francisco, California, assigned Army Hospital, Fort Bayard, New Mexico; died July 4, 1908, Fort Bayard, New Mexico, private.

DREW, JAMES L.: born October 10, 1869, Powhatan County, Virginia; enlisted June 17, 1897, Richmond, Virginia, horse trainer, assigned I Troop, Ninth U.S. Cavalry; married June 12, 1889, Goochland County, Virginia, to Eloise J. Moseley; discharged June 16, 1900, Fort Duchesne, Utah, sergeant, excellent; enlisted September 15, 1900, Cincinnati, Ohio, soldier, assigned I Troop, Ninth U.S. Cavalry; discharged November 24, 1902, Presidio of San Francisco, California, sergeant, excellent; enlisted March 28, 1903, Jersey City, New Jersey, clerk, assigned F Troop, Tenth U.S. Cavalry; discharged July, 2, 1905, Fort Washakie, Wyoming, corporal, excellent; filed March 28, 1921, for pension as invalid, New York; died October 10, 1939, New York City, New York; buried October 14, 1939, Forest Lawn Cemetery, Utica, New York.

EDWARDS, SAMUEL W.: BORN November 1875, Austin, Texas; enlisted July 29, 1903, Beaumont, Texas, cook, assigned I Troop, Ninth U.S. Cavalry; discharged July 27, 1906, Jefferson Barracks, Missouri, cook, excellent.

ENOX, JOHN: born October 1882, Savana, Missouri; enlisted March 15, 1904, Presidio of San Francisco, California, butcher, assigned I Troop, Ninth U.S. Cavalry; discharged March 14, 1907, Fort Sheridan, Illinois, private, very good.

FAUCETT, ALEXANDER: born April 1882, White Pine, Tennessee; enlisted March 7, 1904, Middleboro, Kentucky, miner, assigned I Troop, Ninth U.S. Cavalry; discharged February 24, 1905, Jefferson Barracks, Missouri, private, dishonorable.

FEARINGTON, GEORGE W.: born July 11, 1874, Durham, North Carolina; enlisted December 21, 1892, Lexington, Kentucky, laborer, assigned I Troop, Ninth U.S. Cavalry; discharged December 20, 1897, Fort Washakie, Wyoming, private, good; enlisted December 28, 1897, Fort Washakie, Wyoming, soldier, assigned I Troop, Ninth U.S. Cavalry; discharged December 27, 1900, Fort Duchesne, Utah, corporal, very good; enlisted December 28, 1900, soldier, Fort Duchesne, Utah, assigned I Troop, Ninth U.S. Cavalry; shot by Corporal Lockett, November 7, 1902, Presidio of San Francisco, California; competed in rifle competition, August 6, 1903, Whipple Barracks, Arizona Territory; discharged December 27, 1903, Presidio of San Francisco, California, private, good; enlisted January 11, 1904, Presidio of San Francisco, California, soldier, assigned Hospital Corps; discharged January 21, 1907, Angel Island, California; enlisted February 12, 1907, Fort Sheridan, Illinois, assigned I Troop, Ninth U.S. Cavalry; discharged February 11, 1910, Fort D. A. Russell, Wyoming, private, good; enlisted May 4, 1910, Fort Logan, Colorado, soldier, assigned Company F, Twenty-Fifth U.S. Infantry; discharged May 3, 1913, Schofield Barracks, Hawaii Territory, private, very good; enlisted May 7, 1913, Schofield Barracks, Hawaii Territory, assigned Company F, Twenty-Fifth U.S. Infantry; promoted to sergeant, May 29, 1917, Schofield Barracks, Hawaii Territory; retired July 30, 1917, Schofield Barracks, Hawaii Territory; filed for pension as invalid, June 17, 1925, Territory of Hawaii; died November 20, 1933, Oakland, California; buried November 23, 1933, San Francisco National Cemetery, Presidio of San Francisco, California (section C, site 655).

FERGUSON, JULIUS: born March 1879, Brenham, Texas; enlisted July 29, 1903, Beaumont, Texas, laborer, assigned I Troop, Ninth U.S. Cavalry; discharged March 18, 1905, Jefferson Barracks, Missouri, private, excellent.

FISH, MAJOR: born December 1881, Fitzpatrick, Georgia; enlisted Nashville, Tennessee, March 8, 1904, laborer, assigned I Troop, Ninth U.S. Cavalry; discharged March 7, 1907, Fort Sheridan, Illinois, private good.

FRYE, LEO: born February 1870, Cincinnati, Ohio; enlisted March 18, 1901, Dayton, Ohio, assigned I Troop, Ninth U.S. Cavalry; discharged March 17, 1904, Presidio of San Francisco, California, cook, excellent; living 1910, Berkeley, California; living 1911–17, Oakland, California; filed March 3, 1927, for pension as invalid, California; died February 27, 1935, Laytonville, California; buried San Francisco National Cemetery, Presidio of San Francisco, California (section C, site 1263).

GARLAND, EUGENE: born October 1868, Summit, Mississippi; mustered into federal service April 1898 to the Eighth Illinois Volunteer Infantry; mustered out of federal service April 3, 1899; enlisted May 8, 1899, Chicago, Illinois, laborer, assigned I Troop, Ninth U.S. Cavalry; discharged June 18, 1902, Angel Island, California, private, good; enlisted September 11, 1902, Chicago, Illinois, soldier, assigned I Troop, Ninth U.S. Cavalry; discharged September 10, 1905, Jefferson Barracks, Missouri, private, excellent; enlisted September 11, 1908, Camp McGrath, Philippines, soldier, assigned I Troop, Ninth U.S. Cavalry; died October 12, 1908, Camp McGrath, Philippines, private.

GARRETT, WALTER: born February 1879, Christian County, Kentucky; enlisted February 27, 1901, Hopkinsville, Kentucky, farmer, assigned Company G, Twenty-Fourth U.S. Infantry; discharged February 26, 1904, Fort Assiniboine, Montana, private good; enlisted March 3, 1904, Saint Paul, Minnesota, soldier, assigned I Troop, Ninth U.S. Cavalry; discharged March 30, 1905, Jefferson Barracks, Missouri, private, dishonorable.

GIBSON, WILLIAM: born April 1877, Macon, Georgia; enlisted June 18, 1898, Macon, Georgia, laborer, assigned K Troop, Ninth U.S. Cavalry; discharged January 31, 1899, Fort Huachuca, Arizona, private, good;

enlisted February 25, 1899, Fort McPherson, Georgia, soldier, assigned H Troop, Ninth U.S. Cavalry; discharged March 7, 1902, Angel Island, California, private, good; enlisted March 15, 1902, Presidio of San Francisco, California, soldier, assigned I Troop, Ninth U.S. Cavalry; deserted November 12, 1903.

GOODLOE, CHARLES: born April 1881, Columbia, Tennessee; enlisted October 1, 1900, Nashville, Tennessee, laborer, assigned I Troop, Ninth U.S. Cavalry; discharged September 30, 1903, Kaweah, California, private, good; enlisted October 20, 1903, Nashville, Tennessee, soldier, assigned A Troop, Tenth U.S. Cavalry; discharged October 19, 1903, Fort Robinson, Nebraska, private, good.

GRAYSON, JOSEPH H.: born February 1879, Baltimore, Maryland; enlisted May 23, 1900, Baltimore, Maryland, waiter, assigned I Troop, Ninth U.S. Cavalry; discharged May 22, 1903, Presidio of San Francisco, California, private, excellent; enlisted June 6, 1903, Baltimore, Maryland, soldier, assigned I Troop, Ninth U.S. Cavalry; transferred to Hospital Corps; discharged June 5, 1906, Jefferson Barracks, Missouri, private first class, very good; enlisted June 6, 1906, Jefferson Barracks, Missouri, assigned Hospital Corps; discharged June 5, 1909, Presidio, California, private first class, excellent.

GREEN, JAMES: born May 1876, Yorkville, South Carolina; enlisted July 21, 1898, Charlotte, North Carolina, cook, assigned I Troop, Tenth U.S. Cavalry; discharged March 2, 1899, Fort Bliss, Texas, private, good; enlisted May 7, 1900, Baltimore, Maryland, cook, assigned I Troop, Ninth U.S. Cavalry; discharged May 6, 1903, Presidio, California, private, good; enlisted May 16, 1903, Charlotte, North Carolina, soldier, assigned I Troop, Ninth U.S. Cavalry; discharged May 15, 1906, Jefferson Barracks, Missouri, private, good.

GRIFFIN, JOHN A: born February 18, 1876, Henry County, Kentucky; enlisted February 20, 1894, Lexington, Kentucky, laborer, assigned K Troop, Ninth U.S. Cavalry; discharged May 19, 1897, Fort Robinson, Nebraska, private, very good; enlisted, August 18, 1897, Cincinnati, Ohio, soldier, assigned K Troop, Ninth U.S. Cavalry; discharged August 17, 1900, Fort Duchesne, Utah, sergeant, excellent; enlisted November 4, 1900, Lexington, Kentucky, soldier, assigned Company H, Twenty-Fifth U.S. Infantry; discharged November 3, 1903, Fort Reno, Oklahoma, sergeant, excellent; enlisted November 14, 1903, Lexington, Kentucky, soldier, assigned I Troop, Ninth U.S. Cavalry; discharged November 13, 1906, Fort Sheridan, Illinois, sergeant, very good; enlisted November 14, 1906, Fort Sheridan, Illinois, soldier, assigned I Troop, Ninth U.S. Cavalry; discharged December 25, 1906, Chicago, Illinois, private, on account of imprisonment under sentence of civil court, without honor.

HAMES, PERRY: born February 1877, Spartanburg, South Carolina; enlisted March 13, 1901, Norton, Virginia, laborer, assigned I Troop, Ninth U.S. Cavalry; discharged March 12, 1904, Presidio of San Francisco, California, private, good; enlisted, March 15, 1904, Presidio of San Francisco, California, soldier, assigned I Troop, Ninth U.S. Cavalry; discharged March 14, 1907, Fort Sheridan, Illinois, private, good; enlisted October 5, 1907, Jefferson Barracks, Missouri, laborer, assigned U.S. Military Academy, Detachment of Cavalry; discharged September 17, 1910, Fort McDowell, California, private, excellent; enlisted October 11, 1910, Washington Barracks, District of Columbia, soldier, assigned I Troop, Ninth U.S. Cavalry; discharged August 18, 1911, Fort D. A. Russell, Wyoming, private, good.

HAMILTON, WILLIAM: born May 1873, Perry, Georgia; enlisted June 14, 1898, Macon, Georgia, hackman, assigned I Troop, Ninth U.S. Cavalry; discharged February 19, 1899, Fort Duchesne, Utah, private, good; enlisted February 27, 1901, Macon, Georgia, laborer, assigned I Troop, Ninth U.S. Cavalry; discharged April 3, 1903, General Hospital, Fort Bayard, New Mexico Territory, disability, private, good.

HARDEN, GEORGE: born March 1881, Friendsville, Tennessee; enlisted March 13, 1901, Norton, Virginia, laborer, assigned I Troop, Ninth U.S. Cavalry; discharged March 12, 1904, Presidio of San Francisco, California, private, very good.

HARDEN, MAJOR L.: born February 29, 1880, Friendsville, Tennessee; enlisted March 13, 1901, Norton, Virginia, laborer, assigned I Troop, Ninth U.S. Cavalry; discharged March 12, 1904, Presidio of San Francisco, California, private, very good.

HUSE, BEN: born March 1867, Paris, Kentucky; enlisted February 25, 1901, Cynthiana, Kentucky, farmer, assigned I Troop, Ninth U.S. Cavalry; discharged February 24, 1904, Presidio of San Francisco, California, private, very good; resided April 25, 1910, Battle Mountain Sanitorium, Hot Springs, South Dakota, for treatment.

JACKSON, DAVID S.: born May 1878, Falls Church, Virginia; enlisted May 25, 1900, Washington DC, hostler, assigned I Troop, Ninth U.S. Cavalry; discharged May 24, 1903, Presidio of San Francisco, California, saddler, excellent.

JONES, ABNER "PEGGY": born October 23, 1883 (stated August 1882 upon enlistment), Columbus, Ohio; working June 15, 1900, Fort Duchesne, Utah, cook; enlisted May 24, 1901, Calbayog, Philippines, paperhanger, assigned I Troop, Ninth U.S. Cavalry; discharged November 24, 1902, Presidio of San Francisco, California, private, good; lived 1910, Oakland, California, employed as railroad waiter; lived 1920, San Francisco, California, employed as janitor; filed January 30, 1928, for pension as invalid, California; lived 1930, Palo Alto, California, employed as cook; lived 1940, Palo Alto, California, employed as janitor; lived 1950, Oakland, California; died December 12, 1971, Palo Alto, California; buried Chapel of the Chimes, Hayward, California.

JONES, JESSE: born February 1880, Floyd County, Georgia; enlisted February 1, 1902, Williamsburg, Kentucky, coal miner, assigned I Troop, Ninth U.S. Cavalry; discharged November 24, 1902, Presidio of San Francisco, California, private, good.

JONES, WILLIAM S. "JASPER": born November 1864, Manassas, Virginia; enlisted August 19, 1882, Pittsburgh, Pennsylvania, laborer, assigned K Troop, Ninth U.S. Cavalry; discharged August 18, 1887, Fort D. A. Russell, Wyoming, trumpeter, good; enlisted August 20, 1887, Fort D. A. Russell, Wyoming, soldier, assigned K Troop, Ninth U.S. Cavalry; discharged November 19, 1890, Fort Robinson, Nebraska, trumpeter, excellent; enlisted July 2, 1894, Fort Robinson, Nebraska, soldier, assigned I Troop, Ninth U.S. Cavalry; discharged July 1, 1899, Fort Duchesne, Utah, sergeant, excellent; enlisted July 2, 1899, Fort Duchesne, Utah, soldier, assigned I Troop, Ninth U.S. Cavalry; discharged July 1, 1902, San Joaquin, Panay, Philippines, first sergeant, excellent; enlisted July 9, 1902, San Joaquin, Philippines, soldier, assigned I Troop, Ninth U.S. Cavalry; discharged July 8, 1905, Jefferson Barracks, Missouri, first sergeant, excellent; enlisted July 9, 1905, Jefferson Barracks, Missouri, soldier, assigned I Troop, Ninth U.S. Cavalry; discharged July 8, 1908,

Camp McGrath, Philippines, first sergeant, excellent; enlisted July 9, 1908, Camp McGrath, Philippines, soldier, assigned I Troop, Ninth U.S. Cavalry; discharged July 8, 1911, San Antonio, Texas, first sergeant, excellent; enlisted July 9, 1911, Fort D. A. Russell, Wyoming, soldier, assigned I Troop, Ninth U.S. Cavalry; retired June 16, 1913, Nogales, Arizona, first sergeant; living 1920, Cheyenne, Wyoming, employed as boiler wiper for the Union Pacific Railway; died May 5, 1923, Cheyenne, Wyoming; buried Fort D. A. Russell, Wyoming (now Frances E. Warren Air Base Cemetery); filed (Addie Jones) February 7, 1924, for military pension as widow, Wyoming.

LANE, EUGENE F.: enlisted March 13, 1901, Mobile, Alabama, barber, assigned I Troop, Ninth U.S. Cavalry; deserted November 10, 1902, San Francisco, California; dropped from rolls November 19, 1902.

LANGLEY, WIRT L.: born June 15, 1873, Richmond, Virginia; enlisted August 13, 1898, Richmond, Virginia, assigned Company F, Twenty-Fourth U.S. Infantry; discharged February 3, 1899, Fort D. A. Russell, Wyoming, private, good; enlisted May 1, 1899, Richmond, Virginia, assigned I Troop, Ninth U.S. Cavalry; discharged May 3, 1902, Angel Island, private, excellent; married 1905, to Margaret M. Langley; lived 1910, Oakland, California, employed as deputy meat clerk; lived 1920, Oakland, California, employed as post office clerk; lived 1930, Oakland, California, employed as post office clerk; lived 1940, Oakland, California, retired; died June 23, 1962, Oakland, California; buried Golden Gate National Cemetery, San Bruno, California (section 2E, site 3466).

LENOX, ROBERT: born October 12, 1865, Arkansas; enlisted March 11, 1899, Fort L. H. Roots, Arkansas, farmer, assigned H Troop, Tenth U.S. Cavalry; transferred to L Troop, Tenth U.S. Cavalry; discharged March 10, 1902, Manzanillo, Cuba, private, very good; enlisted April 10, 1902, New York City, New York, soldier, assigned I Troop, Ninth U.S. Cavalry; discharged November 24, 1902, Presidio of San Francisco, California, private, good; filed March 7, 1924 for pension as invalid, Arkansas; died November 23, 1953, Goodwin, Arkansas.

LLOYD, WILLIAM H.: born November 29, 1878, Franklin, Tennessee; enlisted September 29, 1900, Memphis, Tennessee, laborer, assigned I Troop, Ninth U.S. Cavalry; hospitalized, July–November 1902, Letterman General Hospital, Presidio of San Francisco, California; discharged

November 24, 1902, Presidio of San Francisco, California, for the good of the service, private, good.

LOCKETT, WALTER: born September 1872, Evansville, Indiana; enlisted January 4, 1895, Evansville, Indiana, farmer, assigned Company B, Twenty-Fourth U.S. Infantry; discharged January 3, 1898, Fort Douglas, Utah, private, very good; enlisted January 19, 1898, Evansville, Indiana, soldier, assigned I Troop, Ninth U.S. Cavalry; discharged January 18, 1901, Fort Duchesne, Utah, corporal, excellent; enlisted January 29, 1901, Denver, Colorado, soldier, assigned I Troop, Ninth U.S. Cavalry; shot Corporal Fearington, November 7, 1902, Presidio of San Francisco, California; dishonorably discharged December 31, 1902, after general court-martial, corporal, Presidio of San Francisco, California; imprisoned 1903, Alcatraz Island, California.

MAJOR, ALFRED: born February 1857, Accomack County, Virginia; enlisted January 15, 1879, Baltimore, Maryland, sailor, assigned C Troop, Ninth U.S. Cavalry; discharged January 14, 1884, Fort Sill, Indian Territory, private, good; enlisted January 29, 1884, Washington DC, soldier, assigned I Troop, Ninth U.S. Cavalry; discharged January 28, 1889, Fort Robinson, Nebraska, saddler, excellent; enlisted February 7, 1889, Fort Robinson, Nebraska, soldier, assigned I Troop, Ninth U.S. Cavalry; discharged February 6, 1894, Fort Robinson, Nebraska, saddler, excellent; enlisted February 15, 1894, Fort Robinson, Nebraska, soldier, assigned I Troop, Ninth U.S. Cavalry; discharged February 14, 1899, Fort Duchesne, Utah, saddler, excellent; enlisted February 15, 1899, Fort Duchesne, Utah, soldier, assigned I Troop, Ninth U.S. Cavalry; discharged February 14, 1902, Tabaco, Philippines, saddler, very good; enlisted February 15, 1902, Tabaco, Philippines, soldier, assigned I Troop, Ninth U.S. Cavalry; arrived June 11, 1903, General Hospital, Fort Bayard, New Mexico; died September 20, 1903, Fort Bayard, New Mexico Territory, private; buried Fort Bayard National Cemetery (section A, row Q, site 13).

MALONE, JOHN L.: born August 1873, Mocksville, North Carolina; enlisted November 28, 1894, Jonesborough, Tennessee, farmer, assigned I Troop, Ninth U.S. Cavalry; discharged November 27, 1897, Fort Washakie, Wyoming, private, very good; enlisted November 28, 1897, Fort Washakie, Wyoming, soldier, assigned I Troop, Ninth U.S. Cavalry; discharged November 27, 1900, Fort Duchesne, Utah, sergeant, excellent; enlisted

February 13, 1901, Greensboro, North Carolina, soldier, assigned I Troop, Ninth U.S. Cavalry; discharged February 12, 1904, Presidio of San Francisco, California, sergeant, excellent; married February 24, 1904, Sophia Malone, San Francisco, California; applied August 12, 1907, for pension as invalid, California; died July 20, 1920, Solano, California; buried Sunrise Memorial Cemetery, Vallejo, California; applied (Sophia Malone) October 12, 1920, as widow for pension.

MCKEE, ABRAHAM: born February 1879, London, Kentucky; enlisted June 4, 1898, London, Kentucky, laborer, assigned I Troop, Ninth U.S. Cavalry; discharged June 3, 1901, Samar, Philippines, private, very good; enlisted June 4, 1901, Samar, Philippines, soldier, assigned I Troop, Ninth U.S. Cavalry; discharged June 3, 1904, Presidio of San Francisco, California, private, good; enlisted June 9, 1904, Presidio of San Francisco, California, soldier, assigned B Troop, Ninth U.S. Cavalry; discharged February 7, 1907, Fort Riley, Kansas, private, very good; enlisted February 8, 1907, Fort Riley, Kansas, soldier, assigned B Troop, Ninth U.S. Cavalry; dishonorably discharged, general court-martial, August 22, 1909, Fort Russell, Wyoming, private, not hail and fit; applied February 12, 1931, for pension as invalid, Texas; applied (Hattie McKee) March 18, 1932, as widow for pension.

MCKENZIE, FRANK: born July 4, 1874, Fort Wingate, New Mexico; enlisted October 17, 1892, Fort Robinson, Nebraska, laborer, assigned E Troop, Ninth U.S. Cavalry; reassigned I Troop, Ninth U.S. Cavalry, 1895; discharged October 16, 1897, Fort Washakie, Wyoming, trumpeter, good; enlisted October 18, 1897, Fort Washakie, Wyoming, soldier, assigned I Troop, Ninth U.S. Cavalry; discharged October 17, 1900, Fort Duchesne, Utah, trumpeter, very good; enlisted October 24, 1900, Denver, Colorado, soldier, assigned I Troop, Ninth U.S. Cavalry; discharged October 25, 1903, Kaweah, California, trumpeter, excellent; enlisted November 5, 1903, San Francisco, California, soldier, assigned I Troop, Ninth U.S. Cavalry; discharged November 4, 1906, Fort Sheridan, Illinois, trumpeter, excellent; enlisted March 16, 1907, Jefferson Barracks, Missouri, assigned Company G, Twenty-Fifth U.S. Infantry; discharged March 15, 1910, Fort George Wright, Washington, musician, excellent; enlisted March 26, 1910, Fort Riley, Kansas, soldier, assigned Company G, Twenty-Fifth U.S. Infantry; discharged December 23, 1912,

Fort George Wright, Washington, musician, excellent; enlisted January 10, 1913, Fort Riley, Kansas, assigned I Troop, Ninth U.S. Cavalry; honorably discharged January 9, 1917; appointed sergeant, October 17, 1918, Camp Stotsenburg, Philippines; appointed color sergeant, May 28, 1919, Camp Stotsenburg, Philippines; retired March 3, 1920; married August 5, 1926, Salt Lake City, Utah, to Ruby Estes McKenzie; died April 22, 1936, Los Angeles California; buried Los Angeles National Cemetery, Los Angeles, California (90, G34).

MERRELL, WILLIAM H.: born November 22, 1880, Horse Cave, Kentucky; enlisted June 28, 1900, Cincinnati, Ohio, laborer, assigned I Troop, Ninth U.S. Cavalry; discharged June 27, 1903, Kaweah, California, private, good; enlisted June 28, 1903, Kaweah, California, soldier, assigned I Troop, Ninth U.S. Cavalry; discharged June 27, 1906, Arcadia, Missouri, private, good; filed February 16, 1926, for pension as invalid, St. Louis, Missouri; living 1930, St. Louis, Missouri, employed as railroad freight loader; registered 1942 for draft, St. Louis, Missouri.

MERRYWEATHER, HENRY M.: born May 1881, Atlanta, Georgia; enlisted July 21, 1903, Chicago, Illinois, cook, assigned I Troop, Ninth U.S. Cavalry; deserted August 2, 1904.

MITCHELL, CORNELIUS: born 1874, Prescott, Arkansas; enlisted July 30, 1898, Frankfort, Kentucky, farmer, assigned B Troop, Tenth U.S. Cavalry; discharged March 6, 1899, Fort Ringgold, Texas, private, good; enlisted May 19, 1900, Frankfort, Kentucky, laborer, assigned I Troop, Ninth U.S. Cavalry; discharged May 18, 1903, Presidio of San Francisco, corporal, very good.

MOSBY, JAMES A.: born January 1876, Quincy, Illinois; discharged April 3, 1899, Eighth North Carolina Volunteer Infantry; enlisted April 11, 1899, Chicago, Illinois, soldier, assigned I Troop, Ninth U.S. Cavalry; discharged April 10, 1902, Lucena, Philippines, private, excellent; enlisted April 11, 1902, Lucena, Philippines, soldier, assigned I Troop, Ninth U.S. Cavalry; discharged April 10, 1905, Jefferson Barracks, Missouri, private, very good.

MOSELY, THOMAS: born April 1875, Brandenburg, Kentucky; enlisted March 26, 1901, laborer, assigned K Troop, Ninth U.S. Cavalry; reassigned November 20, 1903, I Troop, Ninth U.S. Cavalry; discharged March 25, 1904, Presidio of San Francisco, California, private, excellent;

enlisted February 21, 1905, St. Louis, Missouri, laborer, assigned E Troop, Ninth U.S. Cavalry; reassigned Hospital Corps; discharged February 20, 1908, Fort Leavenworth, Kansas, private, good; enlisted February 21, 1908, Fort Leavenworth, Kansas, soldier, assigned Hospital Corps; discharged February 20, 1911, Fort Riley, Kansas, private, very good; enlisted March 25, 1911, Jefferson Barracks, Missouri, soldier, assigned I Troop, Ninth U.S. Cavalry; reassigned Hospital Corps; discharged March 24 1914, Fort McDowell, California, private first class, excellent.

NICHOLAS, WILLIAM H. "NICK": born July 9, 1876, Charlottesville, Virginia; enlisted December 31, 1897, Richmond, Virginia, messenger, assigned Company I, Ninth U.S. Cavalry; discharged December 30, 1900, Fort Duchesne, Utah, sergeant, excellent; enlisted December 31, 1900, Fort Duchesne, Utah, soldier, assigned Company I, Ninth U.S. Cavalry; discharged December 30, 1903, Presidio of San Francisco, California, sergeant, excellent; living 1904, in Three Rivers, California; married, April 26, 1905, to Edythe B. Hinds, Alameda County, California; living 1910, Berkeley, California, employed as waiter in railroad car; living 1920, Berkeley, California, employed post office clerk; filed January 30, 1923, for pension as invalid, California; sentenced, February 27, 1936, five years for stealing U.S. personal property; incarcerated February 27, 1936, McNeil Island Penitentiary, Washington; paroled December 20, 1937; died February 11, 1949, Solano County, California; buried March 15, 1949, Golden Gate National Cemetery, San Bruno, California (section A, block 1, grave 22A).

NORMAN, JAMES: born July 1873, Henry County, Virginia; enlisted March 29, 1899, Roanoke, Virginia, cook, assigned I Troop, Ninth U.S. Cavalry; discharged April 23, 1902, private; enlisted May 20, 1902, San Francisco, California, soldier, assigned I Troop, Ninth U.S. Cavalry; deserted October 28, 1903, Kaweah, California; surrendered from desertion April 27,1904, Presidio of San Francisco, California; discharged without honor, June 25, 1904, Presidio of San Francisco, California; filed November 10, 1930, for pension as invalid, San Francisco, California (denied); died December 31, 1930, San Francisco, California.

PARKER, JEFFERSON: born March 1877, Atlanta, Georgia; enlisted May 12, 1898, Atlanta, Georgia, deliveryman, assigned M Troop, Tenth U.S. Cavalry; discharged February 28, 1899, Fort Clark, Texas, private, good;

enlisted March 10, 1899, Fort Clark, Texas, soldier, assigned Troop M, Tenth U.S. Cavalry; discharged March 9, 1902, Manzanillo, Cuba, private, good; enlisted April 2, 1902, Washington Barracks, District of Columbia, assigned I Troop, Ninth U.S. Cavalry; discharged November 24, 1902, Presidio of San Francisco, private, good; served 1905–11, U.S. Navy, fireman first class, USS *Buffalo*, USS *Lawton*, USS *Rainbow*, USS *Helena*, USS *Independence*, USS *Hull*, USS *West Virginia*; applied March 30, 1926, California, for pension as invalid (approved); living 1943, Los Angeles, California.

PIERCE, SAMUEL: born July 31, 1881, Washington DC; enlisted January 18, 1898, Washington Barracks, District of Columbia, laborer, assigned I Troop, Ninth U.S. Cavalry; discharged January 17, 1901, Fort Duchesne, Utah, corporal, excellent; enlisted January 18, 1901, Fort Duchesne, Utah, soldier, assigned I Troop, Ninth U.S. Cavalry; discharged January 17, 1904, Presidio of San Francisco, California, sergeant, excellent; living 1904, Three Rivers, California; married April 26, 1906, to Joanna A. Hinds, Alameda County, California; living 1910, Berkeley, California, 1910, employed as Pullman porter; married October 10, 1914, to Georgia L. Hendricks; living 1920, Berkeley, California, 1920, employed as Pullman porter; filed December 12, 1922, for pension as invalid (approved); married April 6, 1940, Ella M. Williams, Alameda County, California; living 1940, Berkeley, California, employed factory maintenance; married Georgia L. Henricks, November 22, 1950, Alameda County, California; married Mary C. Weeks, December 8, 1957, Alameda County, California; married Ora Glasman, November 21, 1961, Alameda County, California; died March 19, 1970, Berkeley, California, buried Chapel of the Chimes Memorial Park, Hayward, California.

PITMAN, ISAAC: born 1882, Frankfort, Kentucky; enlisted May 19, 1900, Frankfort, Kentucky, waiter, assigned I Troop, Ninth U.S. Cavalry; discharged May 18, 1903, Presidio of San Francisco, California, private, excellent.

PRICE, CHARLES: born January 1870, Franklin County, Virginia; enlisted June 7, 1898, laborer, assigned I Troop, Ninth U.S. Cavalry; discharged June 6, 1901, Blanca Aurora, Philippines, private, very good; enlisted June 7, 1901, Samar, Philippines, soldier, assigned I Troop, Ninth U.S.

Cavalry; deserted November 9, 1902, San Francisco, California; dropped from roles, November 19, 1902.

RAY, EDWARD M.: born March 1876, Ringgold, Texas; enlisted December 22, 1897, Chicago, Illinois, photographer, assigned Company E, Twenty-Fourth U.S. Infantry; discharged December 21, 1900, San Jose, Nueva Ecija, Philippines, private, good; enlisted July 25, 1902, Manila, Philippines, teamster, assigned I Troop, Ninth U.S. Cavalry; discharged June 24, 1905, Arcadia, Missouri, sergeant, very good.

REDMOND, OSCAR: born June 1875, Nashville, Tennessee; enlisted June 28, 1900, Fort Leavenworth, Kansas, cook, assigned I Troop, Ninth U.S. Cavalry; discharged November 25, 1902, Presidio of San Francisco, California, private, good.

RICE, DON: born February 1882, Jefferson City, Tennessee; enlisted March 7, 1904, Middlesboro, Kentucky, miner, assigned I Troop, Ninth U.S. Cavalry; discharged March 6, 1907, Fort Sheridan, Illinois, private, good.

ROBERTS, MACK: born Anderson County, Tennessee; enlisted August 2, 1903, Lexington, Kentucky, waiter, assigned I Troop, Ninth U.S. Cavalry; discharged September 17, 1903, Presidio of San Francisco, California, disability, private, good.

ROBINSON, CECIL: born 1882, Waters Park, Texas; enlisted July 20, 1903, Austin, Texas, waiter, assigned I Troop, Ninth U.S. Cavalry; discharged July 19, 1906, Jefferson Barracks, Missouri, private, very good.

ROBINSON, JUNE: born 1880, San Antonio, Texas; enlisted July 29, 1903, Beaumont, Texas, Pullman porter, assigned I Troop, Ninth U.S. Cavalry; died August 8, 1903, Presidio of San Francisco, private, tuberculosis; buried at San Francisco National Cemetery, Presidio of San Francisco, California (section NA, site 1343).

SCOTT, ROBERT B.: born January 1882, Richmond, Texas; enlisted July 28, 1903, Houston, Texas, waiter, assigned I Troop, Ninth U.S. Cavalry; discharged July 27, 1906, Jefferson Barracks, Missouri, cook, excellent.

SCOTT, SILAS: born June 1878, Frankfort, Kentucky; enlisted May 7, 1900, Frankfort, Kentucky, laborer, assigned D Troop, Ninth U.S. Cavalry; transferred to I Troop, Ninth U.S. Cavalry; discharged November 25, 1902, Presidio of San Francisco, California, private, good; filed March 15, 1921, for pension as invalid, Ohio.

SHEPHERD, HENRY: born 1878, Albany, Georgia; enlisted August 31, 1900, Albany, Georgia, railroad laborer, assigned Company G, Twenty-Fifth U.S. Infantry; discharged August 29, 1903, Angel Island, California, private, good; enlisted September 1, 1903, Oklahoma City, Oklahoma, soldier, assigned I Troop, Ninth U.S. Cavalry; discharged September 6, 1906, Jefferson Barracks, Missouri, private, very good; enlisted December 11, 1906, Jackson Barracks, Georgia, laborer, assigned H Troop, Ninth U.S. Cavalry; discharged December 10, 1909, Fort D. A. Russell, Wyoming, private, good.

SIMPSON, ED: born November 1879, Spartanburg, South Carolina; enlisted March 13, 1901, Norton, Virginia, laborer, assigned I Troop, Ninth U.S. Cavalry; discharged November 24, 1902, Presidio of San Francisco, California, private, good.

SMELLY, DOCK: born February 1877, Randolph, Alabama; enlisted February 25, 1898, Cleveland, Ohio, laborer, assigned I Troop, Ninth U.S. Cavalry; discharged February 24, 1901, Fort Duchesne, Utah, private, excellent; enlisted February 25, 1901, Fort Duchesne, Utah, soldier, assigned I Troop, Ninth U.S. Cavalry; discharged February 24, 1904, Presidio of San Francisco, California, corporal, excellent; enlisted February 25, 1904, Presidio of San Francisco, California, soldier, assigned I Troop, Ninth U.S. Cavalry; transferred to Troop L, Ninth U.S. Cavalry; discharged February 24, 1907, Fort Sheridan, Illinois, private, good; enlisted February 25, 1907, Fort Sheridan, Illinois, soldier, assigned L Troop, Ninth U.S. Cavalry; discharged February 24, 1910, Fort D. A. Russell, Wyoming, sergeant, excellent; enlisted February 25, 1910, Fort D. A. Russell, Wyoming, soldier, assigned L Troop, Ninth U.S. Cavalry; discharged February 24, 1913, Fort Huachuca, Arizona, sergeant, excellent; living, 1915, Leavenworth, Kansas; living 1920, Bibb, Alabama, employed as driver; living 1930, Bayview, Alabama, employed as coal mine loader.

SMITH, DEE: born March 1875, Nashville, Tennessee; enlisted, March 5, 1898, Nashville, Tennessee, barber, assigned L Troop, Ninth U.S. Cavalry; transferred, March 13, 1898, to I Troop, Ninth U.S. Cavalry; discharged March 4, 1901, Calambanga, Philippines, private, good; enlisted May 6, 1901, New York City, New York, soldier, assigned I Troop, Ninth U.S. Cavalry; discharged May 5, 1904, Presidio of San

Francisco, sergeant, excellent; filed September 26, 1904, for pension as invalid, California (approved); married (as William D. Smith) December 10, 1904, Amelia A. Davis, San Francisco, California; living 1910, Oakland, California, employed as night watchman; living 1920, Oakland, California, employed as street sweeper; died April 17, 1925, Oakland, California; buried at San Francisco National Cemetery, Presidio of San Francisco, California (section A, site 893); filed (Amelia A. Smith) April 23, 1925 for pension as widow, California (approved).

SMITH, JAMES: born 1877, New Orleans, Louisiana; enlisted October 24, 1898, New York City, New York, sailor, assigned Company A, Twenty-Fifth U.S. Infantry; discharged February 28, 1899, Fort Huachuca, Arizona Territory, private, good; enlisted March 6, 1899, New York City, New York, soldier, assigned Company K, Twenty-Fifth U.S. Infantry; discharged April 23, 1902, Angel Island, California, private, very good; enlisted July 14, 1903, Kansas City, Missouri, soldier, assigned I Troop, Ninth U.S. Cavalry; discharged July 13, 1906, Jefferson Barracks, Missouri, private, very good.

STANLEY, THOMAS: born March 1879, Fort Valley, Georgia; enlisted June 10, 1898, Macon, Georgia, laborer, assigned I Troop, Ninth U.S. Cavalry; discharged February 3, 1899, Fort Duchesne, Utah, private, very good; enlisted February 27, 1901, Macon, Georgia, laborer, assigned I Troop, Ninth U.S. Cavalry; discharged February 26, 1904, Presidio of San Francisco, California, private, very good.

STOKES, WILLIAM: born 1881, Dayton, Ohio; enlisted May 15, 1900, Dayton, Ohio, teamster, assigned K Troop, Ninth U.S. Cavalry; discharged May 14, 1903, Presidio of San Francisco, California, private, excellent; enlisted July 20, 1903, Cincinnati, Ohio, soldier, assigned I Troop, Ninth U.S. Cavalry; discharged July 19, 1906, Jefferson Barracks, Missouri, private, very good; enlisted July 26, 1906, Saint Louis, Missouri, soldier, assigned I Troop, Ninth U.S. Cavalry; transferred to L Troop, Ninth U.S. Cavalry; discharged July 25, 1909, Fort D. A. Russell, Wyoming, wagoner, excellent.

STUART, WILL: born October 1878, Blount County, Tennessee; enlisted March 13, 1901, Norton, Virginia, laborer, assigned I Troop, Ninth U.S. Cavalry; discharged March 12, 1904, Presidio of San Francisco, California, wagoner, excellent.

SWAGERTY, JOHN D: born March 1882, Newport, Tennessee; enlisted March 7, 1904, Middlesboro, Kentucky, miner, assigned I Troop, Ninth U.S. Cavalry; discharged March 6, 1907, Fort Sheridan, Illinois, private, excellent.

TAYLOR, HERBERT: born March 1880, Dinwiddie County, Virginia; mustered in July 23, 1898, assigned Company F, Sixth Virginia Volunteer Infantry; mustered out January 26, 1899; enlisted February 9, 1899, Richmond, Virginia, soldier, assigned I Troop, Ninth U.S. Cavalry; discharged February 8, 1902, Tabaco, Philippines, private, very good; enlisted February 12, 1902, Tabaco, Philippines, soldier, assigned I Troop, Ninth U.S. Cavalry; discharged February 11, 1905, Jefferson Barracks, Missouri, corporal, very good; enlisted February 24, 1905, Boston, Massachusetts, soldier, assigned I Troop, Ninth U.S. Cavalry; shot and killed December 25, 1906, Fort Sheridan, Illinois, corporal; buried Fort Sheridan Post Cemetery (section 5, site 420).

TAYLOR, JOSEPH R.: born December 1874, Whitfield, Alabama; enlisted May 23, 1898, Tuskegee, Alabama, carpenter, assigned I Troop, Ninth U.S. Cavalry; discharged May 22, 1901, Calbiga, Samar, Philippines, private, very good; enlisted May 24, 1901, Calbiga, Samar, Philippines, soldier, assigned I Troop, Ninth U.S. Cavalry; discharged May 23, 1904, Presidio of San Francisco, California, cook, excellent; living 1910, Vallejo, California, employed as navy yard laborer; filed November 21, 1922, for pension as invalid (approved).

TERRELL, WILLIAM: born 1872, Taylor County, Georgia; enlisted April 15, 1899, Macon, Georgia, train porter, assigned Company B, Twenty-Fifth U.S. Infantry; discharged April 14, 1902, Gerona, Philippines, private, good; enlisted April 15, 1902, Gerona, Philippines, soldier, assigned Company B, Twenty-Fifth U.S. Infantry; discharged November 26, 1902, Fort Niobrara, Nebraska, private, good; enlisted July 14, 1903, Kansas City, Missouri, soldier, assigned I Troop, Ninth U.S. Cavalry; discharged July 13, 1906, Jefferson Barracks, Missouri, private, very good.

TODD, WILBUR: born April 1877, West Point, Georgia; enlisted April 17, 1899, Charleston, South Carolina, laborer, assigned Company B, Twenty-Fifth U.S. Infantry; discharged May 20, 1902, Angel Island, California, private, very good; enlisted August 20, 1902, Atlanta, Georgia, soldier, assigned Company B, Twenty-Fifth U.S. Infantry; transferred

June 30, 1903, to I Troop, Ninth Cavalry; discharged August 19, 1905, Jefferson Barracks, Missouri, private, very good; enlisted September 20, 1905, Boston, Massachusetts, soldier, assigned Company B, Twenty-Fourth U.S. Infantry; transferred to I Troop, Tenth U.S. Cavalry; transferred to D Troop, Tenth U.S. Cavalry; discharged September 22, 1908, Angel Island, California, private, excellent; enlisted October 24, 1908, Fort Slocum, New York, soldier, assigned Company D, Twenty-Fourth Infantry; discharged October 23, 1911, Fort Meyer, Virginia, private, excellent.

TURPIN, SAMUEL: born June 1876, Chambersburg, Pennsylvania; enlisted May 24, 1899, Chambersburg, Pennsylvania, hostler, assigned I Troop, Ninth U.S. Cavalry; discharged May 3, 1902, private, excellent; enlisted May 14, 1902, Presidio of San Francisco, California, soldier, assigned I Troop, Ninth U.S. Cavalry; died July 23, 1903, Presidio of San Francisco, California, private, aortic regurgitation with acute nephritis; buried at San Francisco National Cemetery (section NA, site 1338).

WALKER, JOHNSEY: born November 1883, Fort Reno, Indian Territory (Oklahoma); enlisted March 31, 1902, Los Angeles, California, station engineer, assigned I Troop, Ninth U.S. Cavalry; discharged March 30, 1905, Jefferson Barracks, Missouri, trumpeter, good; enlisted April 29, 1905, Kansas City, Missouri, soldier, assigned G Troop, Ninth U.S. Cavalry; discharged April 28, 1908, Fort Leavenworth, Kansas, trumpeter, very good; enlisted August 12, 1909, Fort Leavenworth, Kansas, assigned Army Service School Detachment; lived April 28, 1910, Fort Leavenworth, Kansas, employed as officer's servant; married to Julia Walker; deserted June 6, 1910.

WARREN, JOE: born December 1879, Unitia, Tennessee; enlisted March 13, 1901, Norton, Virginia, laborer, assigned I Troop, Ninth U.S. Cavalry; discharged March 12, 1904, Presidio of San Francisco, California, private, very good.

WATTS, JOSEPH: born February 1876, Paris, Kentucky; enlisted May 14, 1898, Lexington, Kentucky, farmer, assigned L Troop, Tenth U.S. Cavalry; discharged February 24, 1899, San Antonio, Texas, private, good; enlisted March 7, 1899, Lexington, Kentucky, assigned I Troop, Tenth U.S. Cavalry; transferred to L Troop, Tenth U.S. Cavalry; discharged March 6, 1902, Manzanillo, Cuba, private, very good; enlisted

April 11, 1902, Lexington, Kentucky, soldier, assigned I Troop Ninth U.S. Cavalry; discharged April 10, 1905, Jefferson Barracks, Missouri, private, very good.

WHITE, SAMUEL: born February 1877, Newport, Tennessee; enlisted March 16, 1901, Middleboro, Kentucky, miner, assigned I Troop, Ninth U.S. Cavalry; discharged November 28, 1902, Presidio of San Francisco, California, for disability, private, good.

WHITFIELD, HENRY: born April 1877, New Bern, North Carolina; mustered into federal service May 12, 1898, Fort Macon, North Carolina, assigned Company C, Third North Carolina Volunteer Infantry; mustered out of federal service February 2, 1899, Macon, Georgia; enlisted Richmond, Virginia, soldier, assigned I Troop, Ninth U.S. Cavalry; discharged March 6, 1902, Tabaco, Philippines, sergeant, good; enlisted March 7, 1902, Tabaco, Philippines, assigned I Troop, Ninth U.S. Cavalry; discharged March 6, 1905, Jefferson Barracks, Missouri, private, good; filed September 26, 1922, for pension as invalid, California (approved); living 1943, Los Angeles, California.

WICKS, EMMANUEL W.: born 1879, Baltimore, Maryland; enlisted July 30, 1900, Chicago, Illinois, laborer, assigned I Troop, Ninth U.S. Cavalry; discharged July 29, 1903, Kaweah, California, private, good.

WILLIAMS, EDWARD A.: born March 1872, Warrington, Florida; enlisted February 19, 1902, cook, Houston, Texas, assigned I Troop, Ninth U.S. Cavalry; deserted November 15, 1902, San Francisco, California; dropped from rolls November 25, 1902.

WILLIAMS, JAMES S.: born January 1875, Brenham, Texas; enlisted July 20, 1903, Austin, Texas, cook, assigned I Troop, Ninth U.S. Cavalry; discharged July 19, 1906, Jefferson Barracks, Missouri, private, very good.

WILLIS, PRESTON: born December 1878, Perryville, Virginia; enlisted February 5, 1901, Dayton, Ohio, laborer, assigned I Troop, Ninth U.S. Cavalry; discharged February 4, 1904, Presidio of San Francisco, California, private, very good; enlisted February 29, 1904, Washington DC, soldier, assigned Company A, Twenty-Fourth U.S. Infantry; deserted August 25, 1904.

WILSON, LEWIS W.: born April 1878, Leesburg, Virginia; enlisted January 25, 1902, Harrisburg, Pennsylvania, laborer, assigned I Troop, Ninth

U.S. Cavalry; discharged November 24, 1902, Presidio of San Francisco, California, private, fair.

WORTHY, ARTHUR B.: born January 1878, Jonesboro, Georgia; enlisted January 13, 1899, Chattanooga, Tennessee, blacksmith, assigned F Troop, Tenth U.S. Cavalry; discharged March 8, 1899, Camp Eagle Pass, Texas, per certificate of disability, private; enlisted September 27, 1900, Fort McPherson, Georgia, laborer, assigned I Troop, Ninth U.S. Cavalry; discharged September 26, 1903, Kaweah, California, private, good; enlisted December 11, 1903, Atlanta, Georgia, soldier, assigned I Troop, Ninth U.S. Cavalry; deserted August 3, 1904; surrendered April 8, 1907, Fort McPherson, Georgia; dishonorable discharge, June 18, 1907, Fort McPherson, Georgia, private, not good; served 1916–24, U.S. Navy, officer's steward second class, aboard USS *Nevada*, USS *Solace*, USS *Aaron*, USS *Roanoke*, USS *Ward*, USS *Laduoset*, USS *Chaumont*, and USS *Bream*; filed January 28, 1928, for pension as invalid, California; registered for draft, 1942, Los Angeles, California; living 1943, Los Angeles, California.

WRIGHT, ALFRED W.: born January 1878, Savannah, Georgia; assigned Company G, Forty-Ninth Volunteer Infantry; discharged June 30, 1901; enlisted February 14, 1902, Savannah, Georgia, laborer, assigned I Troop, Ninth U.S. Cavalry; discharged November 25, 1902, Presidio of San Francisco, California, private, good; filed February 6, 1926, for pension as invalid, Georgia (approved).

YOUNG, ALEXANDER: born April 1879, Scioto County, Ohio; enlisted December 18, 1900, Portsmouth, Ohio, laborer, assigned M Troop, Ninth U.S. Cavalry; discharged December 17, 1903, Presidio of San Francisco, California, private, very good; enlisted January 19, 1904, Columbus, Ohio, soldier, assigned I Troop, Ninth U.S. Cavalry; discharged January 18, 1907, Fort Sheridan, Illinois, private, very good.

YOUNG, THOMAS: born March 1872, Maury County, Tennessee; enlisted October 25, 1892, Nashville, Tennessee, teamster, assigned K Troop, Tenth U.S. Cavalry; discharged October 24, 1897, Fort Custer, Montana, sergeant, excellent; enlisted October 25, 1897, Fort Custer, Montana, soldier, assigned K Troop, Ninth U.S. Cavalry; discharged October 24, 1900, Holguin, Cuba, sergeant, excellent; enlisted January 23,

1901, Nashville, Tennessee, soldier, assigned E Troop, Tenth Cavalry; discharged January 22, 1904, Fort D. A. Russell, Wyoming, sergeant, excellent; enlisted February 29, 1904, Nashville, Tennessee, soldier, assigned I Troop, Ninth U.S. Cavalry; discharged February 28, 1907, Fort Sheridan, Illinois, quartermaster sergeant, excellent.

# Notes

## *Abbreviations*

HL Huntington Library, San Marino CA

NAAMCC National Afro-American Museum and Cultural Center, Wilberforce OH

NARA National Archives and Records Administration, Washington DC

Post Return Returns from U.S. Military Posts, 1800–1916, M617, RG 94, NARA

Regimental Return Returns from the Regular Army Cavalry Regiments, 1833–1916, M744, RG 391, NARA

Register of Enlistments Register of Enlistments in the U.S. Army, 1798–1914, Microfilm M233, RG 94, NARA

TRHSM Three Rivers Historical Society and Museum, Three Rivers CA

## *1. Rowdy Gang of Mine*

1. Letter from Charles Young to Joe Clark, October 15, 1916, Charles Young Collection, NAAMCC.
2. Young to Clark, October 15, 1916, Young Collection, NAAMCC.

*2. Time, Place, Men*

1. Ninth Cavalry Regimental Return, October 1902.
2. Shellum, *Black Officer*, 115–35.
3. General Order No. 56, August 1, 1866, in General Orders and Circulars, 1867, NARA; and Coffman, *Old Army*, 218–20. By August 1866, military departments began recruiting Black soldiers and white officers from the former Civil War volunteer regiments to fill the ranks of the Ninth and Tenth U.S. Cavalry and the Thirty-Eighth, Thirty-Ninth, Fortieth, and Forty-First U.S. Infantry Regiments. In 1869 and subsequent years, Congress moved to reduce the size of the peacetime Regular Army by limiting its enlisted strength to less than thirty thousand men, the strength the army maintained throughout the Indian Wars. This mandate forced the army to reduce the number of infantry regiments to twenty-five but left the number of cavalry regiments at ten. The Ninth and Tenth Cavalry Regiments survived intact, but the Thirty-Ninth and Fortieth Regiments combined to form the new Twenty-Fifth Infantry Regiment, and the Thirty-Eighth and Forty-First Regiments formed the new Twenty-Fourth.
4. Coffman, *Old Army*, 218–20.
5. Ninth Cavalry Regimental Return, October 1902; and Thompson, *Presidio of San Francisco*, 74–75. There was no J Troop. The letter *J* was not used because the capital letters *I* and *J* looked alike and were easily confused.
6. Ninth Cavalry Regimental Return, November 1902. The new military cantonment in Monterey, California, was called the Monterey Military Reservation when the First Squadron arrived in 1902. The name was changed to Ord Barracks on July 13, 1903. Raugh, *Presidio of Monterey*, 8.
7. Ninth Cavalry Regimental Return, November 1902. The other two Black officers, commissioned from the ranks in 1901, were Benjamin O. Davis, Tenth Cavalry; and John E. Green, Twenty-Fifth Infantry. Garrard was known for his defense of Black chaplain Henry V. Plummer in his 1894 court-martial and conviction. His wife, Mary Garrard, had served as an organist in the church with Plummer, was one of Plummer's most outspoken supporters, and testified at the trial as a character witness.
8. Shellum, *Black Officer*, 124–25; and William H. Nicholas to Ada Young, January 1945, Charles Young Collection, NAAMCC (hereafter Nicholas letter, January 1945, Young Collection, NAAMCC).
9. Shellum, *Black Officer*, 124–25; and Nicholas letter, January 1945, Young Collection, NAAMCC.
10. Thompson, *Defender of the Gate*, 1:1–2.
11. Broussard, *Black San Francisco*, 14–21; and U.S. Census 1900, San Fran-

cisco CA, United States of America, Bureau of the Census, Twelfth Census of the United States, Microfilm T623, NARA.

12. *San Francisco Chronicle*, February 8, 1904, 7.
13. *San Francisco Chronicle*, February 8, 1904, 7.
14. Broussard, *Black San Francisco*, 2; and Nicholas letter, January 1945, Young Collection, NAAMCC.
15. Asbury, *Barbary Coast*, 103–5; and Daniels, *Pioneer Urbanites*, 79.
16. Shellum, *Black Cadet*, 3–28.
17. Shellum, *Black Cadet*, 32–130.
18. Shellum, *Black Officer*, 1–158. Company-grade officers are those in the ranks of second lieutenant, first lieutenant, and captain. Field-grade officers include majors, lieutenant colonels, and colonels.
19. Nicholas letter, January 1945, Young Collection, NAAMCC.
20. Heitman, *Historical Register*, 1:779; and Shellum, *Black Officer*, 99–100.
21. Nicholas letter, January 1945, Young Collection, NAAMCC; and Samuel B. Pearson to Ada Young, May 3, 1926, Charles Young Collection, NAAMCC.
22. Nicholas letter, January 1945, Young Collection, NAAMCC.
23. Nicholas letter, January 1945, Young Collection, NAAMCC; and Samuel B. Pearson to Ada Young, March 17, 1922, Charles Young Collection, NAAMCC.
24. Enlistment of William S. Jones, August 19, 1882, Register of Enlistments. Enlistment terms were five years until 1893, when they became three years.
25. Enlistment of William S. Jones, August 20, 1887, Register of Enlistments; and Shellum, *Black Officer*, 9–28. Jones was discharged early under Special Order 81, Department of the Platte.
26. Enlistment of William S. Jones, July 2, 1894, Register of Enlistments; and Hebard, *Washakie*, 17–19. Chief Washakie led his Eastern Band of Shoshones from 1840 to 1900 and received a military burial with full honors at Fort Washakie.
27. Ninth Cavalry Regimental Return, April–November 1898; U.S. Census 1900, Fort Duchesne, Utah, United States of America, Bureau of the Census, Twelfth Census of the United States, Microfilm T623, NARA (hereafter Fort Duchesne Census, 1900); and enlistment of William S. Jones, July 2, 1899, Register of Enlistments. According to regulation, the troop commander recommended his nomination for first sergeant to the regimental commander, who then approved the choice and signed the promotion certificate.
28. Enlistment of William S. Jones, July 9, 1902, Register of Enlistments.

29. Enlistment of George Brown, July 22, 1879, Register of Enlistments.
30. Enlistment of George Brown, August 2, 1884, Register of Enlistments; and Ninth Cavalry Regimental Return, January–March 1885.
31. Enlistment of George Brown, August 6, 1889, Register of Enlistments; and Ninth Cavalry Regimental Return, January 1890.
32. Enlistment of George Brown, August 8, 1894, Register of Enlistments.
33. Ninth Cavalry Regimental Return, November 1889; and Moss, *Officers' Manual*, 57.
34. Enlistment of Frank McKenzie, October 17, 1892, Register of Enlistments. In some of his early enlistment papers, McKenzie is spelled as McKinzie. I chose to use McKenzie throughout.
35. Enlistment of Edward McKenzie, December 11, 1866, Register of Enlistments. When Edward McKenzie's wife filed for a pension in 1930, the clerk listed the husband's military units in the paperwork. In addition to the Fortieth, Twenty-Fourth, and Ninth Regiments, the clerk listed and then crossed out "G 54th Mass Inf." It is possible Edward McKenzie served in some capacity in the Fifty-Fourth Massachusetts Infantry during the Civil War, though there is no written record of this.
36. Enlistments of Edward McKenzie, January 4, 1870; April 12, 1875; June 8, 1880; and June 8, 1885, Register of Enlistments. Normally, the enlistment officer would have assigned him to his former company and regiment. Edward McKenzie must have presented himself as a civilian, as noted by the listed occupation (laborer), and the officer assigned him to the Ninth.
37. Enlistments of Frank McKenzie, October 17, 1892, and October 18, 1897, Register of Enlistments.
38. Enlistment of Frank McKenzie, October 24, 1900, Register of Enlistments.
39. Enlistment of Alfred Major, January 15, 1879, Register of Enlistments.
40. Enlistment of Alfred Major, January 29, 1884, Register of Enlistments.
41. Enlistments of Alfred Major, February 7, 1889, and February 15, 1894, Register of Enlistments.
42. Enlistment of Alfred Major, February 15, 1899, Register of Enlistments. After his promotion to first lieutenant, the Ninth moved Young to fill a vacancy in I Troop. Young was promoted to first lieutenant on December 22, 1896, filling a vacancy with the Seventh U.S. Cavalry but only on paper. He was serving at Wilberforce University at the time and never physically served with the Seventh Cavalry. As soon as a vacancy opened in I Troop, he was transferred on paper back to the Ninth Cavalry. Shellum, *Black Officer*, 65–68.
43. Nicholas letter, January 1945, Young Collection, NAAMCC.

44. Enlistment of Wilson Cary, May 9, 1898, Register of Enlistments.
45. Enlistment of Wilson Cary, May 12, 1899, Register of Enlistments.
46. Nicholas letter, January 1945, Young Collection, NAAMCC; and Shellum, *Black Officer*, 94–96. Like Young, it had taken Guilfoyle five years to graduate from the academy because of academic difficulties.
47. Enlistments of Wilson Cary, May 12, 1899, and May 12, 1902, Register of Enlistments.
48. Enlistment of William H. Nicholas, December 31, 1897, Register of Enlistments; and Ninth Cavalry Regimental Return, April–July 1898.
49. Enlistment of William H. Nicholas, December 31, 1900, Register of Enlistments.
50. Shellum, *Black Officer*, 118–26.
51. Enlistment of Samuel Pierce, January 18, 1898, Register of Enlistments. The Register of Enlistments listed his age as twenty-one years and five months, putting his birthdate as July 1877. But his later documents list his real birthday as July 31, 1881. He lied about his birthdate so he could join the army at age seventeen. This was not unusual at a time when few Blacks had written birth records.
52. Enlistment of Samuel Pierce, January 18, 1898, Register of Enlistments.
53. Enlistment of Samuel Pierce, January 18, 1901, Register of Enlistments.
54. Enlistment of John L. Malone, November 28, 1894, Register of Enlistments.
55. Enlistment of John L. Malone, November 28, 1897, Register of Enlistments; and Fort Duchesne Census, 1900.
56. I Troop, Ninth Cavalry Returns, February–August 1901.
57. Enlistment of George W. Fearington, December 21, 1892, Register of Enlistments.
58. Enlistment of George W. Fearington, December 28, 1900, Register of Enlistments.
59. Enlistment of Joseph R. Taylor, May 23, 1898, Register of Enlistments.
60. Enlistments of Joseph R. Taylor, May 23, 1898, and May 24, 1901, Register of Enlistments.
61. Enlistment of Dock Smelly, February 25, 1898, Register of Enlistments.
62. Enlistment of Herbert Taylor, February 9, 1899, Register of Enlistments.
63. Enlistment of Herbert Taylor, February 9, 1899, Register of Enlistments; and U.S. Census, 1900, Fort Duchesne, Utah.
64. Enlistment of Herbert Taylor, February 12, 1902, Register of Enlistments.
65. Nicholas letter, January 1945, Young Collection, NAAMCC; and California Death Index, 1940–1997, Sacramento, California, Ancestry.com.

66. Nicholas letter, January 1945, Young Collection, NAAMCC; and California Death Index, 1940–1997, Sacramento, California, Ancestry.com.
67. Nicholas letter, January 1945, Young Collection, NAAMCC. Nicholas also mentioned an incident where Abner Jones refused to cook for Lieutenant Pearson.

### 3. *Settling In*

1. Ninth Cavalry Regimental Return, October 1902. Both Young and Pearson served with I Troop when it arrived in San Francisco. Second Lt. Hamilton Bowie was assigned as the second lieutenant on paper but was serving on detached duty at Zamboanga in the Philippines in October 1902.
2. Heitman, *Historical Register*, 2:624; and General Order No. 108, October 25, 1902, in General Orders and Circulars, 1903, NARA.
3. "Army food service," 8, undated, accessed October 10, 2023, www.quartermaster.army.mil/qm_functional_areas/Culinary_service.pdf; and *Manual for Army Cooks*.
4. Moss, *Officers' Manual*, 305. By army regulation, a cavalry troop was supplied with two G trumpets with F slides.
5. Moss, *Officers' Manual*, 178–79.
6. *Military Laws of the United States*, 231–35.
7. *Military Laws of the United States*, 231–35.
8. Brady, *Skagway*, 229.
9. Ninth Cavalry Regimental Return, November 1902; and General Order No. 108, October 25, 1902, in General Orders and Circulars, 1902, NARA.
10. Enlistment of William H. Lloyd, September 29, 1900, Register of Enlistments; and U.S. General Hospital San Francisco Return, November 1902.
11. Ninth Cavalry Regimental Return, November 1902.
12. *Annual Report of the War Department*, 1902, 9:25–26.
13. *Annual Report of the War Department*, 1902, 9:25–26.
14. *The Examiner* (San Francisco), November 8, 1902, 2.
15. Enlistments of Schuyler C. Black, June 2, 1898; February 17, 1899; and March 19, 1902, Register of Enlistments. In 1899 the assignment officer, Capt. Owen J. Sweet, should have assigned Black to his previous regiment by army regulations.
16. Enlistments of Charles Price, June 7, 1898, and June 7, 1901, Register of Enlistments.
17. Enlistment of Eugene F. Lane, March 13, 1901, Register of Enlistments.
18. Enlistment of Edward A. Williams, February 19, 1902, Register of Enlistments.

19. *The Examiner* (San Francisco), November 8, 1902, 2. The reporter called the weapon used a rifle. I Troop had Krag-Jørgensen carbines, which were shorter versions of the same model rifle.
20. *The Examiner* (San Francisco), November 8, 1902, 2.
21. *San Francisco Call*, November 8, 1902, 14.
22. *San Francisco Chronicle*, November 8, 1902, 9.
23. *San Francisco Chronicle*, November 8, 1902, 9.
24. *San Francisco Call*, November 22, 1902, 11; and *San Francisco Call*, December 21, 1902, 30.
25. *San Francisco Call*, November 11, 1902, 6. The newspaper wrongly reported that Fleming was a Regular Army soldier and that his court-martial board included volunteer officers. Fleming was a volunteer soldier, and his board included Regular Army officers. Fleming's conviction was voided because of the Supreme Court's decision in the case of McClaughry vs. Deming, 186 U.S. 49 (1902).
26. *San Francisco Call*, November 17, 1902, 5.
27. *San Francisco Call*, December 28, 1902, 36; and *San Francisco Call*, February 21, 1903, 14.
28. Ninth Cavalry Regimental Return, October–November 1902.
29. Thompson, *Defender of the Gate*, 1:426.
30. One theory dates to the Revolutionary War and the application of clay to the uniform piping, and another refers to the Mexican War, citing the dust that coated their uniforms like flour when they marched.
31. Thompson, *Presidio of San Francisco*, 64–69.
32. Thompson, *Presidio of San Francisco*, 68.
33. *San Francisco Call*, November 17, 1902, 10.
34. Young served as the lone Black Regular Army officer from 1894 to 1901, the year Benjamin O. Davis and John E. Green were awarded commissions from the enlisted ranks.
35. Thompson, *Defender of the Gate*, 1:92; and *Tulare County Times*, February 25, 1904. The only description of Young's quarters is from the newspaper article. It is described as "the spacious quarters of Captain Young at the junction of the broad carriage road running westward through the Presidio, and the main street, running north and south." There are two cottages on that corner, Quarters 11 and 12. On a 1909 Post Engineer Office map of the post, Quarters 11 is designated for a captain and Quarters 12 for a major; so Young was likely assigned to Quarters 11.
36. *Seattle Republican*, December 26, 1902, 1. Lieutenant Tillman was an 1897 graduate of the South Carolina Military Academy. U.S. Select Military Registers, Army, 1902–1903, Ancestry.com.

37. *Seattle Republican*, December 26, 1902, 1.
38. Alexander Piper to Ada Young, July 13, 1939, Charles Young Collection, NAAMCC.
39. Winser, "Memories," 198, HL; and Coffman, *Old Army*, 276.
40. Buecker, *Fort Robinson*, 159; and Coffman, *Old Army*, 276.
41. Piper to Young, July 13, 1939, Young Collection, NAAMCC.
42. *Military Laws of the United States, 1901*, 313. A cavalry captain made $2,000 a year and an infantry captain $1,800. This basic pay of captains does not include longevity pay.
43. Ninth Cavalry Regimental Return, November 1902; and Presidio of San Francisco Post Return, November 1902.
44. Ninth Cavalry Regimental Return, November 1902.
45. *San Francisco Call*, May 30, 1903, 16; and Rommel, "Army Remount Problem," 112–13.
46. Farren, "Cavalrymen and Their Horses," 54.
47. *San Francisco Call*, December 11, 1903, 11.
48. *San Francisco Call*, December 11, 1903, 11.
49. Farren, "Cavalrymen and Their Horses," 55.
50. Thompson, *Defender of the Gate*, 1:430.
51. *Tulare County Times*, February 25, 1904.
52. Broussard, *Black San Francisco*, 2; and Nicholas letter, January 1945, Young Collection, NAAMCC.
53. Shellum, *Black Cadet*, 24–25.
54. Shellum, *Black Officer*, 61–62; and Lewis, *W.E.B. Du Bois*, 62.
55. Lottie Pearl Mitchell Papers, Western Reserve Historical Society.
56. Hill and Hatch, *History of African American Theatre*, 130–32; and Cullen, Hackman, and McNeilly, *Vaudeville, Old and New*, 518–21.
57. Johnson, *Black Manhattan*, 129–30; and Burnett, *Florida's Past*, 50–54.
58. Fortune, *Outlook*, 359; Gatewood, *Aristocrats of Color*, 174; and Moses, *Golden Age*, 216.
59. Dineen-Wimberly, "To Carry 'the Black Man's Burden,'" 70.
60. Fletcher, *America's First Black General*, 28; and Shellum, *Black Officer*, 116.
61. Beasley, *Negro Trail Blazers*, 300.
62. *San Francisco Chronicle*, December 30, 1902, 1.
63. *San Francisco Chronicle*, December 30, 1902, 1.

### 4. *Presidio Garrison*

1. Ninth Cavalry Regimental Return, January 1903; and Presidio of San Francisco Post Return, January 1903.

2. *San Francisco Call*, January 9, 1903, 1.
3. *San Francisco Call*, January 9, 1903, 1; and Washington, *Up from Slavery*, 57–61, 110–19.
4. *San Francisco Call*, January 9, 1903, 1; and *San Francisco Call*, January 13, 1903, 10.
5. *San Francisco Call*, January 9, 1903, 1; and *San Francisco Call*, January 13, 1903, 10.
6. *San Francisco Call*, January 13, 1903, 10.
7. *San Francisco Call*, January 13, 1903, 10.
8. Charles Young to B. T. Washington, March 9, 1899, Booker T. Washington Papers, Library of Congress; Washington to Young, February 22, 1899, NAAMCC; Charles Young to B. T. Washington, March 31, 1899, Booker T. Washington Papers, Library of Congress; and Fletcher, "Black Volunteers," 51–52.
9. Du Bois, *Souls of Black Folk*, chap. 3.
10. "The Assembly," *Stanford Alumnus* 5, no. 15 (December 16, 1903): 22; and Johnson, "Invisible Men," 14–16.
11. *San Francisco Chronicle*, February 1, 1903, 14; and Ninth Cavalry Regimental Return, March 1903.
12. Willis E. Davis to Charles Young, February 5, 1903, Charles Young Collection, NAAMCC. Willis E. Davis was the president of the San Francico Art Association. In the run-up to the San Francisco event, the newspaper reported a New Orleans secret order called the Seven Wise Men had declined to extend an invitation to Miss Alice Roosevelt to protest the president's "policy toward the negro." Miss Roosevelt had planned to attend the event as a guest of John McIlhenny, a former member of Roosevelt's Rough Riders. *San Francisco Call*, January 30, 1903, 5.
13. *San Francisco Call*, April 3, 1903, 9; and *San Francisco Examiner*, April 3, 1903, 14.
14. *San Francisco Call*, April 3, 1903, 9; and *San Francisco Examiner*, April 3, 1903, 14. Private Brice was assigned to K Troop, and Lieutenant Camp, assigned as the squadron adjutant, temporarily commanded M Troop for the ailing Captain Cornish.
15. *San Francisco Chronicle*, April 24, 1903, 5; enlistment of Samuel W. Dillahunty, October 2, 1900, Register of Enlistments; and enlistment of Thomas Mosely, March 26, 1901, Register of Enlistments.
16. *San Francisco Call*, May 17, 1903, 23; and Ninth Cavalry Regimental Return, May 1903.
17. *San Francisco Call*, June 30, 1903, 14.
18. *San Francisco Call*, June 30, 1903, 14.

19. *San Francisco Call*, December 20, 1903, 11; and *San Francisco Call*, December 4, 1903, 16.
20. *San Francisco Call*, May 29, 1903, 10; and enlistment of Albert Daspit, December 3, 1900, Register of Enlistments. Daspit had served in the Ninth U.S. Volunteer Infantry during the Spanish-American War.
21. Ninth Cavalry Regimental Return, April 1903.
22. Thompson, *Defenders of the Gate*, 1:273–76.
23. Presidio of San Francisco Post Return, October 1903; and Thompson, *Defenders of the Gate*, 1:426–31.
24. Lockwood, "Uncle Sam's Troopers," 356.
25. Ninth Cavalry Regimental Return, April 1903.
26. Ninth Cavalry Regimental Return, April 1903.
27. Ninth Cavalry Regimental Return, April–May 1903.
28. Ninth Cavalry Regimental Return, April 1903.
29. Ninth Cavalry Regimental Return, April 1903. The other two assigned commanders, Capt. George F. Hamilton of A Troop and Capt. William Kelly, Jr., of D Troop, served on detached service as professors at West Point.
30. Ninth Cavalry Regimental Return, April 1903.
31. Ninth Cavalry Regimental Return, April 1903. Capt. John F. Nance, assigned to K Troop in early April, was on two months' leave, and the fourth captain's slot was vacant. Lieutenant Rubottom of K Troop was on court-martial duty at the Presidio, and 1st Lt. Hamilton Bowie was serving as a general's aide in Denver.
32. Ninth Cavalry Regimental Return, April and September 1903.
33. Ninth Cavalry Regimental Return, May 1903. Also, enlistments of James Green, May 7, 1900, and May 16, 1903; Cornelius Mitchell, May 19, 1900; Robert Dennison, May 19, 1900, and July 3, 1903; and Isaac Pitman, May 19, 1900—all in Register of Enlistments.
34. *San Francisco Chronicle*, May 30, 1903, 16. The specifications were as follows: "All animals must be under 8 years old, the cavalry horses to be between 950 and 1150 pounds in weight and between 15 1/4 and 16 hands high. Artillery horses must be about the same height but weighing between 1150 and 1200 pounds."
35. *San Francisco Call*, May 13, 1903, 1.
36. Film and description of the visit of President Theodore Roosevelt to San Francisco in May 1903, Library of Congress American Memory Website, https://www/loc.gov/item/00694419; and Nicholas letter, January 1945, Young Collection, NAAMCC.
37. *San Francisco Examiner*, May 13, 1903, 6.

38. *San Francisco Examiner*, May 13, 1903, 6; and film and description of President Roosevelt's visit, 1903, Library of Congress.
39. Film and description of President Roosevelt's visit, Library of Congress.
40. *San Francisco Examiner*, May 15, 1903, 1, 4.
41. *San Francisco Examiner*, May 15, 1903, 4.
42. *San Francisco Chronicle*, May 16, 1903, 1.
43. *San Francisco Chronicle*, May 15, 11, and May 18, 1903, 1; and *San Francisco Call*, May 16, 1903, 4.
44. Roosevelt, "The Rough Riders," 420–40.
45. Morgan, *William McKinley*, 66–67, 193, 236, 479.

### *5. Park Guardians*

1. Nicholas letter, January 1945, Young Collection, NAAMCC; and Meyerson, *Nature's Army*, 233, 235.
2. Nicholas letter, January 1945, Young Collection, NAAMCC; and Ninth Cavalry Regimental Return, March–October 1903.
3. Sergeant Nicholas to Ada Young, March 3, 1945, Charles Young Collection, NAAMCC; and Moss, *Officers' Manual*, 306.
4. Young, *Report of the Acting Superintendent of Sequoia*, 16, NPS (hereafter referred to as Young, *Sequoia Report*); and Farren, "Cavalrymen and Their Horses," 56. According to Young's final report, stops and distances marched were as follows:

    1st day, to Uncle Tom's Cabin, 17 miles
    2nd day, to Mayfield, 22 miles
    3rd day, to San Jose, 18 miles
    4th day, to Gilroy, 32 miles
    5th day, to Bell's Station, 21 miles
    6th day, to San Luis house, 20 miles
    7th day, to Los Banos, 16 miles
    8th day, to Dos Palos or "Hog Ranch," 20 miles
    9th day, to the "ditch" [irrigation] beyond Firebaugh, 14 miles
    10th day, to Madera, 30 miles
    11th day, to Fresno, 20 miles
    12th day, to King's River Bridge, 18 miles
    13th day, rested and washed clothing
    14th day, to Visalia, 18 miles
    15th day, to Lemon Cove, 18 miles
    16th day, to Kaweah Post Office, 15 miles

5. Young, *Sequoia Report*, 15. A Dougherty wagon was a horse- or mule-drawn wagon with doors on the side, transverse seats, and canvas sides

that could be rolled up. An escort wagon was a standard, four-mule wagon that could haul an average load of twenty-five hundred pounds.

6. Young, *Sequoia Report*, 15.
7. "Two Troops Camped in Fresno Yesterday," *Fresno Morning Republican*, May 31, 1903, 1.
8. "A Colored Captain," *Fresno Morning Republican*, May 31, 1903, 1.
9. "Saw Philippine Service," *Fresno Morning Republican*, May 31, 1903, 1.
10. "He Never Worries," *Fresno Morning Republican*, May 31, 1903, 1.
11. "Lectured on Minstrels," *Fresno Morning Republican*, May 31, 1903, 1.
12. "Entertained by Militia," *Fresno Morning Republican*, May 31, 1903, 1.
13. "Troopers Made Trouble," *Fresno Morning Republican*, May 31, 1903, 1.
14. "Troopers Made Trouble," *Fresno Morning Republican*, May 31, 1903, 1.
15. *Daily Visalia Delta*, June 3, 1903, 1; and Heitman, *Historical Register*, 1:331, 792. Pilcher was from Tennessee and served as a volunteer officer in the First Tennessee Infantry during the Spanish-American War and Thirty-Seventh Volunteer Infantry during the Philippine-American War. Cox was from Georgia; attended West Point from 1889 to 1890; served as a private, corporal, and sergeant in the Fourth Cavalry from 1998 to 1901; and was commissioned a second lieutenant in the Ninth Cavalry in 1901.
16. *Tulare County Times*, June 4, 1903, 2.
17. *Daily Visalia Delta*, June 3, 1903, 1.
18. *Tulare County Times*, June 4, 1903, 2.
19. Heitman, *Historical Register*, 1:792.
20. Heitman, *Historical Register*, 1:331. Cox was born in Georgia but appointed to West Point from Texas.
21. Heitman, *Historical Register*, 1:546.
22. Ninth Cavalry Regimental Return, April–May 1903.
23. Fort Ringgold, Texas, Post Return, October 1898; and U.S. Census, 1900, Fort Liscum, Alaska, Bureau of Census, Twelfth Census of the United States, T623, NARA. Arwine's father was a doctor, and his grandfather fought in the Mexican War.
24. *Official Register of the United States*, 1903, 402; and Ashburn, *History of the Medical Department*.
25. Emerson, *Encyclopedia*, 183.
26. *Daily Visalia Delta*, June 3, 1903, 1; and Eldridge, *In the Summer of 1903*, 4.
27. Diary of Ranger Ernest Britten, June 3, 1903, Sequoia National Park Archive, NPS (hereafter referred to as Britten Diary).
28. Britten Diary, June 4, 1903; Young, *Sequoia Report*, 4–5; and Eldridge, *In the Summer of 1903*, 6.

29. Britten Diary, June 4, 1903; Young, *Sequoia Report*, 4–5; and Eldridge, *In the Summer of 1903*, 6.
30. The Panamanian government ratified the treaty in 1903, the U.S. Senate did in 1904, and Goethals was assigned as chief engineer in 1907.
31. Eldridge, *In the Summer of 1903*, 8.
32. Young, *Sequoia Report*, 5–6; O'Connell, *Co-operative Dreams*, 46–157; and Eldridge, *In the Summer of 1903*, 7.
33. Ranger Ernest Britten to the Secretary of the Interior, April 28, 1903, and May 9, 1903, Pay Roll of Persons Employed on Repairing Road to Giant Forest, Sequoia National Park during the month of May 1903, Letters Received by the Officer of the Secretary of the Interior relating to Sequoia and General Grant National Parks, 1890–1907, RG 79, NARA (hereafter referred to as Letters Received from Sequoia and General Grant National Parks).
34. Telegram from Captain Young to Secretary of the Interior, June 3, 1903; Letter from Captain Young to Secretary of the Interior, June 10, 1903, Letters Received from Sequoia and General Grant National Parks; and Britten Diary, June 5, 1903.
35. Young to Secretary of the Interior, June 3, 1903; and Young to Secretary of the Interior, June 10, 1903, Letters Received from Sequoia and General Grant National Parks.
36. Young, *Sequoia Report*, 5; Nicholas letter, January 1945, Young Collection, NAAMCC; and Eldridge, *In the Summer of 1903*, 8.
37. Pay Roll of Persons Employed on Repairing Road to Giant Forest, Sequoia National Park, during the month of June 1903, Letters Received from Sequoia and General Grant National Parks. Another gang foreman, Walter Fry, became the first civilian superintendent of Sequoia National Park in 1916, the year the National Park Service was created.
38. Nicholas letter, January 1945, Young Collection, NAAMCC; and Eldridge, *In the Summer of 1903*, 9. According to the payrolls for the summer of 1903, Henry Vehrs was listed as the powderman.
39. *San Francisco Chronicle*, January 10, 1904, 1. The full-page newspaper description of the event appeared on the front page complete with illustrations and photos.
40. *San Francisco Chronicle*, January 10, 1904, 1.
41. Enlistments of William S. Jones, August 19, 1882; and William H. Merrell, June 28, 1900—both in Register of Enlistments. There was no trace of a soldier named Aiken in either I or M Troops, so the reporter must have been mistaken.

42. *San Francisco Chronicle*, January 10, 1904, 1.
43. *San Francisco Chronicle*, January 10, 1904, 1.
44. Pay Roll of Persons Employed on Improvement of General Grant National Park during the month of July 1903; and Letter from Captain Young to the Secretary of the Interior, August 29, 1903, Letters Received from Sequoia and General Grant National Parks.
45. Young to the Secretary of the Interior, August 29, 1903, Letters Received from Sequoia and General Grant National Parks; and Britten Diary, July 6, 1903.
46. Ninth Cavalry Regimental Return, July 1903.
47. Nicholas letter, January 1945, Young Collection, NAAMCC. It was the highest mountain in the United States until the addition of Alaska.
48. Letter from Young to Secretary of the Interior, August 29, 1903, Letters Received from Sequoia and General Grant National Parks; and Eldridge, *In the Summer of 1903*, 9.
49. *Daily Visalia Delta*, August 9, 1903, 2; *Daily Visalia Delta*, August 15, 1903, 1; and Eldridge, *In the Summer of 1903*, 9.
50. Nicholas letter, January 1945, Young Collection, NAAMCC; and Eldridge, *In the Summer of 1903*, 9.
51. Eldridge, *In the Summer of 1903*, 4; and Jacoby, *Crimes against Nature*, 82.
52. Eldridge, *In the Summer of 1903*, 4.
53. *Daily Visalia Delta*, August 9, 1903, 2; and Eldridge, *In the Summer of 1903*, 9.
54. Young, *Sequoia Report*, 5; and Eldridge, *In the Summer of 1903*, 6.
55. Young, *Sequoia Report*, 5; Eldridge, *In the Summer of 1903*, 6; and Britten, *Pioneers in Paradise*, 50–51.
56. Britten, *Pioneers in Paradise*, 252; and Pay Roll of Persons Employed on Repairing Road to Giant Forest, Sequoia National Park, during the month of August 1903, Letters Received from Sequoia and General Grant National Parks.
57. Britten, *Pioneers in Paradise*, 252.
58. Young, *Sequoia Report*, 4, 8–9.
59. Young, *Sequoia Report*, 8–9; and Eldridge, *In the Summer of 1903*, 15.
60. Young, *Sequoia Report*, 8–9; Nicholas letter, January 1945, Young Collection, NAAMCC; and Eldridge, *In the Summer of 1903*, 15–16. One large private tract still lies within the park's boundaries.
61. Wisner, "Memories," 196–203. The copy from the Three Rivers Historical Museum has different page numbers than a draft I acquired from the

Huntington Library, which has page numbers 92–96. The Three Rivers' copy was acquired by Jay O'Connell from the Huntington Library.

62. Nicholas letter, January 1945, Young Collection, NAAMCC.
63. Winser, "Memories," 197, HL.
64. Winser, "Memories," 199, HL.
65. Winser, "Memories," 196, HL.
66. Winser, "Memories," 196, HL.
67. Winser, "Memories," 201, HL; and letters from Mary Blanche and Philip Winser to Ada Young, July 20, 1934, Charles Young Collection, NAAMCC. The friendship endured after Young's death, and both Philip and Blanche traded letters with Ada Young for thirty years after their brief acquaintance.
68. Britten Diary, September 5, 1903.
69. Britten, *Pioneers in Paradise*, 251. According to Sophie Britten, the daughter-in-law of Ernest Britten, the money belt was lost in a fire at the home of his sister Eureka Williams in La Canada, where he had left it for safekeeping. It disappeared during the confusion when the housefire was being extinguished.
70. Winser, "Memories," 197, HL.

### *6. Celebration and Departure*

1. Nicholas letter, January 1945, Young Collection, NAAMCC.
2. *Daily Visalia Delta*, August 29, 1903, 1. The party from Visalia included Maj. George W. Stewart, Capt. M. N. Byrnes, W. G. Dozier, W. St. J. Caudron, W. R. Spaulding, and A. Lewis.
3. Nicholas letter, January 1945, Young Collection, NAAMCC.
4. *Daily Visalia Delta*, August 29, 1903, 1.
5. Nicholas letter, January 1945, Young Collection, NAAMCC; and Eldridge, *In the Summer of 1903*, 1. Young used the terms "Redwood" and "Sequoia" interchangeably. Sergeant Nicholas remembered the poem reading

   *After the Forest Road was made,*
   *We sat beneath the Redwood Shade,*
   *And Feasted from Boxes laid,*
   *On well-worked Shovel, Pick, and Spade.*
6. Winser, "Memories," 198, HL.
7. Nicholas letter, January 1945, Young Collection, NAAMCC.
8. Winser, "Memories," 198, HL.
9. *Daily Visalia Delta*, October 1, 1903, 1; and Eldridge, *In the Summer of 1903*, 1.
10. *Daily Visalia Delta*, October 1, 1903, 1.

11. *Daily Visalia Delta*, October 1, 1903, 1.
12. *Daily Visalia Delta*, October 1, 1903, 1.
13. Young and his men dedicated the Booker T. Washington Tree in 1903, but sometime after that, the name plate fell off the tree and was forgotten. In 1999 Floyd Thomas of the National Afro-American History Museum and Cultural Center in Wilberforce, Ohio, asked Ward Eldridge, curator at Sequoia, if he had ever heard of the Booker T. Washington Tree. Eldridge could not locate the tree. In 2000, using a fax of a picture Thomas sent, Eldridge located the tree near Moro Rock. It still had one of the nails from the original sign embedded in it. Eldridge, Thomas, and the author were all present for the rededication of the Booker T. Washington Tree in 2003. The author, Thomas, and Neely Moody, the inspector general of the Defense Intelligence Agency, planted the seed of having the tree finally dedicated to Young in 2004 with the deputy director of the National Park Service, who attended the ceremony. The lion's share of credit for publicizing the efforts of Charles Young and the Buffalo Soldiers at Sequoia for many years prior to that goes to George Palmer.
14. Winser, "Memories," 198, HL; and Eldridge, *In the Summer of 1903*, 11. The author was present for the dedication of the Col. Charles Young Tree on August 28, 2004.
15. Young, *Sequoia Report*, 10; Eldridge, *In the Summer of 1903*, 11; Shellum, *Black Cadet*, 9–15, 26; and Brooks, *Odd Fellows in America*, 12, 164. The first African American Lodge 646 of the Grand United Order of the Odd Fellows in America was established in New York City by Peter Ogden in 1843. Lodge 2302, to which Gabriel Young belonged, was established on October 10, 1881, in Ripley, Ohio.
16. Young, *Sequoia Report*, 10; Britten Diary, September 7 and 10, 1903; and Eldridge, *In the Summer of 1903*, 11. In his diary, Chief Ranger Britten noted that he carried the supplies to the Sherman tree to build the fence on September 7, and the work was completed on September 10, 1903.
17. Young, *Sequoia Report*, 5–7.
18. Young, *Sequoia Report*, 5–7.
19. Ninth Cavalry Regimental Return, May–October 1903; and "Army Slang" in Moss, *Officers' Manual*, 306.
20. Fort Ringgold Post Return, October 1898–August 1899.
21. Ninth Cavalry Regimental Return, May–October 1903.
22. Ninth Cavalry Regimental Return, May–October 1903; and Young, *Sequoia Report*, 16.
23. Ninth Cavalry Regimental Return, May–October 1903.

24. *Daily Visalia Delta*, June 23, 1903, 1; and *Daily Visalia Delta*, August 28, 1903, 1.
25. *Daily Visalia Delta*, August 28, 1903, 1.
26. Fort Ringgold Post Return, October 1898–August 1899; and *Daily Visalia Delta*, October 13, 1903, 1. Young was born in 1864 and Arwine in 1868.
27. Ninth Cavalry Regimental Return, June 1903. Also, enlistments of Joseph H. Grayson, June 6, 1903; David S. Jackson, May 25, 1900; James W. Benson, June 3, 1900; and William H. Merrell, June 28, 1903—all in Record of Enlistments.
28. Ninth Cavalry Regimental Return, July 1903; and enlistment of Samuel Turpin, May 14, 1902, Record of Enlistments. Turpin, who had served as a corporal for Young in the Philippines, had spent forty-five days in the hospital in 1901 for this same issue.
29. Ninth Cavalry Regimental Return, July 1903. Also, enlistments of Lee Bell, July 2, 1903; William Allen, July 26, 1900; and Emmanuel W. Wicks, July 30, 1900—all in Register of Enlistments.
30. Ninth Cavalry Regimental Return, July 1903. Also, enlistments of James Smith, July 14, 1903; William Terrell, July 14, 1903; and William Stokes, July 20, 1903—all in Register of Enlistments.
31. Ninth Cavalry Regimental Return, July 1903.
32. Ninth Cavalry Regimental Return, August–September 1903; and Rocketto, "Short History," 1–3.
33. Ninth Cavalry Regimental Return, August–September 1903; and Rocketto, "Short History," 1–3.
34. Ninth Cavalry Regimental Return, August 1903.
35. Ninth Cavalry Regimental Return, September 1903.
36. Ninth Cavalry Regimental Return, October 1903; and enlistment of Frank McKenzie, November 5, 1903, Register of Enlistments.
37. Major General MacArthur to the Adjutant General of the U.S.A., September 19, 1903; and Acting Secretary of War to the Secretary of the Interior, September 30, 1903, Letters Received from Sequoia and General Grant National Parks.
38. *Daily Visalia Delta*, September 2, 1903, 2; and Department of California to Capt. Lester W. Cornish, September 9, 1903, in Young, *Sequoia Report*, appendix D.
39. *Daily Visalia Delta*, September 8, 1903, 1; and Nicholas letter, January 1945, Young Collection, NAAMCC.
40. *Daily Visalia Delta*, September 8, 1903, 1; and Nicholas letter, January 1945, Young Collection, NAAMCC.
41. Nicholas letter, January 1945, Young Collection, NAAMCC; and *Daily Visalia Delta*, September 22, 1903, 1.

42. Pay Roll of Persons Employed on Improvement of Sequoia National Park during the month of September 1903; and Captain Young to the Secretary of the Interior, September 30, 1903, Letters Received from Sequoia and General Grant National Parks.
43. Telegram from Captain Young to the Acting Secretary of the Interior, October 9, 1903, Letters Received from Sequoia and General Grant National Parks.
44. Captain Young to the Secretary of the Interior, October 20, 1903, Letters Received from Sequoia and General Grant National Parks.
45. Captain Young to the Secretary of the Interior, October 20, 1903, Letters Received from Sequoia and General Grant National Parks. Since he would likely be gone by the time they arrived, Young asked that the funds for October be sent to Ranger Britten for delivery.
46. Captain Cornish to the Secretary of the Interior, October 12, 1903, Letters Received from Sequoia and General Grant National Parks.
47. Britten Diary, October 29 and 31, 1903.
48. Britten Diary, November 2, 1903; and Ninth Cavalry Regimental Return, November 1903. Major Garrard, the previous squadron commander, was promoted to lieutenant colonel in April 1903 and transferred to the Fourteenth U.S. Cavalry, though he remained attached to the Ninth Cavalry for duty as the acting superintendent of Yosemite National Park until early November 1903.
49. Ninth Cavalry Regimental Return, November 1903; and *Daily Visalia Delta*, November 4, 1903.
50. Ninth Cavalry Regimental Return, July 1903; and *Daily Visalia Delta*, November 3, 1903.
51. Ninth Cavalry Regimental Return, July 1903; and *Daily Visalia Delta*, November 3, 1903.
52. *Daily Visalia Delta*, November 4, 1903, 1; and Eldridge, *In the Summer of 1903*, 16.
53. *Daily Visalia Delta*, November 4, 1903, 1; and Eldridge, *In the Summer of 1903*, 16.
54. Ninth Cavalry Regimental Return, November 1903.
55. Ninth Cavalry Regimental Return, November 1903.
56. Britten, *Pioneers in Paradise*, 252.
57. *Tulare County Times*, November 5, 1903, 1.
58. *Tulare County Times*, November 5, 1903, 1.
59. Ninth Cavalry Regimental Return, November 1903; and Meyerson, *Nature's Army*, 234–35.

60. Ninth Cavalry Regimental Return, November 1903; and *Tulare County Times*, November 12, 1903, 1.
61. *Tulare County Times*, November 5, 1903, 2; and *Tulare County Times*, November 12, 1903, 1.
62. *Tulare County Times*, November 5, 1903, 2.
63. *Tulare County Times*, November 5, 1903, 2.
64. Britten Diary, November 14–16, 1903; and *Daily Visalia Delta*, November 20, 1903, 1.
65. Britten Diary, November 18, 1903; Ranger Britten to Interior Department, December 5, 1903; and Acting Secretary of the Interior to Ranger Britten, December 22, 1903, Letters Received from Sequoia and General Grant National Parks; and Batter, "Tule Elk."
66. Britten Diary, November 19, 1903; and *Daily Visalia Delta*, November 20, 1903, 1.
67. Visalia Board of Trade Certificate, Charles Young Collection, NAAMCC.

### *7. Return to Garrison Life*

1. Ninth Cavalry Regimental Return, December 1903.
2. Ninth Cavalry Regimental Return, December 1903. The third, Maj. George H. Morgan, served on detached duty at the University of Minnesota as the professor of military science and tactics.
3. West Point Association of Graduates, USMA *Annual Report*, 1936, 103–4; Heitman, *Historical Register*, 1:217; McChristian, "'Dress on the Colors,'" in Glasrud and Searles, *Buffalo Soldiers*, 89; Kinevan, *Frontier Cavalryman*, 125, 306n54; and Langellier, *Scouting*, 116. Remington was a fellow student and friend of John Bigelow's brother, Poultney, at Yale and later became friends with John while he served with the Tenth Cavalry.
4. West Point Association of Graduates, USMA *Annual Report*, 1936, 103–4; Heitman, *Historical Register*, 1:217; McChristian, "'Dress on the Colors,'" in Glasrud and Searles, *Buffalo Soldiers*, 89; and Kinevan, *Frontier Cavalryman*, 125, 306n54.
5. West Point Association of Graduates, USMA *Annual Report*, 1936, 103–4; Heitman, *Historical Register*, 1:217; Kinevan, *Frontier Cavalryman*, 235–37; and Glass, *History of the Tenth Cavalry*, 34.
6. Kinevan, *Frontier Cavalryman*, 238–39; and Ninth Regimental Return, December 1903.
7. West Point Association of Graduates, *Register of Graduates*, 2681; Samuel Pearson to Ada Young, March 17, 1922, Charles Young Collection, NAAMCC; and Shellum, *Black Officer*, 94–95.

8. Ord Barracks Post Return, August 1903; and *Monterey New Era*, November 12, 1902. The name was changed to Presidio of Monterey by paragraph 1, General Order No. 142, War Department, August 30, 1904, in General Orders and Circulars, 1904, NARA.
9. Raugh, "Buffalo Soldiers," 2–3.
10. Bureau of Census, "Statistics of Population: Cities, Towns, Villages, and Boroughs," Census of the United States, 1900, 439, table 8, NARA, www2.census.gov/library/publications/decennial/1900/volume-1/volume-1-p9.pdf; and Ord Barracks Post Return, December 1903.
11. Monterey Post Return, June 1903; Ord Barracks Post Return, July 1903; *Monterey New Era*, October 14, 1903; and Raugh, "Buffalo Soldiers," 2–3.
12. Ord Barracks Post Return, December 1903; and Raugh, "Buffalo Soldiers," 2–3.
13. "The Assembly," *Stanford Alumnus* 5, no. 15 (December 16, 1903): 1.
14. "The Assembly," 1.
15. "The Assembly," 1. The sculptor Young refers to must be Meta Warrick Fuller.
16. "The Assembly," 1.
17. Shellum, *Black Officers*, 61–65.
18. *San Francisco Call*, December 10, 1903, 6; and "Quotes by David Starr Jordan," Stanford Eugenics History Project, accessed October 12, 2023, https://www.stanfordeugenics.com/jordan-quotes.
19. Winser, "Memories," 199, HL.
20. Letter from Professor Max Farrand, Stanford University, to Capt. Charles Young, February 20, 1904, Charles Young Collection, NAAMCC. Farrand was a history professor, and Allardice was a professor of mathematics.
21. Young, *Sequoia Report*, 1–18.
22. Young, *Sequoia Report*, 1–18.
23. *San Francisco Call*, November 9, 1903, 3.
24. *San Francisco Call*, December 18, 1903, 8.
25. *Tulare County Times*, December 31, 1903.
26. *San Francisco Call*, November 20, 1903, 12.
27. *San Francisco Call*, November 20, 1903, 12.
28. *Annual Report of the War Department*, 1904, 1:289.
29. *San Francisco Call*, November 24, 1903, 9.
30. *San Francisco Call*, November 24, 1903, 9.
31. *San Francisco Call*, November 24, 1903, 9; and Ninth Regimental Return, May 1903–June 1904.
32. *San Francisco Call*, November 21, 1903, 16.

33. Presidio of San Francisco Letterman General Hospital Return, September–November 1902.
34. *San Francisco Call*, November 21, 1902, 16.
35. *San Francisco Call*, December 3, 1902, 16; and *San Francisco Call*, February 9, 1904, 10.
36. Dobak and Phillips, *Black Regulars*, 148–49.
37. *San Francisco Call*, December 6, 1903, 31; *San Francisco Call*, December 16, 1903, 7; and *San Francisco Call*, December 20, 1903, 45.
38. *San Francisco Call*, December 13, 1903, 31.
39. *San Francisco Call*, December 22, 1903, 11.
40. *San Francisco Call*, December 13, 1903, 31.
41. *San Francisco Call*, December 22, 1903, 11.
42. *San Francisco Call*, December 23, 1903, 10.
43. Ninth Regimental Return, December 1903; and Nicholas letter, January 1945, Young Collection, NAAMCC.
44. Nicholas letter, January 1945, Young Collection, NAAMCC. Emphasis in original.
45. *San Francisco Call*, December 17, 1903, 7.
46. Ninth Cavalry Regimental Return, December 1903.
47. Ninth Cavalry Regimental Return, December 1903.
48. Enlistment of George W. Fearington, January 11, 1904, Register of Enlistments; and *Miliary Laws of the United States*, 354–56.
49. *San Francisco Call*, December 3, 1903, 10; and enlistment of Jerome Paton, February 2, 1901, Register of Enlistments.
50. Enlistment of Arthur B. Worthy, December 11, 1903, Register of Enlistments.
51. Enlistment of John B. Scott, July 28, 1903, Register of Enlistments.

### *8. Racism, Routine, Change*

1. *San Francisco Call*, January 7, 1904, 4.
2. *San Francisco Call*, January 7, 1904, 4.
3. *San Francisco Call*, January 7, 1904, 4.
4. Turk, "United States Navy," 92–96.
5. *San Francisco Call*, December 30, 1903, 1; and *San Francisco Call*, January 8, 1904, 7.
6. *San Francisco Call*, December 30, 1903, 1; and *San Francisco Call*, January 8, 1904, 7.
7. *San Francisco Call*, February 3, 1904, 9.
8. *San Francisco Call*, February 3, 1904, 9.
9. *San Francisco Call*, February 11, 1904, 16.

10. *San Francisco Call*, March 9, 1904, 5.
11. *San Francisco Call*, March 24, 1904, 5.
12. *San Francisco Call*, March 24, 1904, 5. Young is mounted on a black horse while his men are riding a mix of white and dark horses. Soldiers at this time received both the older blue wool uniforms and the newer tan khakis issued for service in the Philippines.
13. *San Francisco Call*, March 31, 1904, 16.
14. *San Francisco Call*, March 31, 1904, 16.
15. *San Francisco Call*, March 31, 1904, 16.
16. *San Francisco Call*, April 28, 1904, 7.
17. *San Francisco Call*, December 6, 20, 1904.
18. *San Francisco Call*, January 27, 1904, 9; *San Francisco Call*, January 28, 1904, 11; and *San Francisco Call*, January 29, 1903, 9.
19. *San Francisco Call*, January 29, 1904, 11.
20. *San Francisco Call*, April 29, 1904, 10.
21. *San Francisco Chronicle*, January 4, 1904, 4; and *San Francisco Call*, January 5, 1904, 10.
22. *San Francisco Call*, January 4, 1904, 4; and *San Francisco Call*, January 5, 1904, 10.
23. *San Francisco Chronicle*, January 4, 1904, 12; and *San Francisco Chronicle*, January 5, 1904, 9.
24. *San Francisco Call*, January 4, 1904, 4; and *San Francisco Call*, January 5, 1904, 10.
25. *San Francisco Call*, January 4, 1904, 4; and *San Francisco Call*, January 5, 1904, 10.
26. *San Francisco Call*, January 6, 1904, 9; and *San Francisco Call*, January 7, 1904, 4.
27. *San Francisco Call*, January 9, 1904, 4.
28. *San Francisco Call*, January 23, 1904, 7.
29. *San Francisco Call*, January 23, 1904, 7.
30. Ninth Cavalry Regimental Return, December 1904.
31. Ninth Cavalry Regimental Return, March 1904.
32. Enlistments of Alexander Young, December 18, 1900, and January 19, 1904, Register of Enlistments. Also, enlistments of John A. Griffin, February 20, 1894; August 18, 1897; November 4, 1900; and November 14, 1903, Register of Enlistments.
33. Enlistments of Alexander Faucett, March 7, 1904; Don Rice, March 7, 1904; John D. Swagerty, March 7, 1904; Major Fish, March 8, 1904; and John Enox, March 15, 1904—all in Register of Enlistments.

34. Enlistments of Edward F. Brockenborough, January 26, 1898; February 11, 1901; and February 11, 1904, Register of Enlistments. Also enlistments of Walter Garrett, February 27, 1901, and March 3, 1904, Register of Enlistments.
35. Enlistments of Thomas Young, October 25, 1892; October 25, 1897; January 23, 1901; and February 29, 1904, Register of Enlistments.
36. Enlistments of Thomas Young, October 25, 1892; October 25, 1897; January 23, 1901; and February 29, 1904, Register of Enlistments.
37. *San Francisco Call*, December 18, 1903, 8; and *Tulare County Times*, February 4, 1904, 1.
38. *Tulare County Times*, February 4, 1904, 1. The newspaper misidentified the acting superintendent at Yellowstone as Maj. Hiram M. Chittenden. Chittenden was the senior engineer in Yellowstone from 1899 to 1906 responsible for building the permanent post of Fort Yellowstone. The acting superintendent at Yellowstone from 1901 to 1907 was Maj. John Pitcher.
39. Heitman, *Historical Register*, 1:793; West Point Association of Graduates, *Register of Graduates*, 2680; and *San Francisco Call*, February 11, 1904, 16.
40. Nicholas letter, January 1945, Young Collection, NAAMCC.
41. Nicholas letter, January 1945, Young Collection, NAAMCC.
42. Nicholas letter, January 1945, Young Collection, NAAMCC; and Tulare County Recorder's Officer, 119/231 book and page, February 4, 1904, deed. Described as: "East ½ of East ½ of Section 22, the NW ¼ and West ½ of the SW ¼ of Section 23, and the South ½ of the NE ¼ of Section 23 (except south and east of the river and south of a line running east from Bluff Rock) = 480 acres. Sold to Charles Young by Marion E. Griffes for $10 gold coin. This is the Thorn Ranch, shown on the 1892 Historical Atlas as belonging to Marion E. Griffes; on the 1920 Tulare County map as belonging to M.L. Thorn."
43. Nicholas letter, January 1945, Young Collection, NAAMCC. Nicholas ended his enlistment in December 1903, and Pierce ended his enlistment in January 1904.
44. Alexander, *Battles and Victories*, 178–87, 253. Lt. Gen. Phillip Sheridan appointed Allensworth the first Black chaplain of the African American Twenty-Fourth Infantry Regiment in 1886. Allensworth had served the Union during the Civil War as a civilian nurse and later in the navy as a crew member of a gunboat. After the war, he became a Baptist minister. Allensworth served as a captain from 1886 to 1904, was promoted to major in 1904, and was promoted to lieutenant colonel upon retirement in 1906 because of his military service during the Civil War. He was not a

line officer like Charles Young. Line officers were in the cavalry, infantry, and artillery branches.

45. Glasrud and Searles, *Buffalo Soldiers in the West*, 76–80.
46. The content of the letters exchanged between Young and the Winsers were reproduced word for word in Philip Winser's "Memories," written in the early 1930s.
47. Winser, "Memories," 199, HL.
48. Winser, "Memories," 199, HL.
49. Winser, "Memories," 199, HL.
50. Winser, "Memories," 199–201, HL; and email from Sophia Britten, July 19, 2022.
51. Winser, "Memories," 200, HL; and Lewis, *W.E.B. Du Bois*, 2, 19.
52. Winser, "Memories," 200, HL.
53. Winser, "Memories," 198, HL.
54. Winser, "Memories," 198, HL.
55. Winser, "Memories," 198–99, HL.
56. *Cleveland Gazette*, August 29, 1903, 1.
57. Personal interview with Mrs. Mary E. Henderson, March 1970, as quoted in Coursey, "Life of Edwin Bancroft Henderson," 22–23.
58. Winser, "Memories," 198, HL.
59. Letter from Harry Atwood, undated, Charles Young Collection, NAAMCC.
60. Marriage certificate of Charles Young and Ada Mills, filed in Alameda County, California, on February 20, 1904, book 31, p. 407; and *San Francisco Call*, February 18, 1904, 6.
61. *San Francisco Chronicle*, February 19, 1904, 5; and Young marriage certificate, NAAMCC.
62. *San Francisco Examiner*, February 20, 1904, 10.
63. *San Francisco Chronicle*, February 19, 1904, 5; Young marriage certificate, NAAMCC; and obituary of Ada Mills Young, *Xenia (OH) Daily Gazette*, November 21, 1953.
64. Bond Day, "Study of Some Negro-White Families," Caroline Bond Day Papers 20–22, Peabody Museum, Harvard University; and Jack, "Kentucky Ridge Mine."
65. *San Francisco Chronicle*, February 19, 1904, 5. Two homes described as "cottages" on the corner of Presidio Boulevard and Funston Avenue, Quarters 11 and 12, were built during the Civil War when the post expanded. I concluded the residence was Quarters 11 since the 1909 District Engineer Officer map of the post shows Quarters 11 (then called Quarters 6) as quarters for a captain and Quarters 12 (then Quarters 7) as quarters for a major.

66. Winser, "Memories," 200, HL.
67. Shellum, *Black Officer*, 160–81.
68. John Hay, Secretary of State, to William P. Powell, Minister to Haiti, 23 April 1904, Diplomatic Instructions of the Department of State, 1801–1906, Haiti and Santo Domingo, Records Group 59, NARA; and Ninth Cavalry Regimental Return, May 1904.
69. *San Francisco Call*, May 1, 1904, 44.
70. Ninth Cavalry Regimental Return, May 1904.

### *9. Park Duty and Encampment*

1. *San Francisco Call*, March 30, 1904, 16; and Raugh, "Buffalo Soldiers," 3.
2. *San Francisco Call*, April 12, 1904, 5.
3. Ninth Cavalry Regimental Return, May–June 1904; and *Tulare County Times*, May 12, 1904, 5.
4. Ninth Regimental Return, May 1904; and Post Return of Sequoia Detachment, First Squadron, Ninth Cavalry, May 1904.
5. Ninth Cavalry Regimental Return, October 1903 and May 1904; and Post Return of Sequoia Detachment, First Squadron, Ninth Cavalry, May 1904.
6. Ninth Cavalry Regimental Return, May 1904; and Post Return of Sequoia Detachment, First Squadron, Ninth Cavalry, May 1904. Capt. George W. Read, the B Troop commander, was on detached service in Washington DC from May to August 1904, and Capt. William Kelly, Jr., the D Troop commander, was on detached service as an instructor at West Point from 1903 to 1907.
7. Ninth Cavalry Regimental Return, May 1904; and Post Return of Sequoia Detachment, First Squadron, Ninth Cavalry, June–September 1904.
8. Ninth Cavalry Regimental Return, May 1904; and Post Return of Sequoia Detachment, First Squadron, Ninth Cavalry, August–September 1904.
9. Ninth Cavalry Regimental Return, May 1904; and Post Return of Sequoia Detachment, First Squadron, Ninth Cavalry, June–September 1904.
10. Ninth Cavalry Regimental Return, May 1904; and Post Return of Sequoia Detachment, First Squadron, Ninth Cavalry, September 1904.
11. Ninth Cavalry Regimental Return, October 1904; Post Return of Sequoia Detachment, First Squadron, Ninth Cavalry, September–October 1904; and Presidio of Monterey Post Return, September–October 1904. The name of the post was changed from Ord Barracks to Presidio of Monterey by the War Department on August 30, 1904. To avoid confusion between the Presidio of San Francisco and the Presidio of Monterey, Ord Barracks is used throughout this chapter.

12. *Tulare County Times*, May 26, 1904, 1; *Daily Visalia Delta*, October 15, 1904, 1; and *Tulare County Times*, December 15, 1904, 1.
13. Ninth Cavalry Regimental Return, May 1904; and Special Field Return of the First Squadron (Troops C and D), Ninth Cavalry at Camp A. E. Wood, California, May 1904.
14. Meyerson, *Nature's Army*, 235.
15. Meyerson, *Nature's Army*, 235.
16. Special Field Return of the First Squadron (Troops C and D), Ninth Cavalry at Camp A. E. Wood, California, May 1904. Meyerson misidentifies these two as Troops K and L.
17. "Willard Herman McCornack," *Assembly Magazine (West Point, NY)* 7, no. 1 (April 1948): 8–9; and Meyerson, *Nature's Army*, 235.
18. Special Field Return of the First Squadron (Troops C and D), Ninth Cavalry at Camp A. E. Wood, California, May 1904; and Heitman, *Historical Register*, 1:525.
19. Special Field Return of the First Squadron (Troops C and D), Ninth Cavalry at Camp A. E. Wood, California, May 1904.
20. Ninth Cavalry Regimental Return, May 1904; and Post Return of Sequoia Detachment, First Squadron, Ninth Cavalry, May 1904.
21. Special Field Return of the First Squadron (Troops C and D), Ninth Cavalry at Camp A. E. Wood, California, June 1904.
22. Meyerson, *Nature's Army*, 235–36.
23. Ninth Cavalry Regimental Return, October 1904; and Special Field Return of the First Squadron (Troops C and D), Ninth Cavalry at Camp A. E. Wood, California, October 1904.
24. *San Francisco Call*, October 18, 1904, 7.
25. *San Francisco Call*, October 18, 1904, 7.
26. *The Californian* (Salinas), October 20, 1904, 1; *San Francisco Call*, October 21, 1904, 5; and *San Francisco Chronicle*, October 21, 1904, 3.
27. *The Californian* (Salinas), October 20, 1904, 1; *San Francisco Call*, October 21, 1904, 5; and *San Francisco Chronicle*, October 21, 1904, 3.
28. *San Francisco Examiner*, October 21, 1904, 1. Private Brooks was misidentified as Butler.
29. *San Francisco Call*, October 22, 1904, 3.
30. *Tacoma (WA) Daily Ledger*, October 22, 1904, 6.
31. *The Californian* (Salinas), October 26, 1904, 6.
32. *Santa Cruz Sentinel*, October 23, 1904, 1.
33. *The Californian* (Salinas), October 26, 1904, 6.
34. Enlistment of Albert Johnson, February 16, 1902, Register of Enlistments; and Ninth Cavalry Regimental Return, June–August 1904.

35. Enlistment of William H Brooks, April 15, 1904, Register of Enlistments; and Ninth Cavalry Regimental Return, October 1904.
36. Enlistment of Daniel S. Allen, February 26, 1902, Register of Enlistments; *Salinas (CA) Daily Index*, December 7, 1904, 3; *Salinas (CA) Daily Index*, December 16, 1904, 3; and Ninth Cavalry Regimental Return, January 1905.
37. Ninth Cavalry Regimental Return, February–May 1904.
38. *San Francisco Call*, May 8, 1904, 8.
39. *San Francisco Call*, May 31, 1904, 6.
40. *San Francisco Call*, June 8, 1904, 16.
41. *San Francisco Call*, July 5, 1904, 9.
42. *San Francisco Call*, April 6, 1904, 8; and *San Francisco Examiner*, April 6, 1904, 8.
43. *San Francisco Call*, June 12, 1904, 27; and Ninth Cavalry Regimental Return, July 1904.
44. *San Francisco Call*, June 19, 1904, 30; and Ninth Cavalry Regimental Return for November 1903, April 1904, and June 1904.
45. *San Francisco Call*, June 29, 1904, 9.
46. Lowe, *Camp Atascadero*, 3–4.
47. *San Francisco Call*, June 29, 1904, 9.
48. *San Francisco Call*, July 3, 1904, 44.
49. *Morning Tribune* (San Luis Obispo), July 7, 1904, 4; and Lowe, *Camp Atascadero*, 8–10.
50. *Morning Tribune* (San Luis Obispo), July 7, 1904; Ninth Cavalry Regimental Return, July 1904; and enlistment of Lewis W. Young, July 22, 1903, Register of Enlistments.
51. Lowe, *Camp Atascadero*, 9–18.
52. Lowe, *Camp Atascadero*, 9–18.
53. Lowe, *Camp Atascadero*, 15.
54. *San Francisco Call*, August 26, 1904, 2.
55. Ninth Cavalry Regimental Return, July–August 1904; and Lowe, *Camp Atascadero*, 81–88.
56. Ninth Cavalry Regimental Return, September 1904; and enlistment of Arthur Worthy, December 11, 1903, Register of Enlistments. Worthy surrendered to the authorities in Georgia in 1907, was court-martialed and dishonorably discharged, and later served in the U.S. Navy as an officer's steward on several ships from 1916 to 1924.
57. Ninth Regimental Return, September to October 1904; and Lowe, *Camp Atascadero*, 60–61.
58. *San Francisco Call*, October 8, 1904, 2; and Lowe, *Camp Atascadero*, 60–65.

## 10. *Rotation Issue*

1. Ninth Cavalry Regimental Return, October 1904; and *San Francisco Call*, October 8, 1904, 14.
2. Ninth Cavalry Regimental Return, October 1904; and *San Francisco Call*, October 8, 1904, 14.
3. Ninth Cavalry Regimental Return, October 1904.
4. Ninth Cavalry Regimental Return, October–November 1904.
5. Presidio of San Francisco Post Return, October–November 1904; and Field Return of the Third Squadron, Fourth Cavalry, October 20, 1904.
6. *San Francisco Call*, October 1904 to October 1905; and Fourth Cavalry Regimental Returns, October 1904-October 1905.
7. *Salt Lake City Tribune*, October 8, 1896, 1; and *The Appeal* (St. Paul MN), May 17, 1902, 2.
8. *Minneapolis Daily Times*, April 19, 1902, 10; *Saint Paul Globe*, May 12, 1902, 4; and *Minneapolis Daily Times*, June 4, 1902, 5.
9. *Saint Paul Globe*, May 12, 1902, 4; and *Star Tribune* (Minneapolis), June 1, 1902, 5.
10. Fort Niobrara Post Return, July 1906; and Fort Brown Post Return, July 1906.
11. Coffman, *Regulars*, 127–28.
12. Coffman, *Regulars*, 129.
13. Coffman, *Regulars*, 129.
14. Coffman, *Regulars*, 129–30.
15. Coffman, *Regulars*, 129–31.
16. Coffman, *Regulars*, 130–31.

## 11. *Postscript*

1. Presidio of San Francisco Post Return, May 1905; and Fourth Cavalry Regimental Return, May 1905. The Presidio of Monterey had five troops assigned: E, F, G, H, and I. The Presidio of San Francisco had three troops: K, L, and M.
2. Fourth Cavalry Regimental Returns, April–November 1905.
3. Fourth Cavalry Regimental Returns, May–November 1905.
4. Fourth Cavalry Regimental Returns, September–November 1905; and Thirteenth Cavalry Regimental Return, November 1905. After promotion to major in October 1905, Benson was assigned to the Thirteenth Cavalry from November to December 1905. Yet the record shows he was back at Wawona, California, on November 2, 1905, and on detached service in

California on December 2, 1905. It appears as if the assignment to the Thirteenth was on paper only, and he never left California.

5. Presidio of Monterey Post Returns, November to December 1905.
6. Ninth Cavalry Regimental Return, February 1906.
7. Presidio of San Francisco Post Return, April 1906.
8. Presidio of San Francisco Post Return, May 1906; and Fourteenth Cavalry Regimental Return, May 1906.
9. Sequoia Detachment Post Returns, May–October 1891 and October–November 1891; Yosemite National Park Post Returns, May–November 1895, May–October 1896, and May–October 1897; and West Point Association of Graduates, USMA *Annual Report*, 1925, 174–75.
10. Meyerson, *Nature's Army*, 238.
11. Camp Yosemite Post Returns, 1906–8.
12. West Point Association of Graduates, USMA *Annual Report*, 1925, 175–76.
13. Post Return of Camp Yosemite, October 1908; and West Point Association of Graduates, USMA *Annual Report*, 1934, 175–76.
14. Post Returns of Camp Yosemite, 1909–10.
15. Meyerson, *Nature's Army*, 243–44.
16. Meyerson, *Nature's Army*, 145–47, 244. Gabriel Sovulewski died in 1938 and was buried at Yosemite Valley.
17. Post Return of Camp near Giant Forest, Sequoia National Park, May 1906.
18. Camp Sequoia Post Returns, 1907–9.
19. Camp Sequoia Post Returns, 1910.
20. Camp Sequoia Post Returns, 1911; and First Cavalry Regimental Return, October 1911. In October, Hughes returned to Sequoia to be on hand for the department commander's annual inspection tour and to complete his annual report as superintendent.
21. First Cavalry Regimental Returns, September 1911.
22. First Cavalry Regimental Returns, 1912.
23. Hampton, *U.S. Cavalry Saved*, 162. Hugh S. Johnson later headed the New Deal National Recovery Administration.
24. Hampton, *U.S. Cavalry Saved*, 163.
25. First Cavalry Regimental Returns, 1913.
26. Britten, *Pioneers in Paradise*, 253–55.

### 12. *Aftermath*

1. Enlistment of William S. Jones, July 9, 1911, Register of Enlistments.
2. U.S. Census, 1920, Cheyenne, Wyoming, Bureau of Census, Fourteenth Census of the United States, T624, NARA; letter from Samuel B. Pearson

to Ada Young, March 17, 1922, Charles Young Collection, NAAMCC; and filing of Addie Jones, February 7, 1924, for pension as widow, Ancestry.com.

3. Enlistment of George Brown, August 8, 1906, Register of Enlistments; and Ninth Cavalry Regimental Return, February 1908.
4. Enlistments of Frank McKenzie, October 17, 1892; October 18, 1897; October 24, 1900; November 5, 1903; March 16, 1907; March 26, 1910; and January 10, 1913, Register of Enlistments. Also, Ninth Cavalry Regimental Return, March 1920; and appointment to Color Sergeant, May 28, 1919, McKenzie Collection. When he reenlisted in November 1903 at the Presidio of San Francisco, he changed the spelling of his name from McKinzie to McKenzie, which is used throughout this book.
5. Marriage of Frank McKenzie to Ruby Estes, August 5, 1926, Utah, County Marriages, 1887–1937, Ancestry.com; Census of 1930, Salt Lake City, Utah, Ancestry.com; death of Frank McKenzie, Los Angeles, April 22, 1936, and burial at Los Angeles National Cemetery, Ancestry.com; and death of Ruby Estes McKenzie, April 2, 1977, Inglewood, California, and burial at Lincoln Memorial Park, Carson, California, Ancestry.com. In 1930 the couple rented a house in Salt Lake City, and Frank worked for the railroad.
6. Enlistment of George W. Fearington, May 7, 1913, Register of Enlistments; and North Carolina, World War I Service Cards, 1917–1919, for George W. Fearington, Ancestry.com.
7. Record of issue of license to marry, Honolulu, June 15, 1918, Ancestry.com; standard certificate of birth for George Fearington, August 5, 1919, Ancestry.com; filing of George W. Fearington, June 17, 1925, for pension as invalid, Ancestry.com; death of George W. Fearington, November 18, 1933, Alameda County Register of Deaths, Ancestry.com; and Glasson, "National Pension System," 40–62.
8. *Chicago Tribune*, December 26, 1906, 3; and *Chicago Tribune*, April 2, 1907, 9. Griffin was discharged without honor on April 3, 1907.
9. Enlistment of Arthur Worthy, December 11, 1903, Register of Enlistments; Fort McPherson Post Return, March–June 1907; filing of Arthur B. Worthy, January 28, 1928, for pension as invalid, Ancestry.com; and Arthur B. Worthy draft registration, 1942, Ancestry.com. Worthy served from 1916 to 1918 as an officer's steward second class aboard USS *Nevada*, USS *Solace*, USS *Aaron*, USS *Roanoke*, USS *Ward*, USS *Laduoset*, USS *Chaumont*, and USS *Bream*.
10. Enlistment of Jefferson Parker, May 12, 1898, Register of Enlistments; Ninth Cavalry Regimental Return, June 1902; filing of Jefferson Parker,

March 30, 1926, for pension as invalid, Ancestry.com; and letter from John Blakeney to Wirt Langley, January 13, 1943, Charles Young Collection, NAAMCC. According to Parker's pension filing, he served from 1905 to 1911 aboard the USS *Buffalo*, USS *Lawton*, USS *Rainbow*, USS *Helena*, USS *Indianapolis*, USS *Hull*, and USS *West Virginia*.

11. Enlistment of John A. S Blakeney, April 27, 1902, and September 9, 1911, Register of Enlistments; filing of John A. S. Blakeney, November 27, 1914, for pension as invalid, Ancestry.com; Census of Los Angeles, California, 1920, Fourteenth Census of the United States, T624, NARA; and obituary of John A. S. Blakeney, January 27, 1945, Ancestry.com.
12. Blakeney to Langley, January 13, 1943, Young Collection, NAAMCC.
13. Filing of Schuyler Black, August 12, 1930, for pension as invalid, Ancestry.com; Census of 1910, Oakland City, California, Thirteenth Census of the United States, T624, NARA; filing of Joseph R. Taylor, November 21, 1922, for pension as invalid, Ancestry.com; and 1952 Index to Register of Voters, Los Angeles City Precinct No. 1338, Ancestry.com.
14. Enlistment of Lee Bell, July 2, 1900, and July 2, 1903, Register of Enlistments; Census of 1930, Oakland, California, Fifteenth Census of the United States, T624, NARA; and filing of Lee Bell, July 7, 1930, for pension as invalid, Ancestry.com.
15. War Department to Mrs. Samuel B. Pearson, January 14, 1930, Pearson Papers, Three Rivers Historical Museum (hereafter referred to as TRHSM). Pearson visited Young in Liberia in 1913 and at the Young home in Wilberforce, Ohio.
16. Typed summary titled "COL S.B. Pearson News," Pearson Papers, TRHSM.
17. Superintendent John R. White to Editor, *Army and Navy Journal*, October 23, 1929, Pearson Papers, Three Rivers Historical Museum. John R. White purchased the home of Samuel and Margaret Pearson in 1929.
18. Newspaper clipping and grave photo, Pearson Papers, TRHSM.
19. Shellum, *Black Officer*, 158–81. Samuel Pearson visited Young in Liberia in 1913 and asked to be assigned to his staff in Monrovia.
20. Shellum, *Black Officer*, 182–279.
21. Enlistment of John L. Malone, November 28, 1894, Register of Enlistments; Letterman General Hospital Return, April 1904; and Ninth Cavalry Regimental Returns, May–July 1904. Sometime before he deployed with Young and I Troop to the Philippines in 1901, Malone was busted to private and served as such throughout two years of campaigning on the island. He was still useful as a member of I Troop since Young sent him on detached service under Quartermaster Sergeant Brown to San Francisco from April to August 1901 to care for the troop's new horses. He was

still a private when he redeployed to San Francisco in late 1902, though soon after arrival he earned his sergeant stripes again.

22. Enlistment of John L. Malone, February 13, 1901, Register of Enlistments; *San Francisco Call*, February 24, 1904, 13; and filing of John L. Malone, August 12, 1907, for pension as invalid, Ancestry.com.
23. Census of 1910, Vallejo City, California, Thirteenth Census of the United States, T624, NARA; 1915 Vallejo City Directory, U.S. City Directories, 1822–1995, Ancestry.com; and Census of 1920, Vallejo City, California, Fourteenth Census of the United States, T624, NARA. In 1910 Malone owned a house at 526 Indiana Street, and in 1920 he owned a house at 526 Tennessee Street. Sophia was working as a chambermaid at a hotel. She must have had children from a previous marriage, since a granddaughter named Susie Barrow lived with them in early 1920.
24. John L. Malone died July 20, 1920, per California Death Index, 1905–1939, Ancestry.com; and filing of Sophia Malone, October 12, 1920, for pension as widow, Ancestry.com.
25. Enlistments of Dee Smith, March 5, 1898, and May 6, 1901, Register of Enlistments; Ninth Regimental Returns, September–October 1898; and Report of Interment, William D. Smith, April 17, 1925, Ancestry.com.
26. Ninth Cavalry Regimental Returns, September–October 1898; filing of William D. Smith, December 12, 1922, for pension as invalid, Ancestry.com; and Glasson, "National Pension System," 40–62.
27. *San Francisco Call*, December 10, 1904, 14; Census of 1910, Oakland City, California, Thirteenth Census of the United States, T624, NARA; and Census of 1920, Oakland City, California, Fourteenth Census of the United States, T624, NARA. In 1910 Smith owned a house at 1326 Moss Avenue and in 1920 owned a house at 5410 Holland Street.
28. Filing of William D. Smith, December 12, 1922, for pension as invalid, Ancestry.com; filing of Amelia A. Smith, April 23, 1925, Ancestry.com; Census of 1940, Berkeley City, California, Sixteenth Census of the United States, T624, NARA; and report of interment, William D. Smith, October 8, 1956, Ancestry.com. This last document noted that during his military service he used Dee Smith as his official name and later changed it to William D. Smith. I visited the San Francisco National Cemetery in April 2023 and observed that Amelia's name was chiseled onto the back side of William D. Smith's gravestone.
29. Enlistment of Leo Frye, March 18, 1901, Register of Enlistments.
30. Census of 1910, Oakland, California, Thirteenth Census of the United States, T624, NARA; 1915 Oakland City Directory, U.S. City Directories, 1822–1995, Ancestry.com; filing of Leo Frye, March 3, 1927,

for pension as invalid, Ancestry.com; and Leo Frye, National Cemetery Administration, U.S. Veteran's Gravesites, 1775–2019, Ancestry.com. Frye lived at 6138 Freemont Street in Oakland, California, from 1915 to 1917.

31. Enlistments of Henry Whitfield, March 7, 1899, and March 7, 1902, Register of Enlistments; Ninth Cavalry Regimental Return, July 1903; Ninth Cavalry Regimental Return, March 1905; and letter from Charles Young to Joe Clark, October 15, 1916, Charles Young Collection, NAAMCC.

32. Young to Clark, October 15, 1916, Young Collection, NAAMCC; and filing of Henry Whitfield, September 26, 1922, for pension as invalid, Ancestry.com.

33. Enlistments of James Norman, March 29, 1899, and May 20, 1902, Register of Enlistments; Ninth Cavalry Regimental Return, October 1903; Ninth Cavalry Regimental Return, June 1904; and Young to Clark, October 15, 1916, Young Collection, NAAMCC.

34. Census of 1920, San Francisco, California, Fourteenth Census of the United States, T624, NARA; and Census of 1930, San Francisco, California, Fifteenth Census of the United States, T624, NARA. He lived at 1515 Lombard Street in 1920 and at 1556 Green Street in 1930 in San Francisco, California.

35. Filing of James Norman, November 10, 1930, for pension as invalid, Ancestry.com; and filing of Minnie A. Raymond, February 3, 1931, for pension as invalid, Ancestry.com.

36. Nicholas letter, January 1945, Young Collection, NAAMCC. This property later became the Thorn Ranch, a cattle ranch owned and operated by three generations of the Craig S. Thorn family.

37. Nicholas letter, January 1945, Young Collection, NAAMCC; and *Daily Visalia Delta*, November 11, 1920, 1. Young had bought the ranch to serve as his home and headquarters for an anticipated second tour as the superintendent of Sequoia National Park. Once he accepted the attaché assignment to Hispaniola, he sold the property.

38. Marriage of William H. Nicholas and Edythe B. Hinds, April 25, 1905, Index to Marriage Licenses and Certificates, No. 11, Alameda County, Ancestry.com; Voter Registration List for 1908, Second Ward, Precinct No. 3, Alameda County, California, Ancestry.com; Census of 1910, Berkeley City, California, Thirteenth Census of the United States, T624, NARA; Census of 1920, Berkeley City, California, Fourteenth Census of the United States, T624, NARA; pension filing of William H. Nicholas, January 30, 1923, Ancestry.com; and Record of Prisoners Received at McNeil Island Penitentiary, William Henry Nicholas, March 14, 1936, Ancestry.com. In 1910 and 1920, Nicholas owned a house at 1234 Ashby Avenue.

39. Letters from William Nicholas to Ada Young dated April 3, 1944; January 1945; and April 3, 1945, Charles Young Collection, NAAMCC. Also, record of interment in the Golden Gate National Cemetery, William H. Nicholas, April 20, 1949, Ancestry.com.
40. Enlistments of Wirt L. Langley, August 13, 1898, and May 1, 1899, Register of Enlistments. Langley may have served an additional enlistment in the army, since his Veterans Administration paperwork indicated he ended his service on February 25, 1905.
41. Census of 1910, Oakland, California, Thirteenth Census of the United States, T624, NARA; Census of 1920, San Francisco, California, Fourteenth Census of the United States, T624, NARA; 1924 and 1930 Oakland City Directory, U.S. City Directories, 1822–1995, Ancestry.com; and Census of 1930, Fifteenth Census of the United States, T624, NARA. He lived at 6140 Freemont Street in Oakland, California.
42. Nicholas letter, January 1945, Young Collection, NAAMCC; and marriage of Samuel Pierce and Johanna A. Hinds, April 26, 1906, Ancestry.com.
43. Marriage of Samuel Pierce and Johanna A. Hinds, April 26, 1906, Ancestry.com; Census of 1910, Berkeley City, California, Thirteenth Census of the United States, T624, NARA; *Oakland Tribune*, October 29, 1910, 5; *Oakland Tribune*, October 22, 1914, 4; and Census of 1920, Berkeley City, California, Fourteenth Census of the United States, T624, NARA. In 1910 and 1920, Pierce owned a house at 1248 Ashby Street in Berkeley, California.
44. Census of 1920, Berkeley City, California, Fourteenth Census of the United States, T624, NARA; pension filing of Samuel Pierce, December 12, 1922, Ancestry.com; Census of 1940, Berkeley City, California, Sixteenth Census of the United States, T624, NARA; and marriage of Samuel Pierce and Ella Maude Williams, April 6, 1940, Ancestry.com.
45. Photo of Samuel Pierce, 1947, Sequoia National Park Archives, NPS.
46. See appendix A for an explanation of "Fiddlers' Green."
47. Application for headstone for Samuel Pierce, May 27, 1970, Ancestry.com.
48. Census of 1910, Oakland, California, Thirteenth Census of the United States, T624, NARA; Census of 1920, San Francisco, California, Fourteenth Census of the United States, T624, NARA; and 1912, 1913, 1914, 1915, and 1918 Oakland City Directory, U.S. City Directories, 1822–1995, Ancestry.com.
49. Census of 1930, Fifteenth Census of the United States, T624, NARA; and pension filing as invalid of Abner Jones, June 30, 1928. Jones lived at 1051 Fife Avenue in Palo Alto, California.
50. Census of 1940, Palo Alto, California, Sixteenth Census of the

United States, T624, NARA; 1951 Oakland Directory, U.S. City Directories, 1822–1995, Ancestry.com; and *Oakland Tribune*, December 14, 1971, 22. In the 1950s and at his death, Jones lived at 3440 Hannah Street in Oakland.

*Appendix A*

1. Stodter, "Fiddlers' Green," 196–97. I use the 1923 spelling of "Fiddlers' Green" though it is also spelled "Fiddler's Green."
2. John H. Stodter, U.S. Military Academy (USMA) class of 1922, must have heard the story as a child or from his father, Charles E. Stodter, USMA class of 1896, who was stationed at Fort D. A. Russell from 1910 to 1917, at the time Samuel B. Pearson was there.
3. Stodter, "Fiddlers' Green," 196–97.
4. Rutherford, *Rudyard Kipling*, 55–57.
5. Paul M. Crosby, "Legend of Fiddler's Green," *Armor Magazine*, November–December 1965, 7–11.

# Bibliography


*Archives and Manuscript Materials*

Bond Day, Caroline. Papers. Peabody Museum Archives. Harvard University, Cambridge MA.

Colorado Springs Fine Arts Center, Colorado Springs.

Photo Collection.

Du Bois, W. E. B. Papers. University of Massachusetts, Amherst.

McKenzie, Frank. Papers. Frank McKenzie Collection, Private collection, Las Vegas.

Mitchell, Lottie Pearl. Papers. Western Reserve Historical Society, Cleveland.

National Afro-American Museum and Cultural Center, Wilberforce OH (NAAMCC).

Charles Young Collection.

National Archives and Records Administration, Washington DC (NARA).

Annual Reports of the War Department.

Bureau of Census, Census of the United States, 1900, 1910, 1920, 1930, 1940, 1950.

Congressional Documents.

General Index to Compiled Service Records of Volunteer Soldiers Who Served during the War with Spain, Adjutant General's Office, 1780–1917, RG 94, M871.

General Orders and Circulars, Adjutant General's Office. Published annually, U.S. Government Printing Office, Washington DC.

Letters Received by the Appointment, Commission, and Personnel Branch, Adjutant General's Office, RG 94.

Register of Enlistments in the U.S. Army, Records of the Adjutant General's Office, 1798–1914, RG 94, M233.
Returns from the Regular Cavalry Regiments, 1833–1916, RG 391, M744.
Returns from the Regular Infantry Regiments, 1833–1916, RG 94, M744.
Returns from U.S. Military Posts, 1800–1916, RG 94, M617.
National Park Service, Washington DC (NPS).
Golden Gate National Recreation Area Archives.
Historic Preservation Fund.
Sequoia National Park Archives.
Pearson, Samuel B. Papers. Three Rivers Historical Society and Museum, Three Rivers CA.
Special Collections. U.S. Military Academy, West Point NY.
John Bigelow, Jr., Papers.
Charles Young Papers.
Washington, Booker T. Papers. Library of Congress, Washington DC.

### *Published Works*

Alexander, Charles. *Battles and Victories of Charles Allensworth*. Boston: Sherman, French, & Company, 1914.
*Annual Report of the Department of the Interior, Miscellaneous Reports, Part II, 1903*. Washington DC: Government Printing Office, 1903.
*Annual Report of the War Department*. Vol. 1. Washington DC: Government Printing Office, 1904.
*Annual Report of the War Department*. Vol. 9. Washington DC: Government Printing Office, 1902.
Asbury, Herbert. *The Barbary Coast: An Informal History of the San Francisco Underworld*. New York: Alfred A. Knopf, 1933.
Ashburn, Percy M. *A History of the Medical Department of the United States Army*. New York: Houghton Mifflin, 1929.
Batter, Tom. "The Tule Elk, a California Comeback Story." California Department of Fish & Wildlife, May 6, 2014. https://calwil.wordpress.com/2014/05/06/the-tule-elk-a-california-comeback-story/.
Beasley, Delilah L. *Negro Trail Blazers of California*. Los Angeles: Times Mirror Print and Binding House, 1919.
Bielakowski, Alexander M. *U.S. Cavalryman, 1891–1920*. Oxford: Osprey Publishing, 2004.
Bond Day, Caroline. *A Study of Some Negro-White Families in the United States*. Cambridge MA: Peabody Museum of Harvard University, 1932.
Brady, William J. "Jeff." *Skagway: City of the New Century*. Skagway AK: Lynn Canal Publishing, 2013.

Britten, Sophie. *Pioneers in Paradise: Historical and Biographical Record of Early Days in Three Rivers, California, 1850s to 1950s*. Indianapolis: Dog Ear Publishing, 2013.

Brooks, Charles H. *The Official History and Manual of the Grand United Order of the Odd Fellows in America*. Philadelphia: Odd Fellows' Journal Print, 1902.

Broussard, Albert S. *Black San Francisco: The Struggle for Racial Equality in the West, 1900–1954*. Lawrence: University Press of Kansas, 1993.

Brownell, Susan. *The 1904 Anthropology Days and Olympic Games: Sport, Race, and American Imperialism*. Lincoln: University of Nebraska Press, 2008.

Buecker, Thomas R. *Fort Robinson and the American West, 1874–1899*. Norman: University of Oklahoma Press, 1999.

Burnett, Gene. *Florida's Past: People and Events That Shaped the State*. Sarasota: Pineapple Press, 1996.

Cirillo, Vincent J. *Bullets and Bacilli: The Spanish-American War and Military Medicine*. Rutgers NJ: Rutgers University Press, 2003.

Coffman, Edward M. *The Old Army: Portrait of the American Army in Peacetime, 1784–1898*. New York: Oxford University Press, 1986.

———. *The Regulars: The American Army, 1898–1941*. Cambridge MA: Belknap Press of Harvard University, 2004.

Coumbe, Arthur T. *A History of the U.S. Army Officer Corps, 1900–1990*. Carlisle PA: U.S. Army War College Press, 2014.

Coursey, Leon D. "The Life of Edwin Bancroft Henderson and his Professional Contributions to Physical Education." PhD diss., Ohio State University, 1971.

Crosby, Paul M. "Legend of Fiddler's Green." *Armor Magazine*, November–December 1965, 7–11.

Cullen, Frank, Florence Hackman, and Donald McNeilly. *Vaudeville, Old and New: An Encyclopedia of Variety Performers*. Oxon, UK: Routledge, 2007.

Cullum, George W. *Biographical Register of the Officers and Graduates of the U.S. Military Academy*. Vol. 4, *1890–1900*. Cambridge MA: Riverside Press, 1901.

Cunningham, Roger D. "'We Are an Orderly Body of Men': Virginia's Black 'Immunes' in the Spanish-American War." *Historic Alexandria Quarterly*, Summer 2001.

Daniels, Douglas H. *Pioneer Urbanites: A Social and Cultural History of Black San Francisco*. Berkeley: University of California Press, 1990.

Dineen-Wimberly, Ingrid. "To Carry 'the Black Man's Burden': T. Thomas Fortune's Vision of African American Colonization of the Philippines in 1902 and 1903." *International Journal of Business and Social Science* 5, no. 10 (November 2014).

Dobak, William A., and Thomas D. Phillips. *Black Regulars, 1866–1898*. Norman: University of Oklahoma Press, 2001.

Du Bois, W. E. B. *The Souls of Black Folk*. Chicago: A. C. McClurg, 1903.

Eldridge, Ward. *In the Summer of 1903: Colonel Charles Young and the Buffalo Soldiers in Sequoia National Park*. Three Rivers CA: Sequoia National History Association, 2003.

Emerson, William K. *Encyclopedia of United States Army Insignia and Uniforms*. Norman: University of Oklahoma Press, 1966.

Farren, Lee. "Cavalrymen and Their Horses during the American Indian Wars." *Symphony in the Flint Hills Field Journal*, 1913.

Fletcher, Marvin E. *America's First Black General: Benjamin O. Davis, Sr., 1880–1970*. Lawrence: University of Kansas Press, 1989.

———. "The Black Volunteers in the Spanish-American War." *Military Affairs* 38, no. 2 (April 1974): 48–53.

Fortune, Timothy Thomas. Letter to the editor. *The Outlook* 62, no. 1 (May 6, 1899).

Gatewood, Willard B. *Aristocrats of Color: The Black Elite, 1880–1920*. Fayetteville: University of Arkansas Press, 2000.

Glasrud, Bruce A., and Micheal N. Searles, eds. *Buffalo Soldiers in the West: A Black Soldiers Anthology*. College Station: Texas A&M University, 2007.

Glass, Edward L. N. *The History of the Tenth Cavalry, 1866–1921*. Fort Collins CO: Old Army Press, 1972.

Glasson, William H. "The National Pension System as Applied to the Civil War and the War with Spain." *The Annals of the American Academy of Political Science* 92 (March 1902): 40–62.

Grunigen, Delores, and Jay O'Connell. *A Strength Born of Giants: The Life and Times of Dr. Forest Grunigen*. Van Nuys CA: Raven River Press, 2002.

Hampton, H. Duane. *How the U.S. Cavalry Saved Our National Parks*. Bloomington: Indiana University Press, 1971.

Hebard, Grace R. *Washakie: Chief of the Shoshones*. Lincoln: University of Nebraska Press, 1995.

Heitman, Francis B. *Historical Register and Dictionary of the U.S. Army*. Vols. 1 and 2. Washington DC: Government Printing Office, 1903.

Hershler, N. *Soldier's Handbook for Use in the Army of the United States*. Washington DC: Government Printing Office, 1902.

Hill, Errol G., and James V. Hatch. *A History of African American Theatre*. Cambridge: Cambridge University Press, 2005.

Jack, Linda K. "The Kentucky Ridge Mine: Colonel English's Enterprise." *The Union*, November 12, 2021.

Jacoby, Karl. *Crimes against Nature: Squatters, Poachers, Thieves, and the Hidden History of American Conservation*. Berkeley: University of California Press, 2014.

Johnson, James W. *Black Manhattan*. New York: Da Capo Press, 1991.

Johnson, Shelton. *Gloryland*. San Francisco, CA: Sierra Club Books, 2009.

———. "Invisible Men: Buffalo Soldiers of the Sierra Nevada." Accessed October 10, 2021. http://buffalosoldier.us/images/Sheldon_Jonson_National_Parks.pdf.

Kenner, Charles L. *Buffalo Soldiers and Officers of the Ninth Cavalry, 1867–1898: Black and White Together*. Norman: University of Oklahoma Press, 2014.

Kilroy, David P. *For Race and Country: The Life and Career of Charles Young*. Westport CT: Praeger, 2003.

Kinevan, Marcos. *Frontier Cavalryman: Lieutenant John Bigelow with the Buffalo Soldiers in Texas*. El Paso: Texas Western Press, 1998.

Lamm, Alan K. "Buffalo Soldier Chaplains of the Old West." In Glasrud and Searles, *Buffalo Soldiers in the West*, 68–83.

Langellier, John P. *Scouting with the Buffalo Soldiers: Lieutenant Powhatan Clarke, Frederic Remington, and the Tenth U.S. Cavalry in eh Southwest*. Denton: University of North Texas Press, 2020.

Leckie, William H. *The Buffalo Soldiers: A Narrative of the Negro Cavalry*. Norman: University of Oklahoma Press, 1967.

Lewis, David Levering. *W.E.B. Du Bois: The Fight for Equality and the American Century, 1919–1963*. New York: Henry Holt, 2000.

Linn, Brian M. *Guardians of Empire: The U.S. Army and the Pacific, 1902–1940*. Chapel Hill: University of North Carolina Press, 1997.

———. *The Philippine War, 1899–1902*. Lawrence: University Press of Kansas, 2000.

Lockwood, J. A. "Uncle Sam's Troopers in the National Parks of California." *Overland Monthly and Out West Magazine* 33, no. 196 (April 1899): 366–68.

Lowe, Dorothy. *Camp Atascadero: First Joint Maneuvers, United States Army and California's National Guard, 1904–1912*. Atascadero, CA: Wilkins Printing, 2004.

MacGregor, Morris J., and Bernard C. Nalty. *Blacks in the U.S. Armed Forces: Basic Documents*. Wilmington DE: Scholarly Resources, 1977.

*Manual for Army Cooks*. Washington DC: Government Printing Office, 1896.

*A Manual for Courts-Martial and of Procedure under Military Law*. Washington DC: Government Printing Office, 1898.

McChristian, Douglas C. "'Dress on the Colors, Boys!' Black Noncommissioned Officers in the Regular Army, 1866–98." In Glasrud and Searles, *Buffalo Soldiers in the West*, 84–95.

McLean, Ridley. "Historical Sketch of Military Law." *Journal of Criminal Law and Criminology* 8, no. 1 (1917).
Meyerson, Harvey. *Nature's Army: When Soldiers Fought for Yosemite*. Lawrence: University of Kansas Press, 2020.
*Military Laws of the United States*. 4th ed. Washington DC: Government Printing Office, 1901.
Morgan, H. Wayne. *William McKinley and His America*. Syracuse NY: Syracuse University Press, 1963.
Moses, Wilson J. *The Golden Age of Black Nationalism*. Oxford: Oxford University Press, 1988.
Moss, James A. *Officers' Manual*. 5th ed. Menasha WI: George Banta Publishing, 1917.
Muller, William G. *The Twenty-Fourth Infantry: Past and Present*. Fort Collins CO: Old Army Press, 1972.
O'Connell, Jay. "Charles Young: The Road through Sequoia." Three Rivers Historical Society and Museum, 1996.
———. *Co-operative Dreams: A History of the Kaweah Colony*. Van Nuys CA: Raven River Press, 1999.
Office of the Quartermaster General, comp. *Regulations and Decisions Pertaining to the Uniform of the Army of the United States*. Washington DC: Government Printing Office, 1897.
*Official Register of the United States: Officers and Employees in the Civil, Military, and Naval Service*. Vol. 1, *Legislative, Executive, and Judicial*. Washington DC: Government Printing Office, 1903.
Peterson, Harold L. *The American Sword, 1775–1945*. Mineola NY: Dover Publications, 1954.
Purnell, John H. "Colonel Charles Young, U.S.A., Soldier, Diplomat, Philanthropist, Man of Culture." *The Oracle*, Winter 1979.
Raugh, Harold E., Jr. "Buffalo Soldiers at the Presidio of Monterey: A Legacy of Professionalism and Price." Presidio of Monterey, CA: Defense Language Institute Foreign Language Center, 2015. Copy in author's collection.
———. *Presidio of Monterey*. Charleston: Arcadia Publishing, 2004.
*Regulations for the Army of the United States, 1895, with Appendix, Separately Indexed, Showing Changes to January 1, 1899*. Washington DC: Government Printing Office, 1899.
*Regulations for the Army of the United States, 1901, with Appendix, Separately Indexed, Showing Changes to June 30, 1902*. Washington DC: Government Printing Office, 1902.

Rocketto, Hap. "A Short History of the National Trophy Team Rifle Match." Civilian Marksmanship Program, December 2011. https://thecmp.org/wp-content/uploads/NTTMatchHistory.pdf.

Rodenbough, Theodore F., and William L. Haskin. *Army of the United States.* New York: Argonaut Press, 1966.

Rommel, George M. *The Army Remount Problem.* U.S. Department of Agriculture, Bureau of Animal Industry, Circular 186. Washington DC: Government Printing Office, 1911.

Roosevelt, Theodore. "The Rough Riders." *Scribner's Magazine* 25, no. 4 (1899): 420–40.

Rust, Thomas C. *Watching over Yellowstone.* Lawrence: University of Kansas Press, 2020.

Rutherford, Andrew. *Rudyard Kipling: War Stories and Poems.* Oxford: Oxford University Press, 1990.

Sawyer, Charles W. *Our Rifles.* Vol. 3. Boston: Cornhill, 1920.

Schubert, Frank N. *Black Valor: Buffalo Soldiers and the Medal of Honor, 1870–1890.* Wilmington DE: Scholarly Resources, 1997.

———. *Voices of the Buffalo Soldier: Records, Reports, and Recollections of Military Life and Service in the West.* Albuquerque: University of New Mexico Press, 2003.

Scott, Edward Van Zile. *The Unwept: Black American Soldiers and the Spanish-American War.* Montgomery AL: River City Publishing, 1996.

Scott, Emmett J. *Scott's Official History of the American Negro in the World War.* Chicago: Homewood Press, 1919.

Shellum, Brian G. *Black Cadet in a White Bastion: Charles Young at West Point.* Lincoln: University of Nebraska Press, 2006.

———. *Black Officer in a Buffalo Soldier Regiment: The Military Career of Charles Young.* Lincoln: University of Nebraska Press, 2010.

Skirbunt, Peter. "McKinley: From Commissary Sergeant to U.S. President." Defense Commissary Agency, November 3, 2016. https://www.commissaries.com/our-agency/newsroom/news-releases/mckinley-commissary-sergeant-us-president.

Smith, Bolling W., and William C. Gaines. "Coast Artillery Organization: A Brief Overview." In *American Seacoast Defenses: Reference Guide*, edited by Mark A Berhow, 417–32. McLean VA: Coast Defense Study Group, 2022. https://cdsg.org/wp-content/uploads/pdfs/FORTS/CACunits/CACorg2011.pdf.

Steward, T. G. *The Colored Regulars in the United States Army.* Philadelphia: A. M. E. Book Concern, 1904.

Stodter, John H. "Fiddlers' Green and Other Cavalry Songs." *Cavalry Journal*, April 1923, 196–97.

Thompson, Erwin N. *Defender of the Gate: The Presidio of San Francisco: A History from 1846 to 1995*. Vol. 1. San Francisco: National Park Service, 1997.

———. *Presidio of San Francisco: An Outline of Its Evolution as a U.S. Army Post, 1847–1990*. San Francisco: National Park Service, 1992.

Turk, Richard W. "The United States Navy and the 'Taking' of Panama, 1901–1903." *Military Affairs* 38, no. 3 (October 1974): 92–96.

Utley, Robert M. *Frontier Regulars: The United States Army and the Indian, 1866–1891*. New York: Macmillan, 1973.

Washington, Booker T. *Up from Slavery: An Autobiography*. New York: Doubleday, 1901.

Weigley, Russell F. *The History of the United States Army*. New York: Macmillan, 1967.

West Point Association of Graduates. *Register of Graduates and Former Cadets of the United States Military Academy*. West Point: Association of Graduates, 2000.

———. *USMA Annual Report*. West Point: Association of Graduates Library, West Point, 1925.

———. *USMA Annual Report*. West Point: Association of Graduates Library, West Point, 1934.

———. *USMA Annual Report*. West Point: Association of Graduates Library, West Point, 1936.

Winser, Philip. "Memories." Unpublished manuscript, 1931. Huntington Library, San Marino CA, and Three Rivers Historical Museum, Three Rivers, CA.

Young, Charles. *Report of the Acting Superintendent of the Sequoia and General Grant National Parks, in the State of California, to the Secretary of the Interior*. Washington DC: Government Printing Office, 1903. NPS.

# Index

Printed in the USA
CPSIA information can be obtained
at www.ICGtesting.com
CBHW020129090624
9645CB00003B/13

9 781496 238511